THE EXPECTANT MOTHER DISINFORMATION HANDBOOK

ROBERT GUFFEY

GUTTER MYSTIC BOOKS

Gutter Mystic Books
2006 Idlewilde Run Dr.
Austin, Texas 78744

Cover Art by Gavriel Quiroga

Interior Layout by Lori Michelle
www.TheAuthorsAlley.com

For more information, address:
john@madnessheart.press

www.madnessheart.press

ORIGAMI BABY

According to Dr. Kogoro Ogawa, noted expert in medical anomalies of Japan, in the year 1866 AD, Yoshiko Takiyama of Usuitoge gave birth to what appeared to be a carefully folded piece of paper in the shape of a rose.

To everybody's surprise, that's precisely what it was. Seconds after birth, the origami rose unfolded and bloomed into a paper baby. The baby was just like any other; it certainly cried and fussed like one. Every time it kicked, the baby would make a crinkly sound like somebody crumpling up a newspaper. The mother named her Bara.

Defying all expert prognoses and predictions, Bara went on to live a healthy life for almost five years, and would no doubt have continued to do so if the child had not been kidnapped by a greedy carnival owner traveling through Yoshiko's village. Alas, one fateful evening, curious patrons snuck into the carnival after dark to get a better look and drew too close to the child's bed with a lit cigar. Not a single speck of Bara's ashes remain.

We report this curious event in these pages for a good reason: so that all of you reading this will appreciate the advanced medical care of the twenty-first century. Today's doctors would have detected the true nature of the origami baby within the first trimester, and the parents would have then taken precautions to prevent such a thing from entering our world. God does not approve of preventing a child's birth, except of course when the child represents a "statistical outlier"[1] in regards to His plans for us.

As Dr. Ogawa himself once wrote, "Some creatures are for too strange and fragile to live in a world such as ours."

1) The accepted definition of "statistical outlier" is as follows: "In statistics, an 'outlier' is an observation that is numerically distant from the rest of the data."

ONEIROPAEDION
(ARTIFICIAL BABIES PART I)

In 1962 Roy Orbison recorded the popular rock song "Dream Baby," written by a prolific songwriter and dancer named Cindy Walker. The song, far from being just a catchy ditty, was born out of a genuine phenomenon. In 2006, the same year of her death, Walker told an *L.A. Times* reporter that she was inspired to write the song while researching a rare medical condition called *oneirokyesis* by the ancient Greeks. This condition occurs when the mother imagines she's pregnant so strongly that she exhibits all the signs of a genuine pregnancy. Some people think this is the same as *pseudocyesis*, also known as a "hysterical pregnancy," in which a woman will exhibit such classic symptoms as morning sickness, amenorrhoea, tender breasts, and weight gain—almost everything associated with pregnancy, in fact, except for the presence of a fetus. The phenomenon under discussion here, however, is radically different from *pseudocyesis*.

In cases such as these, the delusion of the woman is even stronger, so much so that she *actually gives birth* to the child at the end of nine months. Such a child will only be revealed to be an *oneriopaedion* when the mother shifts her attention away from the child, or leaves his or her vicinity for a great length of time. Some *oneriopaedions* have been known to lead a normal existence until the onset of puberty, or even later, before vanishing into nothingness like a mist. In these cases the mother is often so crushed psychologically that she never recovers from the knowledge that her child never even existed in the first place.

Sometimes, the death of the mother will also cause the physical dissolution of the child, resulting in a double blow for the remaining family members.

The ancient Greeks considered an *oneriopaedion* to be at best the prank of a mischievous and uncaring demigod, or, at worst, the curse of an angry god.

The last verifiable *oneiropaedion*, Mr. Oliver Lerch, was born in 1870 in South Bend, Indiana. On December 24th, 1890, at roughly 10:00 P.M., while fetching a pail of water from a well, Mr. Lerch suddenly returned to the immaterial plane from which he had emerged, never to be seen or heard from again. This strange disappearance occurred in front of several respectable witnesses, including the Reverend Samual Mallelieu, all of whom were interviewed extensively by local police. Days later, after being accused of foul play by the police, Oliver's mother admitted she was a virgin but never wanted to accept the obvious truth. Subsequent medical examinations confirmed this was the case. This incident is documented in the police records of South Bend, Indiana, and still discussed in the town to this day.

DER GOLEM
(ARTIFICIAL BABIES PART II)

We, the authors of this handbook, do not recommend the creation of imaginary and/or artificial beings, whether on purpose or by accident. When Man has tried to overstep his God-given boundaries, he has always regretted it. Observe the mythological example of Prometheus, the brash human who was punished eternally by the gods for stealing fire from their domain. Or the real-world historical examples of those who have dabbled in black magic and the alchemical arts, infamous and tragic personages such as Rabbi Judah Loew ben Bezalel, Johann Konrad Dippel, and Victor Frankenstein.

Both Dippel and Frankenstein made the mistake of studying the forbidden writings of the ancient Kabbalists, who sought the secrets of creating living beings from primordial matter by deciphering hermetic codes they believed were embedded in the Bible. According to the eminent Argentinian scholar Jorge Luis Borges (in his classic historical text *The Book of Imaginary Beings*): "'Golem' was the name given to the man created by combinations of letters; the word means, literally, a shapeless or lifeless clod [. . .]. The procedures involved cover some twenty-three folio columns and require knowledge of the 'alphabets of the 221 gates,' which must be recited over each of the Golem's organs. The word *Emet*, which means 'Truth,' should be marked on its forehead; to destroy the creature, the first letter must be obliterated, forming the word *Met*, whose meaning is 'death'" (112-14).

Alas, this foolproof safeguard did not protect the aforementioned Rabbi Bezalel, who, according to the Austrian historian Gustav Meyerink, created a golem from clay in order to take over the menial tasks of his synagogue, such as sweeping the floors and making lunch. This artificial being was granted a robotic, pseudo-existence during daylight hours, thanks to a magic tablet placed under its tongue. One evening, the rabbi failed to remove the tablet, and the golem went into an uncontrollable frenzy, maiming and killing many local villagers, until the rabbi managed to wrest the tablet from its mouth, returning the creature to its original primordial form.

Borges's respected colleague, Michael A. Hoffman, president and founder of The Independent History and Research Company, believes the spiritual descendants of Rabbi Bezalel and his ilk repeated the rabbi's unholy mistakes in 1945 and are even now attempting to extend their transgressive researches further. These descendants, who masquerade as "scientists," of course . . .

> [. . .] teeter on the brink of the synthesis of the darkest dream of the Kabbalists, a marriage frantically sought, between E. coli bacteria from the colon of man, the genome code and the power of computer automata, for the creation of the Golem [. . .]. [A] Kabbalistic substance was inside the giant steel bottle weighing nearly half a million pounds which the U.S. government placed near 'ground zero,' on July 16, 1945, immediately preceding the first atomic bomb explosion (creation and destruction of primordial matter), at the 'Trinity Site' in New Mexico.
>
> The U.S. Government has never offered any cogent explanation for exactly what purpose the Golem-proportioned (25 ft. long, 12 ft. in diameter)

> capsule, custom-fabricated at an eastern steel mill and trucked in at great expense by a 64 wheel trailer, served at the Trinity Site. (*Secret Societies and Psychological Warfare* 102-08)

But we, dear friends, armed with *true knowledge*, can make an educated guess. What with unchristian, evil powers of a decidedly Hassidic nature weaving its black magic behind the scenes of the U.S. government, we don't need honest common folk such as yourself mirroring such Luciferian follies. If you are, in fact, infertile and are studying this handbook out of an ineffable longing for something you can never possibly attain, please, for the sake of all that's holy, consider adoption instead.

THE MOONCHILD
(ARTIFICIAL BABIES PART III)

Yet another artificial method for creating a child is that of the Babalon Working, commemorated in a 1929 novel entitled *Moonchild*, written by the black magician Aleister Crowley, and eventually performed by three of his most famous disciples in 1946 in the middle of the Mojave Desert. These three disciples were Jack W. Parsons, L. Ron Hubbard, and Marjorie Cameron.[2)]

The Babalon Working is a complicated method of birth requiring a grueling weekly schedule of magical ceremonies that can last well over a year and culminate in the implantation of an ethereal spirit-being into a woman's otherwise barren womb. This entity, known to occultists as a "Moonchild," will then, theoretically, mature into a spiritually-evolved "demigod" possessed of supernatural powers far greater than any attained by even the most disciplined human yogi or seer. This unique entity, according to Francis King's *The Rites of Modern Occult Magic*, would be considered the incarnation of Babalon, an aspect of "the mother of the universe."

2) Parsons was a rocket scientist who created the fuel that propelled America to the moon and was one of the most prominent founders of Jet Propulsion Laboratory in Pasadena, CA; Hubbard made a name for himself writing pulp science fiction novels in the 1940s and '50s and later founded the Satanic Church of Scientology; and Cameron was a painter, poet and actress whose burnt corpse later starred in Kenneth Anger's 1954 film *Inauguration of the Pleasure Dome*.

All three participants of the Babalon Working came to bad ends. Recently unclassified documents have revealed that Parsons faked his death in 1952 and literally went underground for the U.S. government, working to back-engineer crashed extraterrestrial spacecraft at the top secret S-4 military base in Nevada until dying of cancer in the mid-nineties; he was a virtual prisoner of the U.S. government for almost five decades, in which time he never once saw the rays of the sun. Hubbard died in 1978 when attacked by an army of red ants in South Africa while searching for gold he'd apparently buried during a previous incarnation as Cecil Rhodes. In late 1953, Cameron was burned at the stake in Mexico by a renegade Catholic priest, who was then expelled from the Roman Catholic Church for his "crime," if indeed such an act could be deemed criminal.

THE WOMAN WHO GAVE BIRTH TO A BUILDING

On April 16th, 1999, Mrs. Fiona Naylor of Hoboken, New Jersey thought she was giving birth to quadruplets, but gave birth instead to a three-foot-tall replica of a Bronx brownstone, complete with a full load of almost fifty miniature tenants, operable electricity, and all other utilities. According to the little sign on the iron gate outside, no pets or children were allowed in this building, but nonetheless some of the tenants came readymade with cats hidden inside their bedrooms. The tenants were fully sentient and went about their tiny lives like unemployed homunculi. Most of them spent their days watching TV or arguing passionately with one another. When something would go on the fritz, they would stick their head out the window and complain to Mrs. Naylor, whom they perceived to be their omniscient landlord.

At first, Mrs. Naylor was devastated by this strange twist of fate. After only a few weeks, however, she seemed to adjust. She placed the brownstone inside the crib her grandmother had given her and decided to care for her fifty-plus tenants (including the cats) as if they were her own children—which, according to all the DNA tests, they were.

Mr. Naylor was so disgusted and ashamed by the media attention that he fled the country and never returned. Mrs. Naylor wasn't too upset. She realized she loved her children more than her husband.

After a flurry of attention from various medical journals, Mrs. Naylor changed her last name back to Yulish (her maiden name), then she and her children settled down to a relatively normal life. No scientific expert can explain how this anomaly occurred, but Ms. Yulish has gone on record as stating that she doesn't care the least bit about *hows* or *whys*. She says she and her children are content, and that's all that matters. Who are we to disagree?

According to our sources, Ms. Yulish has been dating again. In fact, she has been seeing someone on a fairly regular basis. Who knows? Perhaps there will be more little brownstones in Ms. Yulish's future.

If so, soon she might be able to throw the most unique and liveliest block party in the history of Hoboken, New Jersey.

VEGETATIVE REPRODUCTION

As hard as it is to accept, it's now possible to eliminate the mother from the birth process entirely. Experiments involving what is known as "vegetative reproduction" have occurred at respectable institutions of learning, such as Oxford in England, as well as in the private sector. Back in 1988, a misogynistic group of all-male terrorists known as The Wild Boys formed a base of operations in the jungles of North Africa, where they practiced this form of reproduction quite regularly. These commandos established secret enclaves from the outskirts of Tangier to the Blue Desert of Silence, but their influence extended far beyond just the African continent.

According to recently declassified CIA documents prepared by an intelligence agent codenamed "Old Bull Lee": "The legend of the wild boys spread, and boys from all over the world ran away to join them. Wild boys appeared in the mountains of Mexico, the jungles of South America and Southeastern Asia [. . .]. The wild boys exchange drugs, weapons, skills on a world-wide network. Some wild-boy tribes travel constantly, taking the best cannabis seeds to the Amazon and bringing back cuttings of the Yage vine for the jungles of Southern Asia and Central Africa [. . .]. A common language based on variable transliteration of a simplified hieroglyphic script is spoken and written by the wild boys. In remote dream rest areas, the boys fashion these glyphs from wood, metal, stone and pottery."

According to one highly placed narcotics official who

once debriefed President Ronald Reagan on this matter, "The wild-boy thing is a cult based on drugs, depravity and violence, more dangerous than the hydrogen bomb."

These Wild Boys were well trained in hand-to-hand combat and had access to advanced technology, such as "gold laser guns" that were, according to one report, capable of shooting highly destructive "arrows of light." It's been documented by African journalists that this terrorist group could travel through the trees on prehensile hemorrhoids; other modes of travel included streamlined gliders and, according to the CIA, hi-tech roller skates.

One particular intelligence document states that the group was divided into numerous "units" for strategic purposes. These units were made up of various Wild Boys, such as "glider boys," "naked blowgun boys," "slingshot boys," "shaman boys," "Juju boys," "dream boys," "weather boys" and the "silent boys of the Blue Desert." The vast majority of these guerrilla warriors were produced from single cells extracted from the intestines of other boys, genetically engineered to perform specific tasks for the overall group.[3)]

The aforementioned CIA report goes on to say: "Each [unit] developed special skills and knowledge until, they evolved into humanoid subspecies. One of the more spectacular units is the dreaded Warrior Ants, made up of boys who have lost both hands in battle [. . .]." The Wild Boys were masters of stealth, and the only warning of their presence was the "overpowering odor [of] roses, carbolic soap, gardenias, jasmine, oil of cloves, ambergris and rectal mucus."

Rumor has it that The Wild Boys insurgency was instrumental in the highly destructive Medical Riots of

---

3) According to the FBI, a Midwestern surgeon named "Dr. Benway" was involved in the black market trafficking of valuable organs used by The Wild Boys for their illicit experiments, but Benway fled the U.S. before he could be arrested. His whereabouts are unknown. He's currently on the FBI's Ten Most Wanted List.

1999, also known as "the week of the Long Scalpels," which started in the Burn Unit of a Midwestern hospital that need not be named here. It is estimated that at least ten thousand doctors, medical bureaucrats, and directors of pharmaceutical companies were massacred by The Wild Boys and their sleeper agents during that one week. The Wild Boys and their sympathizers have not been heard from since. Let's hope their ungodly "vegetative reproduction" techniques have vanished with them.

We here at the offices of *The Expectant Mother Disinformation Handbook* wish to state that we do not approve of The Wild Boys or their treasonous philosophy. If you encounter anyone you suspect of having ties to The Wild Boys, we urge you to contact your local FBI office immediately. This is the phone number for their main office: 714-542-8825.

MARCO POLO'S REPORT CONCERNING FAUNA OF THE INNER WORLD

The exact nature of the fauna produced in the womb during pregnancy is open to debate, but the few facts we know are these:

The womb is, as the great Dr. Kogoro Ogawa once said, "another world unto itself," populated by its own animal life and sociological structures. Some say there is a central sun that exists inside the womb, giving light and life to a miniature world, the entire purpose of which is to tend to the health of the growing fetus.

In 1284, Marco Polo—through ancient and alchemical sorcery unknown to us—was shrunk by Kublai Khan's court seer to the size of a poppy seed and sent inside the womb of Khan's pregnant mistress to chart out the topography of this strange inner world. Many of his findings bordered on the fantastic, but we feel compelled to relate them to you now nonetheless.

Upon arriving in this world, Messr Polo uncovered a city of towering monoliths called Walandra, in which tiny replicas of Khan's mistress sat quietly in a guarded parapet, weaving the Khan's gestating baby from silken spider webs the color of night.

From there, he traveled west, over the Bridge of Sighs, to the Unborn Land. There, he met all the various future selves of Khan's progeny—both male and female—that he or she might one day become.

He briefly dallied on the banks of the River of Blood, and rode the backs of the manphibian rodents that slumber deep beneath the coagulating river, where they can hibernate for months at a time, eventually producing a rare, protein-rich, clear liquid from their multitudinous tear ducts, which the infant will imbibe when he or she at last enters the world without.

He saw the immense man-devouring flowers of Langerhans through a bamboo telescope, but knew enough not to venture too close, due to the warning of the All-Frog, an omnipotent, bloated beast that lay on its back atop a throne of miscarried fetuses, forever predicting certain doom for the inner world on an hourly basis, his croaking prophecies often escaping through the medulla oblongata and floating upwards into the dreaming brain of Khan's mistress.

Messr Polo swam with the lamia of the inner sea, wrestled with the prehistoric reptiles in the Land of Unshadow just beneath the central sun, and scaled the onyx cages within the Arena of Pain, but despite these and other near-misses with death, Polo managed to escape to the outer world eight months later, hidden within a hair follicle of Khan's newborn baby. The seer practiced his magics, returning Polo to his original size. Polo then related all of what you have learned here today, and so much more. These and other adventures are delineated in far greater detail in Polo's journal, *Being the Adventures of Messr Marco Polo in the Inner World of the Womb of Kublai Khan's Lady, the Fair Xanadu Khan.*

THE FETUS WHO SURVIVED HIS MOTHER'S UNTIMELY DEATH

On January 15, 1947, the body of twenty-two year old Elizabeth Short (later to be known as The Black Dahlia) was found in a lot on the corner of 39th and Norton Avenue in the Leimert Park section of Los Angeles. Having been impregnated by Norman Chandler, the publisher of the *Los Angeles Times*, she naturally became the target of a mob hit. Chandler ordered his henchman Bugsy Siegel to take Short for a little ride, which ended with the young woman's body being bisected and her unborn child ripped from her womb.

A local secret society of Theosophical magicians led by Manly P. Hall of The Philosophical Society (located at 3910 Los Feliz Blvd. in L.A., not far from the scene of the crime) immediately recognized the occult significance of this blood sacrifice, and wished to retrieve the fetus from Siegel, believing it to be infused with magical powers. Funded by a cabal of rabbis located in the Dead Sea Desert, a team of alchemists made up of Manly P. Hall (founder of The Philosophical Research Society), John Huston (the director of *The Maltese Falcon*, *The Treasure of the Sierra Madre*, *The Man Who Would Be King*, and other classic films), and George Hodel (an influential physician based in L.A., who specialized in sexually transmitted diseases and performed illegal abortions on behalf of politicians and other prominent businessmen on the side) planned a raid on Siegel's heavily fortified Hill Mansion in Beverly Hills, and murdered Siegel on the night of June 20, 1947 with the help of a U.S. Military M1 Carbine provided by their masters in the Middle East.

After the dark deed was complete, the trio fled back to the underground vaults beneath The Philosophical Research Society and resurrected the fetus, imbuing it with life once more. Though the magicians wished to manipulate this powerful fetus to take control of the world, they didn't count on the progeny of The Black Dahlia retaining the conscience of his mother and betraying the Society at the last second, foiling their iniquitous goals for world domination. Some say the living fetus still stalks the night-shrouded streets of Los Angeles to this day, avenging the random hurts and mutilations and murders of abused women the city over. They say the thought of his mother is never far from his fetal mind. He can sometimes be seen standing on the corner of 39th and Norton, motionless, contemplating a past forever lost to him and mourning a mother forever out of reach.

IN UTERO PREGNANCY

There have been cases, some of them documented and reported extensively in reputable medical journals, in which one's baby will somehow become pregnant while in the womb. In turn, *that* baby might become pregnant and so on: embryos within embryos, resembling living Russian dolls. *In Utero* pregnancy is believed to be a form of parthenogenesis. How this process can occur within humans is still not known. The condition is rare, however, so new mothers need not worry about it too much. It occurs in only 0.8% of females in North America, 0.14% in South America, 0.15% in Central America. Only two cases have been reported in the Arctic Circle within the past 100 years. It has never been known to occur with small animals or insects.

CERAMIC BABIES

People who can't have children will go to extreme lengths in order to attain them, even going so far as to create simulacrums. We've already discussed such beings as golems, tulpas, and the like. However, we have not yet discussed the Ceramic Baby of Bluff Park.

On October 25, 2007, sculptor Matt Wendel, using an esoteric mixture of ceramics and certain hermetic resins found only in the Far East, created a sixteen-foot-tall bright yellow baby that he chose to display in the Ella Reid Rose Garden of the famous Long Beach Museum of Art in Long Beach, California. The Gallery is located on Ocean Boulevard in a historic area that has a world-class—and, therefore, highly *expensive*—view of the Pacific Ocean. Dozens of Craftsmen-era homes face the Museum as well as the exhibit in question, titled by Wendel, simply, *Child.*

A twin of the sculpture, this one colored a bright red, went on display on the very same day at the Werby/Gatov Gallery on the campus of CSU Long Beach only a few miles away. Though the red sculpture elicited no controversy whatsoever, its yellow twin was not so fortunate. The highly conservative residents of the Bluff Park Historic District initiated a petition to have the baby removed, due to the fact that it was naked—and therefore "offensive."

In the 11-7-07 edition of *District Magazine*, Melinda Rooney, the person who started the petition, was quoted by journalist Theo Douglas as saying, "This is a historic neighborhood and it's totally out of character in a historic neighborhood. It totally offends it. The whole neighborhood is going berserk."

Meanwhile, seventy-year-old Elizabeth Handley had this to say: "Everyone's interpretation of art is different. That's what we keep telling ourselves. My opinion is, I don't like the color. I do believe in art and I believe in this art. But it's not appropriate for the neighborhood."

This violent controversy continued to snowball, finally peaking on November 10, 2007. Late in the afternoon, at around 5:00 P.M., the giant yellow baby uprooted itself from its massive square pedestal, kicked its way through the museum's landscaping, then stomped across Ocean Boulevard during rush hour traffic, miraculously causing no damage to any of the oncoming cars or injuries to the drivers and passengers (though traffic was jammed for a while as lookie-loos stopped and stared at the sculpture's sudden rampage).

According to witnesses, the baby crushed Melinda Rooney's historic house with its right fist, plucked out the crabby woman as if she were a plastic monkey in a barrel, then squeezed her head off and dropped the mutilated body on the front lawn. Seconds later, Elizabeth Handley hobbled out of her house with the help of a metal walker in order to see what all the hubbub was about. The child turned its bitter, pained expression on the woman, then slammed its golden foot into her fragile back and squished her into the front lawn with its massive heel until her spine was heard to crack in two by shocked passersby. Several other signers of the petition were ripped to shreds that evening, after which the baby returned to its temporary home on the pedestal located in the luxurious Ella Reid Rose Garden.

The yellow baby was briefly taken into custody by the local police, until its red twin uprooted itself from the campus of CSU Long Beach, stomped across town at around 9:00 P.M., then crashed through the walls of the Long Beach Police Department, releasing its sibling from the massive iron chains in which the law enforcement officers had bound the fussy creature. Though Homeland Security officers stationed at the nearby Long Beach Port, along with brave members of the U.S. Coast Guard, joined forces with local police to halt this rampage, nothing seemed capable of destroying either of the giant infants.

The pair were last seen heading into the Pacific Ocean together at around midnight, hand-in-hand, perhaps intent on finding a quiet place somewhere within the whispering ocean where they could be free to be themselves without worrying about the persecution of little minds and—worse yet—little hearts.

As could be expected, Matt Wendel was questioned by the authorities, but he insisted he had nothing to do with the sudden sentience exhibited by his creations. Some say he programmed the monsters to destroy those who reacted negatively to his art, while others believe that a random electrical storm on the night of November 6th somehow granted the statues a freakish and anomalous simulacrum of human consciousness. Others blame the contents of a mysterious fog that rolled in off the Pacific Ocean only hours before the rampage. Some say the U.S. Navy was testing experimental chemical-biological warfare gases just off the coast that night, and the testing grew out of control, with unforeseen effects. Subsequent attempts by *District Magazine* and other local publications to attain Freedom of Information records regarding these experiments have, predictably, been denied on the grounds that releasing such documents would threaten National Security. This reticence on the part of the military has fueled the bizarre conspiracy theories that swirl around such mysteries.

Perhaps the truth will never be known about that strange night. All that can be known is this: When you're wide awake at two in the morning wishing you'd never gotten pregnant in the first place, just think about how many people want to have babies and can't . . . people so deranged by their failure to procreate that they turn to forbidden black magicks and hermetic, Luciferian formulae to simulate what only the wisdom of God can grant: the sacred ability to create human life.

Wendel's children, no matter where they are right now, no doubt wish they had been allowed to remain as unformed clay that could neither feel pain nor commit it so casually upon others.

The moral is the same that Dr. Baron Von Frankenstein and Prometheus before him learned: The Natural way is the Best and Only way.

THE COMPRACHICOS

Beware the Comprachicos, a band of wandering gypsies who plague every corner of this earth. They are not bound to any one particular country. Reports of their iniquities crop up in folklore from continent to continent all throughout recorded history. They are, according to those whose lives have been destroyed by their evil, traders in stolen fetuses and newborn children. It is said that they kidnap women around their thirtieth week of pregnancy and forcibly remove the almost-grown fetuses from the womb in a manner most unspeakable, often leaving the mother to die. These gypsies practice certain unlawful surgical arts, whereby they carve the living flesh of these children and transform them into monstrous clowns and jesters. The children are then accepted as members of the tribe and forced to perform in gypsy carnivals; many of them no doubt grow old and die without ever knowing their true origins or the devastated and loving parents from whom they had been stolen. Beware the Comprachicos, ladies. Beware.

THE STRANGE CASE OF THE TRANSPARENCY BABY

One case that came across our desk in the fall of 1999 was very unorthodox indeed. An English teacher at UC Santa Cruz made a transparency of his child's ultrasound and projected the image on a whiteboard to make a rhetorical point about the significance of visual images in our "post-postmodern culture." Inexplicably, while the teacher was lecturing about the work of Jean Baudrillard, the image turned its head to observe the students, then shocked everyone in the room by peeling itself off the whiteboard and willing itself into three dimensions.

The image has since gained its own independent life separate from the fetus that spawned it—or, rather, the *image* of the fetus that spawned it. Flesh slowly formed around the sentient image, and the child matured like any other newborn infant. Over the years, it has grown into a healthy and otherwise normal eight-year-old girl. She has been welcomed by the English teacher and his family as a proud addition to their household. All their friends and relatives are under the impression that this "transparency" is a twin of the daughter to whom the teacher's wife gave birth; the family simply allows everyone to think this for convenience sake. This transparency baby has more than proved her worth, surpassing even her own sister in various unexpected ways. She's superior in athletics, mathematics, reading comprehension, history and the sciences. In fact, many of her elementary school teachers say she's one of the brightest and liveliest students they've ever laid eyes on.

SHAKESPEARE CREATED PREGNANCY

According to the respected literary scholar and historian Harold Bloom, the biological process of pregnancy did not exist in humans until William Shakespeare created it in one of his famous plays, circa 1600. The first reference to pregnancy in a Shakespeare play is Act 4, Scene 5 of *Hamlet* (1600). Before that moment, humans had not yet conceived of the notion of procreating via sexual intercourse. Only the legendary bard of Stratford-upon-Avon could dream up such a poetic and yet utilitarian process. Bloom also claims that the Caesarean birth was created by Shakespeare for his famous tragedy *Macbeth* in 1603, despite the fact traditional history states that Julius Caesar, for whom the Caesarian is named, lived well over 1600 years *before* Shakespeare. Of course, traditional historians don't understand that Julius Caesar did not exist as a historical figure until Shakespeare created him as the titular character of his famous 1599 tragedy. How Shakespeare's history could be retroactive is still not known (though it may have something to do with the rarefied field of hyperdimensional physics). Bloom sets forth various theories, each of them eminently reasonable, in his voluminous study published by Riverhead Books, *Shakespeare: The Invention of the Human.*

On a related note, reading Shakespeare aloud to your fetus can also reverse breech births. Bloom discovered that the best plays to read aloud for this purpose are as follows:

Love's Labour's Lost (1595), *A Midsummer Night's Dream* (1595), *Hamlet* (1600), *Measure For Measure* (1603), *Macbeth* (1603), and—maybe—*The Tempest* (1610). Bloom is hesitant to include this last play, for various obscure reasons, amongst Shakespeare's official *pharmacopeia.*

BLACK HOLE SYNDROME

There have only been six reported cases of this syndrome in the last sixty years. In this tragic syndrome, a black hole no larger than the head of a pin can form spontaneously within the brain of the infant. Within seconds, the infant will then fold in upon itself and be sucked into the center of the black hole, leaving no trace of itself behind. (Unlike in other rare conditions such as Quantum Singularity Syndrome, however, the parents will indeed remember that the child did exist at one time.) What happens to the child after the black hole has taken him or her is unknown, but eminent physicists like Stephen Hawking have speculated that the infant's body is most likely stretched to infinite lengths before being torn to shreds and ejected into a sea of quantum foam, through which his or her pulpy remains will then drift for an indefinite period of time, tumbling into an endless series of different universes, all of them far stranger and younger than our own.

QUANTUM SINGULARITY SYNDROME

Here's another rare condition you shouldn't worry about, ladies. Sometimes, in 0.0001% of the infant population, a quantum singularity can form in the general vicinity of the infant, suck the infant out of this space-time continuum, and consequently wipe even the *memory* of the infant out of existence. Reality will then snap back several seconds before the moment of conception, and the whole timeline will begin all over again. This time, however, the child might not even be conceived. Or if it is, it could be a completely different child.

This syndrome is nothing to worry about, ladies, because you won't have any memory of the child ever having existed in the first place. Without the invention of the extremely sophisticated SuperConducting Super Collider at the University of Texas at Austin, we would never have had the capability of knowing that this syndrome even existed.

The SuperConducting Super Collider, of course, is a ring particle accelerator built in 1993, with financial backing from Harvard, in order to create a Higgs boson, a scalar elementary particle once thought to be merely hypothetical.

SCS[4)]

Those of you ladies who only have half an ovary might be asking yourself, "Will this affect my pregnancy?" The truthful answer is: It's a possibility, but an unlikely one. Having half an ovary can indeed lead to the birth of half a child, but only .05% of cases are affected in this curious way. In 1972, for example, Thomas Flanagan of Cleveland, Ohio, was literally born split down the middle. The doctors declared this event a medical miracle. Thankfully, Mr. Flanagan has gone on to lead a normal life as a prominent mathematician. You see, when half of one's organs are absent, one's remaining organs pick up the slack, as it were, and perform 200% of the work. Children born with SCS will usually lead healthy, productive lives, as long as they are allowed to develop normally. Do *not* think of SCS as a disability. For a child born with SCS, he/she knows no other life. To him/her, living with half a body will be

4) Symmetrical Child Syndrome (SCS), so-called because the first known beneficiary of this condition, a man named Darrell Travin—born in Madison, Wisconsin in 1898—ended up in an exhibit in P.T. Barnum's Circus and was subsequently dubbed by Mr. Barnum "The Amazing Symmetrical Man." Part of the show involved Mr. Travin leaning up against a wall, creating the illusion that half of him was stuck inside it. His beloved partner, known as Tululu the Bearded Lady, would also prop him up against a mirror and tell the audience he was the first "perfectly symmetrical" human being. Mr. Travin would then engage in witty banter with the Bearded Lady, often insulting her in clever ways, to which Tululu would respond with sarcastic comments like, "Don't talk out of the side of your mouth!" Mr. Travin was a very popular attraction at P.T. Barnum's Circus for over a decade. He lived until 1931, at which time his body was donated to a hospital in his native Wisconsin.

completely normal. In fact, in 1993, the aforementioned Mr. Flanagan married a non-SCS woman and had a child totally unaffected by SCS. He published a celebrated book about fractal geometry in 2001 and has won several awards in his field. A film about the life of Mr. Flanagan, to be produced by Steven Spielberg, directed by Ron Howard, and starring Tom Hanks, is currently in development even as this is being written.

ULTRA SOUND

You might undergo an ultra sound at some point in the second trimester. What you might see is an X-ray-like photograph of a tiny, skeletal baby. This is bad news, mothers. It indicates that your child will be born *without flesh*. Sad as it is to say, if your ultra sound appears this way, we at *The Expectant Mother Disinformation Handbook* recommend an immediate abortion. Don't delay, ladies. You don't want to give birth to a walking skeleton-child, do you? His or her life will be unlivable in normal society, except on October 31st. No normal person could live off a single night's wages posing as a Halloween door decoration, could they? Surely not. Your path is clear, ladies. Now go do the right thing.

IN UTERO INTERNET CONNECTION—ARE THERE DANGERS?

In recent years, it has become more and more popular to implant subcutaneous wires into the developing fetus that allow him or her to communicate with the mother from inside the womb via the internet. The first *in utero* email was sent out at 02:14 A.M. on March 16th, 2018. Below is a reproduction of this historic message:

From: fetus <yourfetus@gmail.com>
Sent: Friday, March 16, 2018 2:14 AM
To: expectantmotherdisinfo@gmail.com

Subject: Why Did You Bring Me Into This World?

Hi Mom,

It's getting warmer and warmer in here by the minute. Need air conditioning. Do you mind if I punch a hole in your stomach, bitch?

Messages like this can be disturbing to the mother, and have led to many mothers blocking their fetuses from their private email accounts after only a few days. One mother we know woke up one morning to find seventy-six email messages sent by the fetus. Each one was a variation on the same complaint: “I never wanted to be born in the first place.” We find this to be despicable behavior, inexcusable even for a fetus who has not yet been taught basic manners. We recommend holding off wiring your fetus into cyberspace until he or she has been trained in proper internet etiquette. If you’re interested, we here at *The Expectant Mother Disinformation Handbook* offer a wide variety of courses for *in utero* internet etiquette training on-line at <www.inuterointernetettiquettetraining.com>. Other, more positive, emails from fetuses can be found in our companion book, *Messages from the Womb: The Miracle of Communication.*

VACCINES—ARE THEY HEALTHY?

Many people are wondering if childhood vaccines have any connection to autism, Sudden Infant Death Syndrome (SIDS) or Spontaneous Infant Combustion Syndrome (SICS). This latter syndrome is relatively obscure, and usually results in the infant suddenly and unexpectedly bursting into flame at around three months of age. In one case, only a singed pair of diapers and a small pile of gray ash was left behind in the crib. Though a mysterious phenomenon, scientists are trying their best to get a handle on it. Some doctors believe SICS is brought on by overexposure to mercury, and since traces of mercury can be found in almost all childhood vaccines, a small minority of doctors are vigorously attempting to make a correlation between these two facts. We here at *The Expectant Mother Disinformation Handbook* elect to keep an open mind on this subject. Millions of children are injected with mercury-laden vaccines every year, but only a small percentage of these children end up bursting into flame at three months of age. For this reason, some conclude there must be another cause for SICS. Nonetheless, an aversion to childhood vaccines is growing among the U.S. population. More and more Christians seem to connect SICS with these questionable vaccines. We know of at least one case in which a mother claims that her recently deceased infant, a victim of SICS, wrote her an email from The Other Side. The message contained a single sentence: "Thanks for letting those Nazis inject me with mercury, you whore." We can only conclude this is merely an urban legend, as there have never been any proven email communications from beyond the grave.

IS NEIL GAIMAN DANGEROUS TO THE FETUS?[5)]

Many occult experts, including the honorable Christian activist group called Return to Order, have uncovered a number of disturbing subliminal messages embedded in Neil Gaiman's books (as well as in their film and television derivatives) that are clearly Luciferian in nature. The knowledgeable members of Return to Order, whose intimate and firsthand involvement with secret occult orders make them leading authorities on the subject, have determined that reading Gaiman's books (particularly *Good Omens*, a degenerate fantasy novel co-authored with the late Terry Pratchett) to one's developing fetus might desensitize the child to the tools and language of Satanism, while also leaving the doorway of the child's mind wide open to New-Age-style deception. What could be worse than that? Even the dreaded Quantum Singularity Syndrome would be preferable to such an insidious and hopeless fate.

5) It's important to note at this point that some of the chapters in *The Expectant Mother Disinformation Handbook* were inspired by questions that originally came to us via the *EMDH* discussion board on the internet. We thought it would be wise to address some of the most representative questions in the pages of this book for the benefit of our readers. Keep in mind that being concerned about your child's welfare doesn't end with birth. We're not trying to disturb you in any way, of course, but your biggest troubles are just now beginning. We hope that answering these questions in the following pages will help put your mind at ease, as some of these concerns can often cause stress during pregnancy—and stress is something all of us ladies (whether pregnant or not!) should try our best to avoid.

In order to fully understand the true nature of the occult world, a group of devoted Christians—who may or may not be connected to Return to Order—recently decided to hold a séance, invoke a demon known only as Belphegor, and ask the infernal being if it was acquainted with Gaiman's work. Allegedly, the demon confirmed that it was indeed the main source of Gaiman's "creativity." Mind you, no one associated with *The Expectant Mother Disinformation Handbook* attended this particular séance, at least not to our knowledge, but informed sources provided us with all the details one would need to reach a sensible conclusion regarding this subject. The details were juicy. Juicy and damning. Understand: There's no place on God's green Earth that Gaiman can hide from divine judgment. You can take that to the bank.

The founding fathers of Return to Order beseech all good Christians to sign a petition banning the recent television adaptation of *Good Omens* from our sanctified living rooms. For more information about their righteous crusade against the endless blasphemies churned out by the Hollywood sin factory, please visit: <https://www.returntoorder.org/petition/tell-netflix-to-cancel-blasphemous-good-omens/>.

PRENATAL EXPOSURE TO FICTION—IS IT TOO SOON?

Reading to the child while he/she is still in your womb has been known to cause negative, unintended consequences. Some of these consequences might affect the child his or her entire life. Fiction, in particular, is contraindicated. *By no means should the fetus be exposed to fiction in the second trimester*. At this stage in his/her development, the fetus is very susceptible to certain ideas that are phantasmagoric in nature, and thus disconnected from reality.

In one case, a child who was subjected to 140 consecutive readings of Lewis Carroll's *Alice in Wonderland* later developed into a disturbed teenager with a tenuous grip on reality, who to this day suffers from secondary anxiety and delusions of persecution. Another child, who shall remain nameless here, developed a pathological fear of being squashed by a falling two-story house after repeated exposure to L. Frank Baum's *The Wizard of Oz*. To this day, he leaves his house only with great difficulty; alas, this person is equally reluctant to remain *inside* his house for any great length of time, due to the fact that he fears his home will be picked up off the ground by a mysterious meteorological phenomena and dropped on an unsuspecting passerby. These twin fears have led to a most unusual disorder that perfectly melds agoraphobia and claustrophobia at the same time, rendering his daily life untenable. A third child, normal in all other respects, refused to learn how to drive a car for fear of losing control and slamming it into a horse-pond, à la Mr. Toad of Kenneth Grahame's seductive fable, *The Wind in the Willows*.

What more evidence does a responsible parent need? If you're still unconvinced, we recommend visiting the website of Dr. Thomas Radecki's National Coalition on the Connection between Mental Disturbance and Fantasy Fiction (NCCBMDFF). Dr. Radecki's noble researchers can back up the preceding facts with unassailable scientific evidence. All of their sources are reliable and based on the latest, cutting edge research in child rearing. See www.nccbmdff.org.

SHOULD I ALLOW MY FETUS TO HAVE PLAY DATES?

As long as you're certain the parents are responsible people, we at *The Expectant Mother Disinformation Handbook* encourage having your child visit other developing fetuses in their wombs in order to strengthen their social skills. If the purpose of the play date is to watch movies, make sure these films are strictly G-rated. At this stage, the fetuses are too sensitive for stronger fare. And make certain any electronics they plan to use (such as a blu-ray player or an X-Box) do not come into direct contact with the amniotic fluid in the womb of your child's little playmate. Numerous miscarriages have been brought about due to the mishandling of entertainment centers in the womb. Recently, a woman in Los Feliz, CA, was killed when her child somehow got loose from his umbilical cord and plugged it into a wall socket that had been embedded in the womb so the child could watch Nickelodeon during his downtime. We feel such tragedies are easily avoidable. Teach your fetus and his/her friends proper womb safety when handling all electronic equipment, and the play date should go smoothly.

IF I GET BITTEN BY A VAMPIRE WHILE PREGNANT, WILL MY CHILD BECOME A VAMPIRE AS WELL?

Not necessarily! There have been recorded cases of females, transformed into vampires, giving birth to human children. It all depends on when the attack occurs. If you are bitten during your third trimester, for example, the chances of giving birth to a human child are quite high indeed. According to the *Malleus Maleficarum*, in 1894, a woman who lived in a village known as Grautz, located in the treacherous Harz Mountains of Germany, was impregnated by her husband on her wedding night, then attacked by a vampire later that same evening. Fortunately, the woman escaped her attacker and found refuge in a local monastery. Due to persistent prayers, the monks were able to help the mother deliver a perfectly healthy human child. Alas, seconds after birth, the monks were then forced to plant a wooden stake through the mother's heart, cut off her head and burn it to a fine gray ash. However, the child went on to live a healthy and normal life.

If you are bitten by a vampire, do not call 911. The police are not equipped or trained to handle situations like this. Make sure you contact a local Catholic church immediately and request further assistance. There is no known cure for vampirism, but an experienced exorcist can help you deliver a child completely devoid of vampiric symptoms. Once bitten, ladies, remember this piece of advice above all: Though it's too late for you, your child can still be saved.

THE POTENTIAL DANGERS OF 'BRANE WORLDS

Various women will often approach us at conferences and ask us the following question: "Is it possible for my child to fall off the mattress while sleeping, roll under the bed, then tumble through a temporary portal and end up trapped in another dimension?"

The answer is: "Yes, ladies, of course it's possible!" Recent breakthroughs in quantum physics have uncovered the existence of 'brane worlds (short for "membrane worlds"), dimensions that exist *between* dimensions. Proponents of a hyperdimensional model of physics—"string theory" is one such theory—postulate the existence of ten or more dimensions higher than our own. Wormholes, rips in space-time, can form spontaneously anywhere in this or any other universe . . . *including your child's bedroom.*

If such a portal opens, and your child goes through it, you will need to impress upon your husband or Special Partner the importance of entering this portal and exploring the potentially mind-altering terrain of the 'brane world in which your child has been lost. Tie heavy rope around the waist of your husband or Special Partner and help him/her enter the portal while you stay behind and keep a strong grip on the other side of this tether. You don't want your husband (or Special Partner) and child spinning off into the hellish void before you can pull them both back through the portal!

The second your husband (or Special Partner) has successfully located your child amidst the floating heads and melting-watch-landscapes, you must then pull them both back in before the portal closes indefinitely. *A portal that closes cannot be reopened*, so time is of the essence.

Once the family has been reunited, stay well away from the portal and contact Ron Pandolphi at the Central Intelligence Agency. He will be interested.

WHITHER GO THE WORRY?

All pregnant women worry about the same exact issues, no matter the location or even the century. One of the most common questions we get here at *The Expectant Mother Disinformation Handbook* is: "Once the child is born, will I stop worrying?"

The simple answer is, "YES!" You will have serious concerns, of course, but you will not *worry*. Some of you may not believe that. "But where could such a tremendous amount of worry possibly *go*?" you're no doubt wondering. Well, we here at *The Expectant Mother Disinformation Handbook* have an answer to that question.

The worry simply drains out of your body through your pores, forming a viscous black liquid known to scientists as Noctril, which then dissipates upon contact with air and transforms into a gaseous substance that is harmless to humans but can cause wort-like blemishes on cold-blooded creatures such as geckos and salamanders. From these blemishes are derived tonics and herbs that native cultures have used medicinally for centuries to treat stress and headaches. Modern pharmaceutical companies have synthesized these chemicals into many beneficial products such as aspirin and Ibuprofen. So you see, ladies . . . from your worry comes the cure for worry.

WHAT IF I'M POOR, UNDERAGE, AND CAN'T AFFORD TO RAISE A CHILD?

Easy: Pretend the situation isn't happening. Recent studies performed by the prestigious Stanford Research Institute have proven that the human mind has a remarkable amount of control over physical matter. By wishing it to be so, you may induce the embryo's spontaneous disappearance (not an abortion, God forbid, which we would not recommend except under extreme circumstances), thus solving your dilemma once and for all. These SRI experiments indicate that, when you concentrate your mental energies hard enough and long enough on a specific outcome, your wishes do indeed come true.

However, this manipulation is a two-way street. If the embryo wishes for *your* disappearance hard enough and long enough, before you get around to doing the same to him or her, you might vanish and leave your embryo behind. This is why it's important to get the drop on him or her as fast as possible, if that's your wish, or (conversely) to keep the embryo well-fed and as happy as possible. According to the aforementioned SRI studies, one embryo was so displeased with his mother that he wished her into a nearby cornfield, where very unpleasant events occurred to her. It's not a cheerful topic, so we shan't delve any deeper into it in these pages.[6]

6) Suffice it to say the embryo continued to develop outside the mother's body and grew into a malevolent but otherwise healthy child.

THINKING NEGATIVE THOUGHTS

Given what you've read in the previous entry, you might be asking yourself the next logical question: If the mind really has such a powerful control over physical matter, what about *subconscious* thoughts? Let's face it: All of us sometimes entertain negative thoughts, even when we don't really mean them. In a moment of frustration or exhaustion, we might even wish harm upon a loved one. Some of us experience such extreme pain and nausea during pregnancy that we might briefly think something along the line of: "Oh, I wish I'd never gotten pregnant in the first place," or "I sure wish I'd miscarriage just so my life could go back to normal again."

These are dangerous thoughts, ladies. You must not entertain them even for a second, unless you wish to assassinate your child. According to the Stanford Research Institute, most miscarriages are induced by the subconscious desires of the mother. Remember, ladies: If you have a miscarriage, 99.9% of the time it's because *you yourself* brought it about by a fleeting, careless wish. Therefore, ladies, your will power must be strong at all times. Once a wish has entered your mind as a fully formed thought it could be too late for your child.

Too late.

WHAT IF VARIOUS OBJECTS AND PETS START DISAPPEARING AROUND THE NEIGHBORHOOD? IS MY CHILD WISHING THEM AWAY?

Could be. Is your child, still safe in your womb, threatened by the environment that awaits him or her in the outside world? We recommend visiting your obstetrician and having the OBGYN ask the fetus a series of pointed questions. Psychologically, fetuses don't do well with abstract concepts at this stage, so it's best to be as literal and as direct as possible. Ask the fetus, "Are you so threatened by the outside world that awaits you once you're born that you're attempting to make it disappear one piece at a time?" If the fetus says, "Yes, I am," assure the child he or she has nothing to fear. The world is a beautiful place, and he or she will learn to appreciate that once he or she's gotten used to it. Then politely ask the child to retrieve the missing objects and pets from the cornfield, or wherever he or she has hidden them, so that life can go on as usual.

You must make the fetus understand that he or she is not the center of the universe, and therefore must take into consideration the wants and needs of others. There are various ways to accomplish this, the best of which we will cover in the very next chapter.

HOW DO I CONVINCE MY CHILD THAT HE OR SHE IS NOT THE CENTER OF THE UNIVERSE?

A difficult dilemma for sure, but by no means an impossible one for dedicated and sincere parents such as yourselves. One of the best methods is to insert the lens of a projector into the mother's vaginal opening and transmit a series of images onto the walls of the womb using simple glass slides. These slides should depict various and sundry cultures of this diverse biosphere of ours, thus introducing the child to a complex web of multitudinous religious and philosophical beliefs, without which our world would be far less satisfying and interesting—just make sure that all of these religions and philosophies are wholly *Christian* at their core.

Multiculturalism, even if only introduced to the child via prenatal slide shows, is the ultimate cure for solipsism. Your goal as responsible post-postmodern parents is to wipe out any hint of individualism in your child. We're part of a global village—a *Christian* global village, mind you—and we have to learn to live and think and dream within its borders or not at all.

LEGAL, AS OPPOSED TO COLLOQUIAL, DEFINITION OF THE TERM "BABY DADDY"

Since the first edition of this book, a 2008 precedent-setting Supreme Court case has determined that the individual the mother was thinking about during conception is the individual who must take care of the child financially. This is determined through a "thought scanning" process developed by a private corporation called Blackwater (since renamed Academi). This non-lethal "mind reading" technique involves complex and technical methods such as water boarding, spinning and all forms of sensory deprivation. Blackwater's/Academi's accuracy rate has been extremely high, according to their own records.

Mothers should be aware of this significant shift in legal procedure before demanding child support from the biological father. We recommend having a very good lawyer teach you how to navigate through the "thought scanning" procedure in such a way that the final results benefit both you and the child, emotionally *and* financially.

IF I'M PREGNANT, SHOULD I RISK GETTING A TATTOO?

Absolutely not! In fact, if you already have tattoos you *must* remove them as soon as possible. In several infamous cases[7], tattooed women have given birth to children whose virgin flesh has been marred by the same exact tattoos inscribed upon the mother. In the eyes of *The Expectant Mother Disinformation Handbook*, this represents the most heinous form of irresponsibility on the part of a parent. If the child wishes to be tattooed when he or she is twenty-one, he or she can make that decision on his or her own (though we don't recommend it). *The parent should not make that decision for the child.* Just because you got a wee bit tipsy one night when you were sixteen and thought it'd be "cool" and "oh-so-hip" to get a Polynesian hula girl carved into your right bicep doesn't mean your child should be doomed to be delivered into God's world with the same exact image branded on his or her right bicep, does it?

According to the Pope, tattoos are nothing more or less than Lucifer's brand upon his wayward cattle, the evil residue of iniquitous minds made manifest in two dimensions. And who are we to disagree?

Res Ipsa Loquitor.

Now go do the right thing.

---

7) Examples available upon request.

MURDER OR DIVORCE

If you're not yet married when you discover that you're impregnated, you might feel as if you're being rushed into marriage. This could very well be the case. We generally encourage couples to remain together for the child's sake, even if you're miserable. You both created a life together, and now you have to live with it. Face up to your responsibilities. However, the only cases in which we sanction divorce are those in which *death* is the only other option.

So we here at *The Expectant Mother Disinformation Handbook* suggest you two love birds sit down on a quiet night before the Big Day; choose a spot next to a fireplace or a placid lake, and lay all your cards out on the table. Don't be shy of offending your partner. After all, you're a team. You can be upfront with each other. Just be honest and say, "Listen, honey, if this relationship ever disintegrates so horribly that's it's far beyond repair, let's agree right now that you won't murder me and I won't murder you. If you think you're on the verge of killing me, I'll leave right away without a single complaint. And the same will be true for me as well. Let's turn this into a bit of a game, okay? We might as well make this fun. Let's come up with a 'safe word' system. We'll each have a single word, something that's not too complicated, that we'll share with each other. If we ever utter that word during an argument, that's a specific signal to either you or me to pick up the child and leave as soon as possible because we feel we might be on the verge of a homicidal breakdown. If we go out of our way to memorize our safe word, even during a moment of mindless rage we might be able to retrieve the word from our subconscious and blurt it out before we pick up that axe and cut our loved one (or loved ones) to tiny bloody pieces. Right, hon?"

If your partner is reasonable, he or she will smile and say, "That's a swell idea, babe, I'm so glad you thought of it," after which the two of you will seal this important promise with a firm handshake. Once you've gotten the serious business out of the way in a casual and friendly manner, you can then proceed with a perfectly romantic evening.

We recommend words not normally used during high-pitched arguments, such as "effervescent" or "pluperfect," be chosen for your crucial "safe word." The alien quality of such words, retrieved from memory and uttered aloud during a heated moment of passion, helps return the speaker to his or her normal frame of mind.

DREAMS OF THE FORBIDDEN

It's very common for women to dream about acts that are now forbidden due to their pregnancy. For example, many pregnant women of our acquaintance have reported that they will dream about smoking a cigarette, or drinking alcohol, or engaging in homosexual sex, or even less savory acts (depending on the character of the woman). Most modern day psychiatrists will tell you that these dreams are perfectly okay, merely your unconscious having a bit of a harmless, cathartic romp.

We're sorry to report that *WE WON'T* say such a thing.

Recent studies performed by researchers at Columbia University have indicated that such dreams are detrimental to the child, as harmful as the actual enactment of such behavior would be in reality. Fetuses are far more sensitive than fully developed human beings and *experience your dreams right along with you*. Therefore, the next time you smoke a cigarette in your "harmless, cathartic" dream, be well aware that you're sucking in a lungful of cancer-inducing smoke for your unborn child. In this day and age, when we know so much about science, experts like us can now say definitively: *You MUST watch what you dream, ladies*. Dreams are dangerous, particularly those that violate societal strictures, and only bad can come from allowing yourself to indulge in such nonsense on a regular basis.

Eli Lilly, the manufacturers of Prozac® and other groundbreaking beneficial treatments, has now created a fast-acting dream-suppressant called Somnambulex, or

Dream-Away®, that allows you to spend your entire pregnancy unencumbered by the dreary unreality of dreams. This is a serious matter that cannot be ignored, for it's affecting more pregnant women these days than ever before. In this increasingly libertine society, every pervert once relegated to the back alleys now has the freedom to flaunt his or her private obsessions in the open, to wear them proudly on their sleeves for the express purpose of tempting others . . . impressionable young ladies such as YOU.

Sound familiar?

If so, you *MUST* seek out an obstetrician who is sensitive enough to your plight to be willing to write a nine-month-long prescription for Somnambulex. In a media-saturated environment that overtly—as well as *covertly*—encourages dreams of the forbidden, dream-suppression is more crucial for young mothers than ever before.

PRENATAL DRUGS

Stern warnings abound in this book, and for good reason. Many accidents can be avoided with minimal foreknowledge. For example: It's best to keep your prenatal drugs separate from the vitamins your husband or Special Partner takes on a regular basis. One husband of our acquaintance accidentally swallowed some of his wife's prenatal vitamins and ended up sharing some of his wife's symptoms, such as nausea and severe cramping. At first, the doctors believed that the husband was merely suffering from sympathetic pains due to his close proximity with his wife. Alas, this was not the case. *The husband had been impregnated by the prenatal drugs.* As if that wasn't startling enough, the husband then acquired a taste for the drugs and became addicted to them.

Strangely, both husband and wife ended up giving birth on the same exact day: one boy each. A few months later, the husband overdosed on the prenatal drugs (which he was still taking regularly even after the birth), went mad as a result, and kidnapped both boys. With a year-long-supply of prenatal drugs under his arm, the husband fled to the jungles of South America to join The Wild Boys insurgency—at least according to the scrawled note he left behind.

Nobody has seen him or the boys since.

CHOOSING A WEDDING DATE

To this day, historians are confused as to the events of December 18, 1941. Why did Adolf Hitler order the invasion of Moscow during the dead of winter, the worst possible time to stage a full-scale attack of this kind? Years after the end of the war, high officials in the Nazi Party claimed this wrongheaded strategy was brought about by Hitler's fanatical dependence on his personal astrologer. Hitler would follow his astrologer's dictums without question, no matter how dubious the advice.

Some couples have a hard time choosing a day to be married. (Needless to say, if you're not already married it's imperative to do so soon for the benefit of the coming child.) Understandably, couples wish this date to bear some special significance: to coincide with a particular date in history, perhaps, or to fall on the anniversary of their parents' wedding day. Some even resort to paying so-called "psychics" to pick the "perfect date" for them.

Listen, don't be too obsessed with choosing "the perfect day." The only "perfect day" is the one that you create for yourselves.

We here at *The Expectant Mother Disinformation Handbook* suggest taking a lesson from Adolf Hitler: *Do not rely on astrologers*. They are Satan worshippers in disguise. Since Hitler ended up barbecued to a hollow husk beneath the streets of Berlin[8], it's clear to us and any other

8) Of course, some irrational conspiracy theorists insist that it was actually Hitler's doppelganger who was burned in the conflagration, while the real Fuhrer fled Germany on his JU290A6—his special high pressure personal

rational human being that the advice of astrologers isn't exactly reliable. So now let's take our first piece of advice one step further: When choosing a wedding date, simply ask yourselves, "What would Hitler's astrologer have done?" and do the exact opposite.

Picking a wedding day is much like any other worthwhile endeavor in life. Sometimes the practical outweighs the ideal.

---

transport plane—six days after his fifty-sixth birthday. They say he was accompanied by Martin Bormann, Hermann Fegelein, Eva Braun, and his favorite German Shepard, Blondi. They also say he and his inner circle took off from the IKG200 Base at *Ainring Hoerching* Airfield late that evening, alighting in Barcelona, Spain the very next day, and that General Francisco Franco assisted the group in their eventual escape to Colonia Dignidad, a Nazi stronghold in South America that exists to this day. If you wish to rot your brain, see the article "The Flight of the Wolf" by Gregory Douglas in the winter 1992 issue of *The Military Advisor* (Vol. IV, No. I) for more nonsense of this kind, though we urge you not to waste your time with such trash.

MUPPETITIS

The vast majority of Americans assume a "muppet" to be an imaginary creature invented by a famous puppeteer named Jim Henson for two popular American TV shows aimed at children: *Sesame Street* and *The Muppet Show*. This assumption could not be further from the truth. Jim Henson was a humanitarian who created gainful employment for adolescents and young adults suffering from a rare disease called "Muppetitis."

Dr. Thackery T. Lambshead was the first to catalogue this disease back in 1921, though most of the London medical community discredited his findings almost as soon as his controversial monograph was published. Today, the medical community recognizes Dr. Lambshead as a genius who was decades ahead of his time. The disease he discovered, believed by biologists to be caused by a rare genetic mutation, causes a child's arteries and blood to harden while the bones soften and congeal into a whitish protoplasm that resembles cotton stuffing, the kind one might find inside an average teddy bear. This protoplasm does not kill the child, though it may cause him or her to be dangerously fragile, prone to fatal injuries that would be minor to other children. The symptoms of Muppetitis share some similarities with neurofibromatosis, the affliction that plagued John Merrick, also known as "The Elephant Man." Dr. Lambshead discovered that this rare disease causes the child's features to distort into animal-like visages. Children afflicted in this way have resembled frogs, pigs, bears, and even forms of sea life like shrimps (and/or prawns).

Their level of intelligence is, for the most part, unaffected by the illness. Some of these children are far more advanced than those unaffected by this disease. For example, there's a high rate of talented musicians and singers among the afflicted community, though no pathologist or biologist can explain why this should be.

Thanks to their benefactor, Jim Henson, a whole generation of these afflicted children have gone on to achieve great acclaim as movie and television stars. To deflect any unwanted media publicity that might have been generated by widespread public knowledge of their affliction, and above all to protect their coveted privacy, for decades this unusually modest stable of actors have allowed everyone to believe that they were the creation of Mr. Henson alone. While we respect their position, we at *The Expectant Mother Disinformation Handbook* believe these people deserve some applause for overcoming so many hardships in their lives. The more the general public is aware of the true nature of the Muppets' affliction, the more that others in similar (or worse) situations might grow inspired to overcome their own illnesses and difficulties.

If you're concerned about your own child coming down with this unique disease, there are certain signs to watch out for: gradual malleability of bone structure, a diminishment in height, and an unexplainable compulsion to switch from speech to song for no apparent reason. If these three symptoms occur in close proximity to each other, we recommend taking your child to a doctor immediately. If your child tests positive for Muppetitis, you should then call the Jim Henson Studios to see if your child is eligible to apply for a full-time position with benefits. The main information line at the Jim Henson Studios is: 213-960-4096.

DAVIES'S DISEASE

There's almost no end to the horrible mishaps that might befall your child before he or she is even born. Though it's disturbing to hear about such morbid tragedies, think about it this way: The more possibilities you're aware of, the better equipped you will be to deal with them if they occur. The purpose of this handbook is to illuminate, not frighten. If only Frank and Lenore Davies had had access to the type of book you hold in your hand right now!

The disturbing case of Mr. and Mrs. Davies is spoken of only in whispers amongst the biological community. In 1974 Lenore Davies gave birth to an infant whose deformity was so unusual, it has since been christened "Davies's Disease" by medical experts. This child was born with fangs and claws, rather like a feral animal, and immediately developed a taste for human flesh. The child fatally maimed the doctor who delivered it into this world, then escaped from the hospital and proceeded to engage in a homicidal rampage that left dozens injured or killed. This onslaught was not stopped until Mr. Frank Davies led a police taskforce into the storm drains of Los Angeles and confronted the creature in its subterranean lair.

Medical experts determined that the deformity was due to contaminated fertility drugs, all of which were banned once the incident reached the newspapers. Alas, this action was far too late for many families. Babies with similar deformities continued to be born all around the country.

After the death of his child, Mr. Frank Davies lost his

mind and convinced himself that these children represented the next evolutionary step of mankind, rather than weird biological mistakes. He formed a terrorist group for the express purpose of protecting these murderous little creatures from being eliminated by the government. Fortunately, Mr. Davies's interference did not stop a military taskforce from rounding up the diseased infants and shipping them to an internment camp located on a desert island, where they quickly escaped and caused chaos on the mainland before being rounded up again and held indefinitely for medical study.

Mr. Frank Davies has not been seen or heard from since 1978, and no case of Davies's Disease has been reported in the United States since 1987.

THE LIMBO PERIOD

It's only fair to warn you, ladies, that around the twelfth week of pregnancy, there begins what we like to call a "limbo period" in which you will appear to be neither pregnant nor (well, how can we put this delicately?) . . . your usual slim self, shall we say?

In other words, ladies, it will not be *obvious* to the casual passerby that you're pregnant. Most people will assume, naturally, that you're lazy and letting yourself go, just another poor slob who's stuffing the Oreos down her throat while watching the latest installment of her favorite reality TV show. You can't possibly stop each of these people in the street and assure all of them, one on one, that you're actually pregnant and not just gaining weight, correct?

There are three ways of handling this dilemma: 1) Keep your palms cupped over your stomach *at all times*. This is a tried and true phatic[9] method of signaling to the average passerby—at a subliminal level—that the fat on your belly is due to an invading parasite and not an over intake of comestibles. Or, 2) Tape a sign to your back that says, I'M NOT FAT, I'M PREGNANT! Of course, human psychology being what it is, most onlookers who see such a sign taped to your back will immediately assume the opposite of what it claims. Think about it: If you saw some corpulent strumpet wearing a sign that said, I'M NOT FAT, I'M PREGNANT! you'd probably think, *Oh, dear, that poor*

9) A term created by the anthropologist Bronislaw Malinowsky in the 1920s to identify non-verbal communication techniques among tribal cultures.

slob has been stuffing Oreos down her throat while watching the latest installment of her favorite reality TV show and now she's trying to deflect attention from the sad and obvious truth with that big sign on her back. Jesus, I'm glad I'm not her. So instead, if you will really want to convince people, we at *The Expectant Mother Disinformation Handbook* suggest taking the third route: 3) Tape a sign to your back that says, I'M NOT PREGNANT, I'M FAT!

Try it tomorrow morning and just see what happens. We've never had a complaint yet.

THE SCIENCE OF INTENTION

Many young mothers who experience a great deal of discomfort during the first trimester have a tendency to partly blame the father when the pain is at its most intense. This is wrongheaded. Please, ladies, keep in mind the science of intention, also known as the Science of the Will. Professor José Laputa of Columbia University has recently released a ten-year-long study on pregnancy that has far-reaching implications. His findings indicate that women who become pregnant do so because, either consciously or unconsciously, they devoutly *wished* to be pregnant. The converse is true as well: Those women who won't (not "can't" but "*won't*") become pregnant choose this route because, either consciously or unconsciously, they *do not* wish to experience pregnancy. It's all very simple, you see.

Motivations differ from woman to woman, of course. Some women wish to become pregnant in order to prove that they're women; this is both a psychological and biological imperative. Other women, those in their teens and early twenties, wish to become pregnant in order to be taken care of, i.e., to get on welfare and be granted weekly allowances by Big Daddy Government. These sort of women often hail from broken homes in which the mother was on welfare herself, and so they can't imagine any other way to survive in this world. They are not to be blamed.

According to Professor Laputa, women who want to have a child will become pregnant no matter the circumstances surrounding them. If it's not one mate who provides the sperm, then it'll be another one down the line.

So in reality, ladies, it's not fair to expect this *particular* father to accept any of the blame at all. The situation you're experiencing right now would be happening to you in this same exact way, accompanied by pain of the *same exact* intensity, no matter who you had been with sexually. The father, you see, is the irrelevant X-factor in a situation of manifest destiny. The *motivating* force is merely your intention, your will.

This notion disturbs many women, for some reason. You can dispute Professor Laputa's findings all you want, but that doesn't change the fact that Laputa's experiments in the Science of the Will have earned him a Pulitzer nomination on two separate occasions. He's one of the most revered figures in his particular field of study, and we have drawn on his work in this book before (refer back to the chapter entitled "Thinking Negative Thoughts").

The moral of these findings is obvious. You've heard the phrase before: Be careful what you wish for, because you might just get it.

Now stop complaining, ladies, and suck up all that pain. Really, it's not that bad. This is what you wanted, after all, so enjoy it, and leave the X-factor alone.

SUBDERMAL IDENTIFICATION CHIPS

As you've no doubt already heard from a reliable internet news source, or seen on the nightly news, or perhaps even read in a daily newspaper, in this post-911 world, Homeland Security has found it necessary to pass laws that compel all hospitals to implant newborn infants with subdermal identification chips. Some parents are concerned about this development, so concerned they're going out of their way to sue the government to prevent such implantation from occurring.

We here at *The Expectant Mother Disinformation Handbook* are asked about this issue quite a bit, and to be totally honest with you we think you *should* be concerned.

You should be concerned if your child is NOT implanted!

These implants serve one purpose and one purpose only: to protect your child from harm. Do you want your darling cherub, the very same innocent you bore for nine torturous months, to be kidnapped by psycho-sexual maniacs recently released from a local insane asylum via a legalistic loophole initiated by the ACLU or a similar domestic terrorist organization, and sacrificed to dark demons from the Outer Realms? If not, you'll walk proudly up to your OBGYN and say, with a smile on your face, "Sir or madam, please insert a subdermal identification chip into the fruit of my loins and save him or her from otherwise certain doom at the hands of feral strangers!"

Only via these harmless and unobtrusive chips can your stolen child be tracked down and retrieved by the ever-vigilant forces of Homeland Security before time has run out.

SCHIZOPHRENIA & PREGNANCY

The onset of schizophrenia most often occurs in men and women when they reach their early twenties. This can happen in people who have shown no previous evidence of mental disorders. There's no way of predicting the onset of schizophrenia, and there need not be any history of schizophrenia in the family.

Why do we mention schizophrenia in these pages? Young mothers and fathers should know that the onslaught of hormones caused by pregnancy can, in some cases, trigger an initial schizophrenic episode. Pregnancy can be stressful enough, but when a young family has to deal with the onset of schizophrenia in the mother, then this extra difficulty can render the entire experience unbearable. Some fathers flee the situation in despair. We at *The Expectant Mother Disinformation Handbook* are here to assure you that the situation is by no means hopeless. Just because the mother suffers from schizophrenia doesn't mean the child is destined to be schizophrenic as well.

There's a great deal of misinformation floating around out there, mainly due to laziness and ignorance, in regards to schizophrenia. Schizophrenia does *not* equal the onset of multiple personalities. Multiple Personality Disorder is a completely separate disorder. The symptoms exhibited by schizophrenics are not quite as dramatic. Schizophrenics simply misperceive reality, exhibiting obvious signs of paranoia. This paranoia is, more often than not, directed toward those who are most intimate with the sufferer. Pregnant schizophrenics can develop an intense belief, for example, that the father is intending to kill both the mother and the child, or that close friends and family are involved in a conspiracy to steal the child away from the mother.

In 1967, the famous obstetrician Dr. Abraham Sapirstein wrote a monograph about his experiences treating a young pregnant woman in New York, named Rosemary Woodhouse, who came down with a severe case of schizophrenia which ultimately led her to the unwavering belief that Dr. Saperstein was the head of a satanic coven responsible for drugging her with mind-altering herbs. Furthermore, she believed that her husband, the TV actor Guy Woodhouse, had allowed her to be raped by Satan in return for a successful acting career, and that her child was the progeny of this supernatural sex crime.

This is one of the most complicated—and *fully documented*—schizophrenic delusions exhibited by a pregnant woman in recent times. Dr. Sapirstein successfully delivered the child, even while the mother was still suffering from her delusions. With the help of medication and a protracted stay in a respectable mental health care facility in Manhattan, Mrs. Woodhouse gradually came to grips with her paranoia—but, alas, not with her clinical depression. On July 20th, 1969, Mrs. Woodhouse committed suicide by jumping through a closed window on the ninth floor of a hospital in Manhattan. Her son, Adrian, had just celebrated his second birthday. Guy Woodhouse died in a car accident in Los Angeles only a year later, when the TV sitcom named after him had reached its highest ratings ever.

Dr. Sapirstein's book about this case, *Talking Back to Satan*, stayed on the nonfiction bestseller lists for eighteen months straight.

Adrian Woodhouse has since pursued a successful

career in International Relations, and celebrated his 50th birthday in 2017. He has changed his name in an attempt to disassociate himself from the tragic legacy of his parents. He declines all interviews and refuses to talk about his mother.

This only goes to show that the greatest harm comes not from the disease itself, but from the stigma *attached* to schizophrenia due to misinformation and disinformation promulgated by the popular media. Please remember: Schizophrenia is nothing to be ashamed of. It's merely a disease brought on by a chemical imbalance, not a supernatural phenomenon. This isn't the Dark Ages, folks! Rest assured that schizophrenia can be treated with proper medication, which has advanced in leaps and bounds since the well-intentioned but less-than-successful treatment received by poor Mrs. Woodhouse in the late 1960s.

If you're interested to know how schizophrenia can affect the child, rather than the mother, please skip ahead to the chapter entitled "If I've Suffered Schizophrenic Episodes in the Past, How Likely Is It That My Son Or Daughter Will Suffer From Similar Episodes as He Or She Grows Older?"

ADVICE FOR THE EXPECTANT FATHER

Like many expectant fathers, you might feel left out of the entire birthing process. We, the authors of *The Expectant Mother Disinformation Handbook*, are sympathetic to your plight. After having studied this problem for decades, we have an important piece of advice for you. You would do well to take heed of it.

No matter how frustrated you feel, please never consider depleting your meager savings account merely to hire an aging Lithuanian hitman for the purpose of scaling a water tower and picking off the expectant mother with a ZR rifle while she strolls down a street corner in broad daylight at the local Farmer's Market she's been patronizing lately, in order, no doubt, to purchase some strange vegetables she's never eaten before, but is nonetheless craving now, due to the parasitic influence of your unborn child. This is an inconvenient method of assassination. There are other scenarios that are more dignified and less likely to be traced back to the expectant father.[10] We will be covering these methods in great detail in the forthcoming *The Expectant Father Disinformation Handbook*.

---

10) Celestial Seasonings' Honey Vanilla Chamomile Herbal Tea laced with digitalis, for example.

THE MIDWICH DISEASE

Of course, it would be better for you not to know this, but we feel it's our duty to give you *all* the truth, not just some of it.

Though it's not likely to occur, your child could fall victim to the dreaded "Midwich Disease." In September of 1960, a small English village called Midwich was overwhelmed by an anomalous phenomenon—an invisible gas cloud, origin unknown—that resulted in the simultaneous impregnation of every woman in town. Even queerer, all these women gave birth on the same day. After a few years, it became clear that these children weren't quite the same as average children. They had slightly larger craniums, their hair was a shocking white, they seemed to lack emotion, and were unusually intelligent for children of their age. They also possessed strong telepathic and telekinetic powers. After being accused of several incidents of malicious mischief, physical assault and third degree murder, at three years of age all the children were blown up by a mad school teacher named Gordon Zellaby. Members of MI-6 British Intelligence investigated the case, but their findings remain classified to this day.

Thirty-five years later, almost the same exact events occurred in a small town called Midwich located in Northern California. (The significance of the name "Midwich" is unclear.) This time, only ten children were involved, and yet they exhibited the same abilities as their 1960 predecessors. Perhaps most inexplicably, these children *also* ended up being blown up by a mad school teacher, this one named Alan Chafee. Researchers from the CIA[11] and NASA investigated the case; needless to say, their findings remain as classified as that of their British counterparts.

11) Including Special Agent Ron Pandolphi, mentioned previously in the chapter entitled "The Potential Dangers of 'Brane Worlds."

THE UNBEARABLE DISSOLUTION OF HIPNESS

We all have memories of our parents, and hardly any of these memories involve our parents being "hip." Thus, many pregnant young women live in constant fear that the arrival of the Dear One will mark the inevitable conclusion of their existence as "hip" beings.

As hard as it is for us to say, you *should* be scared.

According to Prof. José Laputa of Columbia University, the hormones released during pregnancy are responsible for lowering one's IQ by twenty to twenty-five points. This mysterious process affects both the mother *and* the father; how this occurs is still unknown. In tandem with the dissolution of one's IQ comes a slight disintegration of right brain activity, the exact centers of the brain responsible for recognizing the cutting-edge trends in fashion, slang, popular music, etc. You will soon realize, upon eavesdropping on the conversations of much younger people, that not only do you not recognize the names of the bands under discussion, but that you're not even familiar with the *genres* of music they're excited about.

You MUST accept your destiny. Those who resist, who attempt to *hang on* to the eroding brain cells that still vaguely recognize what is known colloquially as "hipness," will only end up making the situation worse. Remember that one mother on the block who dressed like a teenager from twenty years before and was a constant source of embarrassment to her brood of hip children? That will be

YOU if you don't let go. That area of the brain is inaccessible to you now. Put a flower on its grave. Carve the letters R.I.P. into the fashion centers of your medulla oblongata, mumble a few "Hail, Marys" under your breath, then turn your back on a half-remembered past now receding into the distant mists of memory. Oh, sure, sometimes these dead brain cells will flicker to life like phantom limbs, like the galvanic muscle movement of dead frogs flooded with electricity in a high school laboratory, but understand that these brief moments of recidivism are nothing more than a zombified, undead memory attempting to burst free from a moldering grave. Put a stake through its heart and continue about your unhip day, please. None of us want to witness your pitiful attempts to try and hang on to something that's dead and buried. Just breathe a sigh of relief that you will no longer have to worry about what your peers think of you. Your peers, you see, will *also* be members of this very same undead community of AM-radio-listening parents who mow the lawn in their underwear and rail about the IRS and "loony leftists" to random teenage passersby, who will see your sagging, sweating flesh jiggling in the midday sun and flee as quickly as possible, fearful that The Old Man at the End of the Block will consume their hip young bodies as he's been rumored to have done with so many innocent victims before them. Just forget them and their lingering screams of terror. They are no longer your peers. What does it matter what they think of you? You have different and more demanding concerns now. You're responsible for a life form separate from your own brain and body. The Dear One has an invisible vacuum-like extremity attached to the right side of your brain and is even now sucking all the flair and originality from your soul. Wave goodbye as it leaves. The Fruit of Your Loins has a gun pointed at your forehead, and he or she isn't afraid to use it. Bang Bang, Momma y Papa, Bang Bang.

Listen, you were never even hip in the first place. You

just thought you were. So you're not really losing anything. Go toward the light, honey. Go toward the light. Hear the distant clamor of overweight Republicans pounding on a podium somewhere in the foggy distance, promising the total eradication of all drug-peddling illegal immigrants? You will soon be in the audience, nodding your head and shouting, "Right on, man! Make America Great Again, Again!" Have you ever met anybody who wiggled out of the crushing grip of Fate? We didn't think so. Your Fate is clear to you now.

Embrace it. Embrace it. Embrace it.

IS IT POSSIBLE FOR MY CHILD TO BE POSSESSED BY DEMONIC ENTITIES?

Alas, yes. It is our duty to inform you of a case that occurred in Georgetown, Washington in 1971. A young girl named Regan MacNeil was possessed by a demon named Pazuzu, an ancient Sumerian demigod associated with Satan, that was accidentally released by a Jesuit priest named Father Lankester Merrin during an archaeological dig in Iraq many years before. From beneath the desert, Father Merrin dug up a grotesque statue originally built in honor of Pazuzu. According to secret Vatican records to which we've gained access, releasing the statue caused the release of the demon.

After Father Merrin and a fellow priest named Father Damien Karras successfully ejected Pazuzu from young Ms. MacNeil, Vatican officials returned the statue to its original resting place in the desert, and there it stayed, until U.S. President George Bush inexplicably ordered the invasion of Iraq in March of 2003. President Bush announced to the world that the reason for the war was the removal of all "Weapons of Mass Destruction" from Iraq, but no Weapons of Mass Destruction were ever found in that country. The real reason for the war is still debated by historians and political scientists. According to an anonymous high-ranking Vatican official, the Pazuzu statue was removed from Iraq at some point during the 2003 invasion. No one in the Vatican, however, knows the current whereabouts of Pazuzu.

The moral of this story is obvious, ladies: Don't let a Jesuit with a shovel anywhere near your backyard.

IS IT WISE TO MEDITATE IN ORDER TO DE-STRESS?

ABSOLUTELY NO! Meditation leaves the mind empty, thus open to intrusive demonic forces. We know of one pregnant woman, a faithful follower of Jesus, who relented to media propaganda and tried meditation for only fifteen minutes in January of 1982. Her child is now a full-grown adult and a member of the Mormon Church in Salt Lake City, Utah. Need we say more, ladies?

IS IT POSSIBLE TO BECOME ADDICTED TO PREGNANCY?

Despite all the minor inconveniences and outright pain involved with pregnancy, many women can become *addicted* to being pregnant. In fact, some women will attempt to become impregnated mere seconds after giving birth—and not necessarily with their husband or Special Partner. Don't worry, ladies, *you need not be ashamed of this.* Many women experience this transgressive compulsion. And help *is* available.

Pregnancy is a beautiful and sacred process without which the human race would not survive. It's admirable that you wish to continue this experience perpetually. But remember, you can sometimes have *too much* of a good thing. Now that the birthing process is over, it's time to focus on more important matters (as discussed elsewhere in this book). Keep our slogan in mind: When pregnancy ends, motherhood begins.

If you feel this compulsion to become impregnated overriding your higher nature, we recommend contacting an organization called Pregaholics Anonymous (PA). This organization will invite you to one of their frequent meetings where postpartum ladies like yourself can role play, make babies out of clay, and give birth on a weekly basis with the help of the latest in Augmented Reality technology, in order to channel your frustrations into more benign outlets. The only danger involved with this process is becoming addicted to the role playing, the clay children, the AR technology, and the weekly meetings themselves. But even if this does occur, *you need not be ashamed of it.* Many women experience this transgressive compulsion. And help *is* available. If you're overcome by an irresistible urge to attend *too many* PA meetings, we recommend contacting an organization called Pregaholics Anonymous-Anonymous (PA-A). This organization will invite you to one of their frequent meetings where postpartum ladies such as yourself can . . .

MY HUSBAND AND I ARGUE ALL THE TIME. I DON'T WANT MY CHILD TO GROW UP IN AN ENVIRONMENT LIKE THAT. WHAT CAN MY HUSBAND AND I DO TO PUT AN END TO ALL THIS ARGUING?

Avoid talking to one another as much as possible.

WHAT CAN I AND OTHER CONCERNED PARENTS IN MY NEIGHBORHOOD DO TO HELP PREVENT YOUTH VIOLENCE?

Kill your kids?

FETUSES FROM SPACE (I)

Fetuses from outer space is a phenomenon currently occupying our "indeterminate file." Miraculous occurrences such as these may have taken place, but of course we can't be certain. Only two incidents that have been reported to us are worthy of discussion here. (We wish to assure you that we've decided to include these reports in the spirit of full disclosure, not for sensationalistic purposes.)

According to an anonymous source in the Pentagon, on December 6th of 2001, in the border town of Spin Boldak in southern Afghanistan, a glowing fetus floated down out of the sky and hovered above the heads of eighteen U.S. Marines with 3rd Battalion, 6th Marine Regiment. The fetus immediately identified itself as Captain David Bowman, the last surviving astronaut of a Top Secret mission to Europa, the only planetary body in the Milky Way galaxy other than Earth known to harbor sentient life. The entity identifying itself as Captain Bowman claimed he had been regressed to the fetal stage by highly advanced life forms on Jupiter, spliced with alien DNA, then sent back to Earth to deliver a vital message for all mankind.

The 6th Regiment, thinking this to be a Taliban trick, followed protocol and shot the fetus with 810 rounds from eighteen separate semiautomatic machine guns, then hauled the barely breathing corpse back to base whereupon it was turned over to the CIA and interrogated for any information it might have regarding the current whereabouts of the terrorists responsible for the destruction of the World Trade Center in New York. The fetus sputtered the word "*orithi*" before drowning in a water boarding experiment.

The point is clear: Whether from outer space or not, DO NOT allow your fetuses to play tricks on the U.S. military. Uncle Sam has better things to do, like protecting our freedoms, than to waste time dealing with nonsense. We have been advised by the Pentagon to inform our readership that any fetus caught impersonating a legitimate terrorist will be prosecuted to the fullest extent of the law.

FETUSES FROM SPACE (II)

According to anonymous sources in the National Aeronautical Space Administration, another fetus said to have arrived from outer space identified itself with the unlikely moniker of "Paranex, the Fighting Fetus" on the 23rd of October, 1983. It was well over 100 feet tall and encased in a lustrous golden armor made of an indestructible metal unknown to mankind. It claimed to have been trapped in an explosion resulting from the destruction of a massive starship engine somewhere in the outer arm of the spiral galaxy. The explosion caused a rip in space-time, teleporting Paranex instantly to the general vicinity of Earth. Paranex claimed it had arrived on our planet only due to the mercy of "The Voice," an ethereal, omniscient entity the fetus apparently worshipped as a god.

Paranex landed on Earth in Grenada, an island nation in the southeastern Caribbean Sea, causing a great deal of destruction as a result. According to our sources, Operation Urgent Fury (the codename for the October, 1983 United States invasion of Grenada) was merely a cover for the retrieval of the "Fighting Fetus." Before withdrawing into a state of hibernation in an unidentified military base somewhere beneath Nevada, Paranex announced that it would wake up only when it was ready to be born. Even after twenty-seven years, the most knowledgeable physicists and engineers in the employ of the U.S. military have been unable to penetrate the alien's armor. No one knows what will emerge from the metal cocoon when Paranex finally awakens and allows itself to be born.

COMF-O-MATE™

If, in the thirteenth week of pregnancy, your husband or Special Partner greets you at the door with a smile and says, "Guess what, honey, I bought you a present," then presents you with a pair of COMF-O-MATE™ Pants/Jean Extenders, you should bury your rage and accept the gift in the spirit with which it was intended: the spirit of Love.

In case you're not aware of this amazing device, a COMF-O-MATE™ Pants/Jean Extender (handcrafted in the U.S.A.) adds one full inch to those favorite Levis that used to fit you so well. Even when you're not pregnant, your waist size fluctuates; sometimes you need a little more room. And you don't want to pay for constant alterations. Just unbutton garment. Unzip zipper 2". Insert the metal hook on back side of COMF-O-MATE™ through zipper eyelet. Slip COMF-O-MATE™ button through buttonhole of garment. Slip button on garment through COMF-O-MATE™ buttonhole. COMF-O-MATE™ is now in place. Buckle belt over COMF-O-MATE if desired; sweater or top can cover up COMF-O-MATE™ entirely. COMF-O-MATE™ attaches or removes quickly and easily when needed. Or it can be switched from garment to garment. It's small enough to have on hand after those big lunches or dinners. Excellent for women with monthly water-weight gain. Now you can still wear those jeans that shrunk in the laundry. Attaches easily to the sides of overalls. Also can be used to help keep a loose zipper up. For more information, write to Rich Tuisi Productions, P.O. Box 130, Sheldon, WI 54766-0130.[12)]

12) U.S. Patent No. 4,580,298, Canadian Patent No. 1264102. Other Patents Pending.

THE USES AND MISUSES OF THALIDOMIDE

Many mothers, too numerous to identify by name, have expressed concern about certain maternity drugs recently approved by the Federal Drug Administration. After all, they say, just because the FDA approves a drug doesn't mean it's safe. Look at Thalidomide, they insist. Here's a case of a harmful drug the FDA allowed doctors to prescribe for use by pregnant women to curtail morning sickness and insomnia. As a result, from the late 1950s to the early 1960s, over 10,000 babies were born with *phocomelia*, symptoms of which include flipper-like arms and toes growing from the hips. Thalidomide sufferers were often born with malformed internal organs as well. Many of the victims did not live past childhood.

One particular Thalidomide survivor later grew up to become the legendary Martin Atchet, the punk rock singer in England who wrote "Maxichem (Bollaaaarks!)," a popular song about the dangers of pharmaceutical companies run amok. He also adapted a Sylvia Plath poem about Thalidomide to popular music, setting her haunting words to a hardcore beat; this song briefly hit the Top 40 charts in the UK in 1972. It no doubt remains one of the strangest pop hits in Top 40 radio history.[13)]

13) Sylvia Plath's 1962 poem "Thalidomide" reads as follows:

O half moon—

Half-brain, luminosity—

In more recent years, Mr. Atchet has evolved into quite a vocal political activist, who supports a wide array of alternative health issues and decries what he sees as the growing power of "monolithic pharmaceutical companies" over the lives of working class citizens. He has plans to run for the Mayor of Northampton in 2024. One of his major

---

Negro, masked like a white,

Your dark
Amputations crawl and appall—

Spidery, unsafe.
What glove

What leatheriness
Has protected

Me from that shadow—
The indelible buds,

Knuckles at shoulder-blades, the
Faces that

Shove into being, dragging
The lopped

Blood-caul of absences.
All night I carpenter

A space for the thing I am given,
A love

Of two wet eyes and a screech.
White spit

Of indifference!
The dark fruits revolve and fall.

The glass cracks across,
The image

Flees and aborts like dropped mercury.

political platforms is to abolish the FDA, which he calls "the Fascist Drug Administration." He believes the Thalidomide maternity drug, created by the German pharmaceutical company Chemia Grünenthal, was allowed to enter the above ground drug market on purpose in order to conduct some kind of neo-Nazi mass experiment.

Though we sympathize with Mr. Atchet's unfortunate plight, we believe this is somewhat of an overreaction. Just because an organization makes one simple mistake sixty years ago doesn't mean it's being run by a cartel of malevolent mad scientists. In the wake of the Thalidomide catastrophe, stringent laws were passed by the United States Congress that require ironclad tests for safety and effectiveness before a drug can be sold to pregnant women in the U.S.

Moreover, the FDA has gone out of its way to make up for its initial mistake. Over ten years ago (on May 26, 2006), Thalidomide was approved once more by the FDA for use in treating AIDS patients suffering from Kaposi's sarcoma and newly diagnosed *multiple myeloma* patients. As stunning as it is to consider, in the ensuing sixty years, the Grüenthal Company has apparently worked all the kinks out of the Thalidomide drug. Surely this kind of tenacity and stick-to-it-iveness is to be admired. Anyone can make a mistake; the truly talented *learn* from their mistakes, thus transforming negatives into positives. It wouldn't do you any harm, ladies, to apply this same level of indefatigable purpose to your childrearing strategies.

Mr. Atchet and his followers have expressed concern about the return of Thalidomide to the arena of international health care. These protestors, sadly, are responding more from *emotion* than pure *reason*. They're allowing their negative childhood experiences with this drug to cloud their perception of it. Consider this analogy: If a mugger stabbed you as a child, would you refuse to cut your steak with a knife for the rest of your life? The same analgesic that can manage pain can be used by a despondent individual to commit suicide. The painkiller is not to blame, but the person who has chosen to *misuse* it.

The researchers at Grünenthal are professionals who care about your health. Surely the same people who market the effective over-the-counter painkiller Tramadol know what they're doing. Mr. Atchet, however, thinks otherwise. The singer has said of Tramadol that a "painkiller" known to cause nausea, vomiting, sweating and seizures is "as effective in killing pain as a severe case of the bends"[14], but we here at *The Expectant Mother Disinformation Handbook* prefer not to respond to base sarcasm. All drugs have side effects. If we want to manage pain and raise our quality of living, we sometimes have to learn to live with minor side effects such as these.

In the interests of equal time, it's only fair to allow the scientists responsible for Chemie Grünenthal to speak for themselves. On their home page, they describe themselves as follows:

> We specialise in the field of pain therapy and contraception, and tread trend-setting paths. The development and marketing of innovative formulations for established active substances are aspects on which we particularly focus. The company, founded in 1946, markets its products in approx. 100 countries; in addition, Grünenthal is internationally active, with seven production sites and 26 affiliates. Grünenthal employs approximately 4800 people world-wide—1800 in Germany.
>
> Together with highly specialised partners, we are pressing on with the research and development of new active substances. For this, we are concentrating on selected indications and the latest technological developments. We are intensively searching for innovative ways of improving pain, pain relief and reducing side-effects.

---

14) Quoted in the 2-2-06 edition of *The UK Guardian.*

We here at *The Expectant Mother Disinformation Handbook* strongly believe that the representatives of any major pharmaceutical company who choose to state on their main home page that their central purpose in life is that of "improving pain" are a-okay in our book. Why can't other multinational corporations be more like Chemie Grünenthal and devote their tremendous resources to a goal as noble as "improving pain?" The improvement of pain is exactly what the world needs.

As you can see, a lot has changed since 1962, when Sylvia Plath wrote her famous poem and Thalidomide was rightfully banned. The field of medicine has evolved, and those who were once seen as purveyors of poison have metamorphosed into the world's foremost managers and improvers of pain.

Ladies, let us reiterate that we here at *The Expectant Mother Disinformation Handbook* do not pretend to be the final arbiter of medical knowledge in this world, but nonetheless we think it's only responsible to inform you that any of us would choose the professional opinion of a white coat over the uninformed opinions of countercultural iconoclasts who wish to get back at the world by spreading hysteria and fear.

You have been warned and informed. It's now up to you to make up your *own* mind on this important subject.[15)]

---

15) For further information regarding Chemie Grünenthal, feel free to visit the company's website at <www.grunenthal.com>.

SHOULD MY HUSBAND (OR SPECIAL PARTNER) AND I BE CAREFUL ABOUT WHAT WE SAY TO EACH OTHER WHILE OUR DEAR ONE IS STILL GESTATING IN THE WOMB?

Absolutely, yes! It's been determined scientifically that a fetus can discern specific sounds and words at only three months of age. You must be careful what you say around each other while your child is still developing through such crucial stages. Though we can't condone the majority of what the man wrote, Mr. L. Ron Hubbard does offer some useful advice regarding this sensitive subject in his bestselling book, *Dianetics: The Modern Science of Mental Health*. On p. 281, Mr. Hubbard reveals that many mental illnesses in adulthood can be traced back to traumatic experiences that occurred while the child was still developing in the womb. One of the best examples Mr. Hubbard gives is of the father who beats his pregnant wife while yelling, "Take that! Take it, I tell you. You've got to take it!" Later in life, the child may interpret these words literally and become a Kleptomaniac.

Another illustrious example given by Hubbard is when an expectant father, suspicious that the child is not his, beats the pregnant mother while screaming that he will maim or kill the child if he or she is not "exactly" like the father. Later in life, the child may feel mysteriously compelled to copy his father "exactly" and end up stuck in a profession unsuited to him, never realizing the true source of this neurotic compulsion.

A third example involves the expectant mother who, while sitting on the toilet suffering from constipation, says aloud, "Oh, this is hell. I am all jammed up inside. I feel so stuffy I can't think. This is too terrible to be borne." Later in life, the child may suffer from an extreme inferiority complex because he was told by his mother, at this crucial moment, that he was "too terrible to be born."

A fourth and final example, from the same revelatory chapter, is about the pregnant mother who cheats on her husband or Special Partner by having sex with another man, then (while in bed with the other man) makes disparaging remarks about the true father of her unborn child. If the child in question is then *named* after the father, he will naturally misinterpret the previous insults as having been about *him*, due to the fact that he and the father now share the same moniker. Needless to say, the resultant neuroses can be disastrous and almost impossible to cure in adult life, without tracing the insult to its original source through extensive and costly psychotherapy.

Having been forewarned, ladies, we now request that you and your husband or Special Partner watch what you say just as much as if the unborn child was standing right beside you, in earshot. The solution to this problem is obvious: Simply pretend you're in public *at all times*. This is just proper decorum. After all, these days you never know *who's* listening.

Nor should you.

Think about it: Perhaps this small amount of doubt is exactly what we need to reclaim the manners of a polite society.

NOW THAT OUR SON OR DAUGHTER HAS BEEN DELIVERED SAFELY, WHAT IF MY HUSBAND AND I ARE UNEXPECTEDLY SHOT TO DEATH BY A DESPERATE MUGGER WHILE OUR CHILD IS STILL AN ADOLESCENT, INNOCENT IN THE WAYS OF THE WORLD?

As you're no doubt aware, once your child is born, this is by no means the end of your concerns. A thousand other horrible events could happen to your child between now and his or her high school graduation. One of those horrible events is a sudden mugging in an alleyway that leaves your and your husband's perforated bodies bleeding to death in the garbage while your young child stares on in bewilderment, totally helpless. The child might respond by utilizing the wealth left to him or her in the will to build up a vast weapons array in the cavern beneath your former estate, weave together from scraps a terrifying costume based on an ominous creature of the night, sacrifice every moment of his or her free time studying cutting edge criminology texts and the rarest forms of martial arts taught only by a nameless secret society of monks living in a subterranean temple in Tibet, then return to the neighborhood where the two of you were shot twenty years before and strike fear in the hearts of evildoers everywhere with a relentless one-man—or one-woman—war on the criminal community that gave birth to his or her burning rage, when a few random pieces of lead wrested away the two most precious people in the life of this eternally wounded adolescent.

Or he or she might just withdraw into him or herself for a little bit, get over it pretty quickly, then move on with life and make friends and go off to college and get married and eventually forget you ever existed, like a normal American child.

As you can see, some kids are more sensitive than others and deal with trauma differently. If you don't want him or her dressing up like an ominous creature of the night, however, you might want to fill in that cavern beneath your estate. What's that doing there anyway? Isn't that a safety hazard?

IF MY HUSBAND AND I ARE ABSOLUTELY CERTAIN THAT THE EARTH IS COMING TO AN END SOON, DO YOU RECOMMEND BUILDING A SMALL ROCKET FOR OUR CHILD AND SHOOTING HIM OR HER OUT OF OUR ATMOSPHERE TOWARD AN UNKNOWN DESTINATION SOMEWHERE IN THE VASTNESS OF SPACE?

As stated previously, once your child is born this is by no means the end of your concerns. A thousand other horrible events could happen to your child between now and his or her high school graduation. One of those horrible events is the sudden destruction of planet Earth. If this should occur, and you and your husband are in a privileged enough position to know when and how this catastrophe will take place, we recommend you use whatever specialized knowledge you have between the two of you to construct a rocket ship small enough to contain your baby but also *durable* enough to withstand the rigors of space, then shoot it on a trajectory toward the only planetary body in this galaxy known to harbor life: that's right, the moon from which Capt. David Bowman returned in December of 2001, none other than Europa. In the spaceship, include a post-it note that says, “Received your kind message. We have no idea what ‘orithi’ means. Don’t bother to respond, as we’re dead now. Please take care of our baby. He prefers cool jazz when being rocked, and apricots for lunch. Thank you.”

Then pray.

It’s all in God’s hands now.

WHAT IF AN ANDROGYNOUS-LOOKING MALE WEARING GREEN LEOTARDS FREQUENTLY INVADES MY DAUGHTER'S BEDROOM AND TAKES HER OUT "FLYING" WITH A GROUP OF HOMELESS YOUNG GANGSTERS WITH NO JOBS AND A LOT OF TIME ON THEIR HANDS TO CAUSE NOTHING BUT CHAOS FOR HER AND HER POOR WORRIED PARENTS?

We here at *The Expectant Mother Disinformation Handbook* do not normally advocate violence of any kind, but in this case we'd encourage you to first castrate, then defenestrate this troublesome young man the next time you find him sneaking around in your defenseless daughter's bedroom. If he's still alive after this assault, report him to the Megan's Law website. Some of these metrosexual types can seem younger than they really are, and impressionable girls are the most easily fooled by the act. This is why you, the responsible adult, are there to protect her. Do not *ever* forget that. These days, parents exhibit far too much tolerance toward their children, particularly in regards to the questionable types young girls seem attracted to (thanks to the corrupting influence of the media). Don't be afraid to put your foot down. More often than not, your children *want* you to say no. They only become wild when they don't receive the stern guidance they unconsciously desire.

Remember, ladies: Extreme rebellion is a cry for extreme discipline.

Tell that to the metrosexual imp the next time he and his hooligans drop in to give your daughter some "flying" lessons.

MEGAN'S LAW

The Megan's Law website (<www.registeredoffenders list.org>) is a useful research tool for the twenty-first century parent. Some neophyte parents go out of their way to avoid looking at the site, as the mere mention of the subject matter tends to upset them.

This is no way to raise a child, ladies. In order to best protect your child, you must be intimately aware of the darkness that lies in wait for him or her in the untamed death pit that is the Outside World. You, and *only* you, stand between your child and the bubbling mass of flesh-eating chaos called *Other People.* Remember: The key to successful child rearing is *control.* Other People, however, are entities that cannot be controlled. Therefore, you must limit your child's contact with Other People. Specifically, you must limit their contact with Other People who might harm them.

We realize that being a mother does not make you a telepath or a seer. The only way to predict which stranger might be a threat is to arm yourself with as much information and as many research tools to which the World Wide Web affords you access. One of the best of these tools is: <www.registeredoffenderslist.org >.

Simply click on the above link, then refer to the Megan's Law map. The red dots on the map will indicate the highest concentration of sex offenders in your area. We here at *The Expectant Mother Disinformation Handbook* know of at least one young couple in downtown Long Beach, CA, who did exactly this and discovered *sixty-three* dots in a one-block radius of their apartment building. Not surprisingly, they moved soon afterwards. Without the Megan's Law map, they would never have known.

One woman of our acquaintance discovered a big red dot on her *exact home address*. This is how she discovered that her new husband, whom she had met through the convenient auspices of Facebook and married on the fly in Las Vegas three months earlier, was a convicted child rapist. She requested a divorce via email two weeks later.

Alas, as with any new technology, there are always services and disservices. Some convicted child molesters use the site in order to find like minds to hang out with, to party with, and plot new deviltry together. In fact, if you track the map on a weekly basis you will see the red dots *slowly converging toward one another*. The day they form one giant red dot is the day to begin worrying.

Will it be *your* neighborhood where the big red dot converges?

Remain on-line and *ever vigilant*, parents.

Beware the red dots.

ALCOHOL INTAKE

(This one's directed toward Dad or Special Partner.)

Listen, when Mom says, "God damn, I feel a burning desire to go on a drinking jag right now—I'll fuckin' die if I don't get some alcohol, I tell you," don't worry about it. This is totally normal behavior. In fact, in some primitive cultures (like Ireland, for instance), they believe alcohol helps the birthing process and makes the fetus stronger. In this spirit, we recommend giving Mom a bottle of JD once a month or so and just letting her have at it. Sometimes Mom needs to *forget* she's Mom, and alcohol's the only true cure for painful and inescapable realities.

We all need a little vacation from ourselves once in a while.

It's nothing to be ashamed of.

IS IT TRUE THAT AT THE END OF NINE MONTHS THE STORK WILL DELIVER MY BABY TO ME?

Some of you might think this is a naïve and unlikely question, but you'd be surprised. We get it all the time. The most accurate answer to the question is: In some societies, yes. In almost all cultures other than the United States, there is a prevailing belief that babies are born of mother-earth first. For example, in Germany women do not give birth to babies. Instead, babies emerge from the soil of deep, rocky caves and are then found by storks and delivered to the proper home by some internal instinct in the bird unknown to medical science. In the Pomerania region of Historical Eastern Germany, and still to this day in northern Poland, babies generally rise up out of deep inland lakes, and are then picked up from the surface of the water and delivered to the proper parents. This may sound less grueling for the mother, but in the end the complicated birth process experienced by women in modern day North America is far more preferable than the pagan scenarios described above. As all civilized societies know, the significance of any event is made that much more wondrous by how much pain it took to accomplish it. If there's no effort involved, then what's the point?

True pain is the mark of true experience, ladies.

Let's take a moment to pity the simple and uneducated women of Germany and Northern Poland for being forced to live their lives pain-free for nine whole months while they merely wait for a dirty flower-child to be dropped into their arms by some overgrown pigeon. All without even one second of nausea or bleeding or cramping.

Pray for them, ladies, pray for them.

NORTH AMERICAN PARTHENOGENESIS

That is not to say North America doesn't have its own urban legends involving the creation of babies via parthenogenesis.[16] One of the most persistent of these rumors involves newborn infants emerging fully formed from alleyway trash cans and other waste bins. In this scenario, however, instead of the aforementioned storks, rats and other rodents are said to have delivered the children to the proper doorsteps.

Some parents in urban areas of the United States claim their own children were brought to them in this unorthodox manner. Among the most famous of these children were Mr. Adam Bomb, Ms. Valerie Vomit, Mr. Ray Decay, and Ms. Virus Iris. These and many other peculiar children were born in the early 1980s. We can't say for sure what would provoke parents to make such startling and potentially damaging claims about their own children, but perhaps the resultant publicity was a motivating factor. These unfortunate waifs later starred as themselves in a feature film roughly based on their difficult upbringings. The movie, produced by MGM, was released in 1987 to roundly negative reviews and was a box office failure.

These children would now be around thirty-six years old, but their current whereabouts are unknown. Let's

16) A form of reproduction in which the ovum develops into a new individual without fertilization.

hope they've changed their names and are now attempting to pursue a somewhat godlier path as normal, productive men and women with families of their own.

THE BLOOD-CLOT BOYS

An even stranger form of North American parthenogenesis is that of the Blood-Clot Boy. This incident occurred among the Plains Indians c. 1800. The story began with an old man who was attacked by his crazed son-in-law with a knife. The old man was trying to protect his daughter from being murdered by the boy. The old man survived the assault, just barely, but not before his son-in-law grabbed the old man's daughter and fled the village. The old man managed to gather up a single clot of blood and bring it to the tribal shaman, who then deposited it in a mystical piece of pottery. To the old man's surprise, a boy grew from the clot of blood and swore to gain vengeance on the crazed son-in-law. The old man warned Blood-Clot Boy not to do so, for the son-in-law was far too insane to be dealt with by one frail little boy (this being looked like any other boy, you see). But the old man underestimated the boy's supernatural powers. Blood-Clot Boy headed off into a previously unexplored wilderness and ultimately saved the daughter from the clutches of the crazed son-in-law. When he at last brought the daughter back to the village, the old man gave his permission for Blood-Clot Boy to marry her. He did so, of course, and lived happily ever after.

Another Blood-Clot Boy was born in California around 1840. Some gold miners actually interacted with the boy and wrote about him in their journals. Apparently, a massive and ferocious bear in the Pacific Northwest ate a young girl while she was out picking berries in the forest in the company of her grandmother. The grandmother saved a single clot of blood and brought it back home with her, not telling anyone about it. Over the course of many years, to her surprise, a boy emerged from the clot of blood. This Blood-Clot Boy actually *looked* like a clot of blood given human form. He was bright crimson and his "flesh" had the consistency of viscous liquid. He would froth white when he grew angry, and he could also change his shape at will. On the boy's thirteenth birthday, he vowed to return to the woods and gain vengeance on the monster that had killed the young girl. The old woman begged him not to do it, but he ignored her and did so anyway. He had many grand adventures in the surrounding wilderness before finally tracking down the bear and killing it. When he returned at last, he was five years older. Many of the miners in the local village of Grass Valley saw the strange-looking boy wander into town in the company of his ailing grandmother and asked him how he came to be that way. The boy told them the story, and that's how we know it today.

We have reported this historical incident in these pages merely for your illumination. Don't worry, ladies; no "Blood-Clot Boy" was ever born of a true God-fearing woman. We, of all people, understand today that little boys and girls are far more than just "blood clots."

PRENATAL FINGERPRINTING

Roundabout the thirteenth week is when the child begins to develop fingerprints. Now, as you no doubt already know, your local law enforcement officials will generally visit public classrooms at some point during the first grade and demand that your child allow him or herself to be fingerprinted, so that the police will be able to locate him or her far more easily in the event of a kidnapping.

These days, however, such precautions are taken even earlier. These days, a representative from your local police force will arrive at your home sometime during your thirteenth week and demand prenatal fingerprinting from the developing fetus. *Do not be alarmed.* The fact that these statistics are shared with Homeland Security agents will allow various law enforcement agencies a better chance to identify terrorists disguised as legal or illegal aliens before they have the chance to strike. As hard as it is to believe, there have been several cases of terrorists disguising themselves as developing fetuses in order to sneak their way into America to cause chaos in this great land of ours. Don't you agree that it's your duty, as a loyal U.S. citizen, to prevent another 9/11 from happening? If so, surely you wouldn't begrudge the fine agents of Homeland Security merely performing a task that has been assigned to them by their superiors.

A harmless and unobtrusive probe will be inserted into your vagina, after which this probe will quickly and efficiently read the fingerprints of your unborn child, recording them on a flash drive for future use by Homeland

Security. The entire process will only take ten minutes, tops. If you wish, you may request a small pair of headphones that will pipe muzak versions of popular Lady Gaga songs into your ears while the procedure is under way. This makes the procedure so stress-free that you won't even know it's happening.

Just make sure you ask for identification from the agent before you allow him or her to proceed. Then close your eyes and think of America. And above all, relax.

ARGUING

Some people worry that constant arguing between the parents will be detrimental to the fetus's health. This is not necessarily true. Now, for those of you who've already read the chapter entitled "Should My Husband (or Special Partner) and I Be Careful About What We Say to Each Other While Our Dear One Is Still Gestating in the Womb?" you might be confused and think we're contradicting our own advice.

Allow us to explain: As long as you don't say anything *negative* while arguing, you and your husband or Special Partner can bicker as much as you wish. With the proper programming, parents can be trained to make encouraging remarks to the child even while eviscerating one another. Read, for example, the following transcript made during one of our *Expectant Mother Disinformation Handbook's* fun and effective Positive Arguing Workshops™:

FATHER [grabbing Loved One around the throat]: You can be anything you want to be, baby. Eliminate self-doubt, and you eliminate self-defeat.

MOTHER [with a smile in her voice]: Ah, I see what you mean. I need to tear down the wall that surrounds my potentiality.

FATHER: Here, let me remove it for you. [At this point Husband slams his fist into Mother's face, making her bleed all over the carpet.]

MOTHER: I feel all self-restraint leaking away from me. [Mother knees Husband in the groin and pushes him over a piece of furniture broken during a previous Positive Arguing Workshop™.]

FATHER: Follow your bliss, honey. [Father rises to his feet, removes his belt from his Versace pants, folds it into a loop and then snaps it threateningly as he begins to walk toward Mother ever so slowly.]

MOTHER [crouching into fetal position to protect herself and her unborn child]: A rolling stone grows no moss!

FATHER [whipping Mother's bare back while also kicking her out into the hall]: You can't burn your bridges behind you! [Now Father grabs Mother by the scruff of the neck, then pitches her down the stairs.]

MOTHER [a faint but *positive* whisper rises from the bottom of the staircase]: It could always be worse.

FATHER: But it won't get worse, because we love each other so much. [Father tosses away the belt and helps Mother to her feet. They kiss and make up.]

You see? Father and Mother have been able to release some pent-up tension while also teaching Baby positive life lessons. This is the boon of the fun and effective *Expectant Mother Disinformation Handbook* Positive Arguing Workshop™.

To sign up for a workshop in a city near YOU, simply visit our website at: <www.theexpectantmotherdisinformationhandbook.com>.

WHAT IF A 30-YEAR-OLD UNMARRIED CLERGYMAN WITH A REPUTATION FOR TAKING NUDE PHOTOGRAPHS OF PRE-PUBESCENT GIRLS ASKS TO TAKE MY TEN-YEAR-OLD DAUGHTER ON A SERIES OF LONG BOAT RIDES DOWN THE RIVER THAMES IN ORDER TO READ HER EXCITING STORIES ABOUT A SASSY YOUNG LASS WHO HAS GRAND, UNFORGETTABLE ADVENTURES WHEN SHE DISOBEYS HER PARENTS?

It sounds harmless to us.

TEMPORAL LOBE EPILEPSY

A concerned woman calling herself M. has recently written us and wants to know what to do if her sixteen-year-old child and/or niece begins insisting that she regularly visits another dimension, in which she enjoys fraternizing with animate scarecrows, tone-deaf lions, metallic men of indeterminate sexuality, drunken dwarves, and winged simians dressed like bellhops.

Well, M., your first mode of action should be to determine whether or not your Dear One is fibbing, hallucinating, or telling the truth. When your child is out playing one afternoon, check her bedroom carefully for a dimensional portal (as discussed in the chapter entitled "The Potential Dangers of 'Brane Worlds"). If no evidence is found, you must then search her belongings for illegal drugs such as LSD or peyote buttons. If this leads nowhere, you must confront the child directly. The truth of the situation can be determined with a stern threat of low-level physical violence followed by a vigorous spanking, or perhaps the other way around, depending on what mood you're in. If the child still insists on sticking to this story, you must then shift to the next stage.

If you have a pretty good health care plan, we suggest taking your daughter and/or niece to a reputable neurologist for an MRI.[17] It could be that she's suffering from a chronic neurological condition called Temporal Lobe Epilepsy. This condition has been found to be the

---

17) Magnetic Resonance Imaging.

cause of formerly unexplained paranormal phenomena, including most Bigfoot sightings and all alien abductions. Though we know for a fact that extraterrestrials visit the Earth from time to time, it has never been determined scientifically or in a court of law that they actually abduct humans against their will. According to well-respected cognitive neuroscience researchers like Dr. José Laputa of Columbia University, increases in local electromagnetism can stimulate TLE and cause hallucinations of ostensible paranormal phenomena, such as so-called "alien abductions." Despite the claims of the True Believers, one hundred percent of alien abduction cases have to this date been satisfactorily explained away in this manner.

If dimensional portals, drugs and outright lying have been eliminated as possibilities, these nightmarish straw people and bipedal lions and axe-wielding automata can surely be explained away as unfortunate by-products of Secondarily Generalized Tonic-Clonic Seizures.

Please don't blame yourself. Nothing you did caused this crinkle in your child's brain. Neurological conditions like this could happen to anyone. Just be sure she receives proper medical care and learns to tell the difference between reality and fantasy.

The best way to explain this dichotomy to a child is as a simple mathematical formula:

Your Brain + Seizure = FANTASY.

Your Brain - Seizure = REALITY.

That should clear up all doubt in your Dear One's mind.

And yours as well.

PREGNANCY FARTS

We here at *The Expectant Mother Disinformation Handbook* refuse to shy away from even the most delicate of subjects. When a woman becomes pregnant, she develops what has been categorized by obstetricians as The Pregnancy Fart. The true severity of The Pregnancy Fart has never been accurately described in either colloquial or scientific terms, as the subject is considered to be taboo in Occidental culture. The closest we have ever heard to a precise summation of this phenomena was a single sentence offered to us in a thoughtful missive submitted to us by a young woman in Michigan. The description is as follows: "It's like a *fart* farted."

Unbeknownst to our untrained contributor from the Midwest, this description is actually quite accurate. The true Pregnancy Fart, distinguished from a quotidian fart by its distinctive and pungent odor, emerges from the developing anus of the embryo and then seeks egress via the most convenient route available to it: what Dr. José Laputa and other obstetricians have called "the mother's second anus, the vagina." The act of passing through the fungi that naturally grows inside the vagina during some pregnancies (see the next chapter for details) can further cause the stench of this embryonic fart to double or even triple in strength. The purpose of the Pregnancy Fart is somewhat akin to a trial run in engineering, or a practice in professional sports, or a rehearsal in acting. The Pregnancy Fart enacts the eventual journey of the fully-grown fetus and thus clears the way like a brushfire. The

Pregnancy Fart is, essentially, the prelude to the actual birth process. This process is merely the way of Nature and should not be considered embarrassing or taboo in any way.

Without Pregnancy Farts, the birthing of your dear innocent child would be fraught with even more danger than it is now—which, as you already know, is considerable. There are so many of these dangers, the possibility of even *one* of them happening should be keeping you up at night, paralyzed and afraid of the future.

THE FUNGI OF USHER

The fungi that appears in the vagina during the thirteenth week of pregnancy can, in some women, quickly get out of control and replicate at a geometric rate. In the case of Ms. Madeline Usher, the anomalous fungi in question extended out of her body, abandoned her body entirely, and proceeded to lead an independent existence, ultimately grafting itself to the walls of the family estate. This case was documented by a nineteenth-century journalist of some distinction named E.A. Poe. Though known more for his flights of fancy, Poe had considerable interest in medical matters and documented this unusual case in an 1845 article entitled "The Fall of the House of Usher," touted by its original publishers as a moralistic tract about the dangers of incest.

The sentient fungi produced by the transgressive union of Ms. Madeline Usher and her brother Roderick is described by Poe as follows:

> [Roderick's] opinion, in its general form, was that of the sentience of all vegetable things. But, in his disordered fancy, the idea has assumed a more daring character, and trespassed, under certain conditions, upon the kingdom of inorganization. I lack words to express the full extent, or the earnest *abandon* of his persuasion. The belief, however, was connected (as I have previously hinted) with the gray stones of the home of his forefathers. The conditions of the sentience had been here, he imagined, fulfilled in the method of collocation of

> these stones—in the order of their arrangement, as well as in that of the many *fungi* which overspread them, and of the decayed trees which stood around—above all, in the long undisturbed endurance of this arrangement, and in its reduplication in the still waters of the tarn. Its evidence—the evidence of the sentience—was to be seen, he said, (and I here started as he spoke,) in the gradual yet certain condensation of an atmosphere of their own about the waters and the walls. The result was discoverable, he added, in that silent, yet importunate and terrible influence which for centuries had molded the destinies of his family, and which made *him* what I now saw him—what he was. Such opinions need no comment, and I will make none.

The unique acidic quality of the fungi in question is now believed by present day mycologists to have been the cause of the mysterious and sudden destruction of the infamous Usher estate. Fortunately, Poe survived the untimely catastrophe, and documented these seemingly paranormal events in such precise detail that the knowledgeable scientists of the twenty-first century can now study these events and recognize them not as the result of paranormal phenomena, but merely as the result of self-replicating prenatal fungi.

Thankfully, proper—indeed, even *minimal*—care and cleaning of the vaginal regions will prevent such extreme cases from ever coming about. For those of you interested in pursuing this subject further, *The Proper Care and Cleaning of the Vaginal Regions Disinformation Handbook* will be appearing in a bookstore near you sooner than later.

CULTURAL DIVERSITY & INFANTICIDE
(INFANTICIDE PART I)

Many mothers worry about the possibility of the father or the physician or a conglomeration of these and other personages stealing the newborn and committing infanticide. The probability of this happening depends on the area of the world in which you're living. There have been various cultures throughout the centuries who have practiced infanticide, for what they felt were ethical and practical reasons. As hard as it is to believe, these practices persist to this day.

In certain provinces in England, such as Northampton, newborns are often throttled for reasons of class distinctions. It is a standard British custom for the lower classes to kill their children, while members of royalty are expected to keep their children alive at all costs, even if they are deformed or mentally deficient.

According to the recent studies of Dr. José Laputa of Columbia University, 34% of infants born to the Hindoos of India are sacrificed to the crocodile god Sobek by drowning them in the Ganges River, believed by Hindoos to be the eternal resting place of Sobek.

In a small village called Pleasant Valley in the Appalachian Mountains, the newborn is buried alive with the mother's corpse if the mother dies during childbirth, because it is believed by many Southern Baptists that only the mother can nurse the child. This is perceived to be a genuine act of mercy toward the infant.

The Jagas, a West African tribe in Angola, kill their newborns because they tend to slow down the women during battle. The tribe is kept populated by stealing the already grown children of neighboring tribes the Jagas have conquered in warfare.

The Mechoopda Indians of Nevada bury their deformed children alive in the hallowed grounds of Las Vegas casinos.

In Snoqualmie, Washington, if the mother has a bad dream the night before the birth, the child is left out in the woods to be eaten by feral animals.

In the Amish community of Nickel Mines, Pennsylvania, newborns who are hunchbacked, lame, dwarfed, crippled, malformed, or who have harelips are dashed against rocks by the feet because these deformities are believed to have been caused by demons.

In Salt Lake City, Utah, a Mormon newborn will be defenestrated if the infant resembles the father too much, due to the belief that whoever the child resembles will die within hours of the birth.

In Riverside, California, an infant born of Scientologists will be killed only if it's unable to perform manual labor by the tenth week.

NAMBLA & THE MOLOCH WORSHIPPERS
(INFANTICIDE PART II)

In Monte Rio, CA, gentile children are often kidnapped by errant groups of Rabbis roundabout Midsummer's Eve (July 15th) and sacrificed to the Great God Moloch by a *minyan*[18)] deep in the redwood forests just outside San Francisco. Such nefarious practices go all the way back to eleventh-century Phoenicia. Sir James Frazier, author of the famous multi-volume history *The Golden Bough*, traced the origins of the Hebrew Passover to the ritual sacrifice of first-born infants; these infants were sacrificed to the dark god Moloch. Moloch still exists to this day, waiting in his lair deep in the redwood forests of Monte Rio to consume the profane flesh of gentile children.

Allen Ginsberg, most famous for having been the poet laureate of the 1960s counterculture, was also a member of NAMBLA (North American Man-Boy Love Association), a group of self-professed pedophiles who gather at public conventions in which they plot new methods of enacting legal protection under the law for their "civil right" to rape innocent children. (See the website <www.nambla.org> for more information.) In his most famous poem, "Howl," Ginsberg includes numerous paeans to the demon Moloch:

---

18) A ***minyan*** is a quorum of ten or more adult Jews who gather together for the express purpose of ritual sacrifice.

> Moloch whose mind is pure machinery! Moloch whose blood is running money! Moloch whose fingers are ten armies! Moloch whose breast is a cannibal dynamo! Moloch whose ear is a smoking tomb! Moloch whose eyes are a thousand blind windows! Moloch whose skyscrapers stand in the long streets like endless Jehovahs! Moloch whose factories dream and croak in the fog! Moloch whose smokestacks and antennae crown the cities! Moloch whose love is endless oil and stone! Moloch whose soul is electricity and banks! Moloch whose poverty is the specter of genius! Moloch whose fate is a cloud of sexless hydrogen! Moloch whose name is the Mind!
>
> Moloch in whom I sit lonely! Moloch in whom I dream Angels! Crazy in Moloch! Cocksucker in Moloch! Lacklove and manless in Moloch!

Significantly, Ginsberg has never denied the fact that he is a Jew. Thus, the logical question must now be asked: Was the poet laureate of the counterculture the core acolyte in a Hassidic cult of flesh-eating pedophiles who stalked the woods outside San Francisco, CA, all throughout the '60s, '70s, '80s, and early '90s? Were the Zodiac killings and the Hillside Strangler murders the result of ancient Jewish blood rituals perpetuated by the deranged poet friends of Allen Ginsberg? If so, did his Jewish cohorts in the media cover up the evidence of this bloody plot?

An independent investigation is needed to get to the bottom of this tragic mystery before more gentile children are lost in the redwood night.

Beware the worshippers of Moloch, ladies, beware the worshippers of Moloch.

A BRIEF VISIT WITH THE LORD OF VAMPIRES

Our special correspondent in Romania took time out of her busy schedule to interview Dracula, the Lord of Vampires. Protected by a crucifix and a necklace adorned with garlic, our interviewer asked Dracula a series of pointed questions about the difficulties of fatherhood. Not many people are aware of the fact that, in 1977, Dracula sired a child named Janus with a human female named Domini. Only minutes after being born, however, Janus was murdered by a Satanist named Anton Lupeski in Boston. In grief, Dracula crushed Lupeski's skull. Dracula fled to his family estate in Romania soon afterwards and was never brought to justice for the crime.

Unbeknownst by the Lord of Vampires, his beloved wife enacted a magical spell to revive Dracula's dead child and merge him with one of God's legion of golden angels. Since that moment, Janus and Dracula have clashed over a panoply of delicate family issues. For example, Dracula's strongest desire is to wipe out all of humanity whereas Janus wishes to protect us and help humanity evolve to our next stage of spiritual evolution. Such extreme differences in opinion can naturally lead to heated family conflicts. So, let's now eavesdrop briefly on the inner thoughts of the self-professed Prince of Darkness regarding these sensitive child-rearing topics . . .

INTERVIEWER: Did it ever occur to you that your child might rebel against your values?

DRACULA: Are you kidding? When I was growing up I was all like, "Lord, if only I had a dad who drank blood, *then* I'd be happy." I figured the kid would love me. We'd both dress in black, go out on the prowl together, feed on the flesh of nubile peasants, etc. What kid *wouldn't* enjoy that? Who could've predicted the whole Jesus freak thing? I blame his mother.

INTERVIEWER: Isn't it natural for a child to rebel?

DRACULA: Hell, no, not when your dad's freakin' Dracula. What could be cooler than that? You know there are thousands of kids who lie awake at night wishing they were the son of the Prince of Darkness?

INTERVIEWER: Really?

DRACULA: I saw a study on it by Dr. José Laputa of Columbia University on the History Channel.

INTERVIEWER: Why do children so often do the exact opposite of what their parents want?

DRACULA: Uh . . . because they're assholes? How the fuck should I know? Do I look like a child psychologist?

INTERVIEWER: No, but you've certainly lived a long time, so you might have insights most other people wouldn't.

DRACULA: Listen, I can't help you, lady. I'm as much in the dark as you are about this shit. You want my advice? Avoid the rhythm method. It don't work.

INTERVIEWER: I see. What kind of birth control *does* Dracula use?

DRACULA: Aw . . . I tried the whole pulling-out thing, but look where that got me. If I have to use a condom, then I guess the Trojan brand Warm Sensations™ Lubricant is my favorite, but most of the time I don't even bother with the shit. It's like sucking somebody's blood with a raincoat on. Who needs it? Anyway, it ruins the mood.

INTERVIEWER: I have to say, that's very irresponsible of you.

DRACULA: So fuck you, I'm the Prince of Darkness. *And*?

INTERVIEWER: Well . . . I guess we're wrapping up the interview now. Is there anything you'd like to say to your son, just in case he's reading this? I understand you've been estranged for quite some time now.

DRACULA: Oh, sure. Uh . . . hey, kid? Guess what? Jesus wants me for a freakin' sunbeam, you prick. Now get out of my way, lady. Your questions are beginning to grate on me. I've got work to do, you breeding whore.

We hope this brief visit with the Lord of Vampires has put some of your own concerns about your child's potential to rebel into a reasonable perspective. We'd like to thank our Romanian correspondent for putting herself in personal danger merely to serve the needs of you, the loyal audience of *The Expectant Mother Disinformation Handbook*.

IF MY CHILD DIES IN THE WOMB, WHAT ARE THE CHANCES OF HIM COMING BACK AS A GHOST?

According to most parapsychologists, embryo-ghosts are rare. In fact, many experts don't even believe such entities exist. There have been some reported cases of fetus-ghosts, but these were later found to be the hallucinations of women suffering from schizophrenia. What this says about the question of humans having souls before they're born is indeterminate.

We *can* say this, however: According to researchers at UCLA's Neuropsychiatric Institute, the younger the ghost, the more likely he or she is to be friendly. The opposite is true as well: The older the ghost, the more likely he or she is to be malevolent. The Neuropsychiatric Institute investigated one reported haunting involving a child-ghost scaring the new tenants of an old house in Culver City, CA. After a great deal of investigation, the UCLA team discovered that this child-ghost did indeed exist and had been named Casper McFadden when alive. Casper was the son of alcoholic parents, the former members of a failed folk band called The Moonshadows, who drowned their sorrows in Jack Daniels and increasing amounts of cocaine mixed with heroin. On top of all this, these middle-aged hippies were experimenting with unusual amounts of LSD. This led the father to go mad one day and kill both his girlfriend and five-year-old son with the jagged edge of a broken JD bottle. The corpse of Casper McFadden was found on top of the kitchen table among all the crack pipes and homemade LSD-synthesizing equipment, with triangular shards of glass sticking out of his limp little head like an inanimate voodoo doll impaled with numerous bloody pins. The mother was found in the corner, clutching her two-pound stash of marijuana to her chest even in death. Apparently, she had been cradling the stash in her arms like a defenseless baby when her Special Partner stabbed her in the throat with the bottle sixteen times, after which he set her—and the marijuana—on fire. The boy's father then went upstairs to the attic, wrote a note addressed to both his EST guru and the Dalai Lama in which he apologized profusely for setting the marijuana on fire, and leapt out the window. He didn't quite die, however, so as the next door neighbors were calling the paramedics for help, the father finished the job by swallowing the shards of the JD bottle that had shattered upon impact and eventually died by choking on glass at the exact moment the paramedics arrived on the scene. The father had just enough time to paint a peace symbol on the driveway using his own blood before life escaped him. He died with a smile on his twisted lips.

Despite this tragic and unfortunate death, Casper McFadden seemed quite friendly upon his return. Apparently, since he didn't realize he was dead, he would try to make friends with the neighborhood children, but they would just run away in fear. This would make Casper quite sad. All he'd ever wanted, even in life, was friends. Sometimes he would manage to convince a small group of live children to let him play with them for a little while, but would then inevitably drive them away by insisting on singing old Simon & Garfunkel songs off-key. Alas, he would be left all alone again.

The UCLA researchers eventually succeeded in convincing Casper that he was dead by enlisting the aid of an experienced exorcist. The exorcist laid out a series of police photographs on top of a Ouija board that documented the position of Casper's lacerated corpse on the bloody kitchen table and said, "Hey, kid! Let me give you a little math lesson: Your hippie dad *plus* a head full of LSD laced with speed *plus* a broken JD bottle *plus* your skull *equals* You Dead. What's hard to get about this?"

Casper burst into tears and dissipated into nothingness, moving on to the white light on the Other Side.

So you see, with even the most violent deaths, salvation is possible. That includes your child just as much as anyone else's. There's no need to worry.

Relax.

USING YOUR CHILD AS AN ASSASSIN

Using your child as an assassin is never a good idea. Though the CIA has indeed trained dolphins to blow up enemy ships with bombs strapped to their backs, we here at *The Expectant Mother Disinformation Handbook* believe it would be immoral to brainwash children into doing the same work, no matter how effective it might seem. True, nobody would suspect a child of such an iniquitous deed, but strapping twelve tons of plastique to a prepubescent child's chest and pointing him in the direction of the local synagogue is, to say the least, rude. We don't advocate violence in any form, but if you insist on committing it, we suggest doing so with your own bare hands. Don't use your children as proxy weapons. Remember: Children are not dolphins.

One of the most infamous cases of child abuse of this kind occurred in Edo-Period Japan (c. 1680), when the infamous Samurai assassin Ogami Itto used his newborn son Ogami Daigoro (a master swordsman before he was four years old) to slaughter about 156 billion people over the course of a few months, despite the fact that only 212 people lived in Japan at that time. No one can explain this discrepancy.

The ultimate fate of Ogami Daigoro is unknown. We suspect he had serious psychological issues, if he managed to survive beyond the age of four and a half.

PRESIDENT GEORGE W. BUSH SHARES HIS PHILOSOPHY REGARDING PREGNANCY, ABORTION, MOTHERHOOD & RELATED TOPICS

In 1993, journalist Kathy Acker recorded a little known speech delivered by the future President of the United States, George W. Bush, in which he shared his innermost thoughts regarding pregnancy, abortion, motherhood, and related topics with an eloquence not associated with him. For those of you laboring under the mistaken impression that George W. Bush is not a gifted speaker, we suspect you'll change your mind after reading the following speech. The mind revealed by these words is both a surprising and insightful one.

> 'God, if these masses of flesh that we call the women of this century—in particular, my daughter, her blood, this part of me that is diseased, whom I've just raped—were made by You:
>
> 'God, listen: I'm going to drag my daughter through every crime that is worse than rape, through every crime that's as yet unknown to man.
>
> 'This is how I'll begin to do in my daughter:
>
> 'One: Reputation. Today, to govern mass opinion is how to control the political body. Every single monk or person in this community is going

to consider the slut as more than outcast, as all that is hateful. From its beginning, America has been a religious civilization.

'As soon as my daughter's dead, she'll be unburiable—no dogs will stick their noses into this cunt—because the stink of rebellion that is named *menstrual blood* never ever leaves skin, even that which is dead.

'It is true that God hath decreed: Let the starving dogs starve.

'It is the physical world that has caused all this. The physical world that is always changing, menstruating, turning to shit and turning its shit and sex, putrefaction into our white minds. All that is flesh will rot; women give birth to flesh.

'Worse than shit or this physical world is that which lies under it: fantasies dreams desire sexuality. All that is the underworld. This underworld is Satan. Our fight, above all, is to defeat the Evil One wherever he has dared to stick his crimson dick.

'Does Satan dare to think that we're a cunt?

'God! Hear me!

'Two: Dear child, Savior of my family (I am calling on You, Jesus Christ), I know You love me with such love that You will answer all of my prayers:

'What I wish most is that my dead daughter becomes pregnant.

'There will be no more abortions.

'May her child look exactly like her so that every time she will look or peer at this brat—she has to look at her own brat—she will see every scratch every purple pulsating pimple every bit of rotting flesh every gorge and abyss in the skin every fester every cancer: may my daughter have borne life only so that every minute she will be confronted by every characteristic that she detects: herself.

'May my daughter go beyond death into the realm of self-hate.

'This isn't a wish: this is how things are. For I and my daughter are of the same blood. Reality is that a child eats out her own mother in the same way that the dogs would eat my daughter if her cunt didn't reek of its own blood.'

At the end of his speech, Bush vomited. 'Now eyes are closing because it's night. I love my mommy so much. All bad conditions will grow worse.'

We would like to thank Kathy Acker for permitting us to reprint this transcript from her Political Science text *My Mother: Demonology*, winner of the 1993 Council on Foreign Relations Arthur Ross Award for Outstanding Contribution to the Understanding of Foreign Policy or International Relations.

REVERSE THINKING

According to *Funk & Wagnalls' Standard Dictionary of Folklore, Mythology, and Legend*:

> Saying or doing something in reverse of its normal order [is] a custom or practice found throughout the world but adapted for different purposes by different peoples. Wherever it is found, imitative magic is probably at its base.
>
> Talking backwards, or saying the opposite of what is meant, is used as a common form of humor among North American Indians, as by the Arapaho Crazy Dancers and several of the Pueblo societies, especially as a typical ceremonial custom. Despite the surface levity, Pueblo clowns are considered as powerful curers in that they recite certain medicinal formulas in reverse order. Among the medieval Jews, the reciting of the opening of *Leviticus*, forwards, then each word backwards, then the whole passage reversed, was thought to be a counter to magic. Among the practices attributed to followers of the Devil in western Europe is the reciting of the Lord's Prayer backwards.
>
> The Mass of St. Secaire, in Gascony, features a backward recitation that brings death to the one against whom revenge is desired. Similar beliefs are found among the Arabs and Buddhists. In the *Katha Sarit Sagara*, the recitation of a given

> formula forwards makes a man invisible, while a backward reading permits him to assume whatever shape he desires.
>
> Doing things backwards likewise has a certain power. Ringing the chime backwards as an alarm is such a custom, as is the flying of a flag in reverse as a sign of distress. These probably are based as much on the idea of reversal of fortune as on the noticeable incongruity of the action. In the United States some maintain that a garment accidentally put on in reverse must not be taken off and put on correctly or ill luck will follow. Medieval Jews deliberately reversed their clothing or walked backwards to reverse a suspected charm against them. Throwing things behind one likewise has a certain efficacy in preventing evil, or as in some folktales in slowing up pursuit.

What the staff of Funk & Wagnalls has left out is the backwards cognitive functions sometimes brought about by pregnancy. A sudden flood of hormones into a female's nervous system can result in a phenomenon psychologists call "reverse thinking." For example, your husband or Special Partner might come home from work and say, "I had a good day at work today" to which you might respond with something like, "So what're you *saying*? Things are so horrible at home that work seems *good* to you now? Are you saying you're going to leave me? You're just going to up and abandon a pregnant wife[19] for some whore at work, just like that, huh, as if I mean *nothing* to you?" followed by several minutes of sobbing. Or your husband or Special Partner might return from grocery shopping and say, "I'm sure glad I got the last batch of good bananas at the grocery store. I know how much you like them," to which you might respond, "So what're you *saying*? That I'm some kind of unnecessary burden to you now? If this whole ordeal is so

19) Or Special Partner.

damn difficult, why don't you just hop on a Greyhound and lose yourself on the East Coast somewhere and become a successful tap dancer and forget all about me? You think I need you and your whining? I can just take my pregnant belly and go elsewhere. I don't need this complaining. Fuck you and your last batch of good bananas!" followed by fragile bric-a-bracs being tossed through the air. Or your husband or Special Partner might return home from the doctor and say, "Oh man, I met an old man in the waiting room today who was suffering from kidney stones and I hear that's the worst pain a man can ever experience. Gee, I hope I never have to go through something as painful as that," to which you might respond, "So what're you *saying*? That giving birth is a walk through the park, tra-la-la? Why don't you try squeezing an eight-pound head out of your vagina if you think it's so easy? Hey, let's demonstrate for a moment, shall we? Here's a pebble of crystal aggregations and here's a wailing human being with spastic limbs. Which do you think is easier to squirt out of a tiny orifice between your legs? Jesus, it doesn't take a genius to figure it out. What the hell is wrong with you, you son of a bitch?" followed by painted fingernails clawing at bare flesh.

You see, interpreting a positive comment negatively is a symptom of "reverse thinking." Though not isolated to pregnant women, "reverse thinking" does indeed seem to manifest most often during this nine-month gestation period. One would think that the proper method to combat "reverse thinking" would be to anticipate its occurrence beforehand, then say the opposite of whatever one really wishes to communicate. Alas, this strategy does not work. When the neurons of a pregnant carbon-based life form find themselves locked in the "reverse thinking" phase, comments of a negative nature are the only ones that are absolutely certain to be taken at face value.

To this day, the only known methods for dealing with "reverse thinking" are 1) wait out the storm patiently until the neurons release themselves from this paralytic state or

2) hop on a Greyhound and lose yourself on the East Coast somewhere and become a successful tap dancer and forget this debacle ever occurred in the first place. Since the second can lead to criminal charges and subsequent jail time, we here at *The Expectant Mother Disinformation Handbook* recommend the former.

FOURTEENTH WEEK DREAMING

During the fourteenth week of pregnancy, blood flow can become inhibited, particularly during REM sleep[20]. If you go to sleep for more than twenty minutes at a time while lying on your left side, you may stop breathing. Therefore, make sure dreaming occurs only when lying on your right side or in a supine position.

A reminder: Don't allow these warnings to disrupt your regular habits too much, ladies. Just relax. Go to sleep and have sweet dreams.

---

20) A stage in the normal sleep cycle during which dreams occur, believed to be crucial for proper central nervous system development.

DJOMAI

During the fourteenth week, 3% of pregnant women will find their fingernails becoming cracked and brittle, eventually crumbling into a fine yellowish-white dust known in Asian countries as *djomai*, a psychoactive powder believed by the Chinese to possess curative properties for clinical depression. Certain aboriginal tribes in Australia give this substance to newborns in order to smoothly transition them from the real-world of the womb to the dream-world of everyday life. This relatively rare substance can fetch an impressive price from both reputable medical labs and underground dealers in illicit narcotics. Contact your local law enforcement agency to notify them that you have this substance in your possession. They will dispose of it in a legal manner.

Your fingernails will inevitably grow back sometime during the third trimester.

WHAT WILL HAPPEN TO MY CHILD'S SOUL IF I CHOOSE TO HAVE AN ABORTION?

A man of our acquaintance, who shall remain anonymous in these pages except for his last name (Gabe), a professional attorney in New York with respectable credentials, sent us a letter years ago informing us of an incredible experience he had back in 1975. After performing several illegal abortions on various girlfriends over the years, one of his lovers finally went mad and demanded he enter the sewers to retrieve the aborted fetus he had flushed down the toilet. He did so, merely to appease her. Upon entering the sewers, however, he discovered a strange colony of abandoned children who rode the backs of albino alligators and insisted on calling him "Father." These children held Gabe in captivity for several years, forcing him to perform backbreaking manual labor for them, until he pulled off a daring escape that left several dozen of these deformed urchins bleeding in the muck-stained water beneath the earth. When he finally reached the surface, he found that twenty years had passed since the night he first entered the sewers. The girlfriend who had forced him down there had been locked away in a mental hospital for decades, whispering his name into the soft walls and never receiving a response.

Gabe insists the children were his own, and has since dealt with his guilt by resuming his law practice and representing activists arrested for blowing up abortion clinics. Whether his strange story is true or not, we here at *The Expectant Mother Disinformation Handbook* certainly applaud him in his work.

PARENTHOOD & AM TALK RADIO

You will experience many changes in your personality upon adopting the proud mantle of parenthood. For example, you will find yourself inexplicably switching on the radio in the afternoon and listening intently to conservative talk radio shows. At first, you will listen to them only when performing meaningless chores, like washing the dishes. You will listen to an endless string of libertarian pronouncements with half a smile on your face, shaking your head in disbelief at the stupidity of their illogic. Slowly, however, you will find yourself looking forward to turning on that radio, to hearing that particular station. You will start doing the dishes even when they're already clean, merely to have an excuse to hear that mid-afternoon team of grating Republican shills berate the helpless and the poor and the illegal immigrants. Soon, you will drop the ruse of doing the dishes. You will turn on the radio and sit right beside it, your ear almost pressed up against the speaker, and you will find yourself softly banging the kitchen counter at the exact moment the irate host bangs his fist against his console. And you will find yourself whispering encouraging words like, "Go to it! Show 'em what for! Somebody needs to say it!" And when you walk outside you will look at the bums on the street and mutter to yourself, "Why isn't anybody doing anything about it? What'm I paying taxes for anyway? Isn't there some island that they can ship 'em all to?" And when one of them walks up to you and asks for a quarter, you'll spit in their face and say, "Why don't you go get a real job, like me?" even though you haven't worked in months. And the brief moments venturing outside will become more and more nerve wracking, as every cell in your body will cry out for more and more vicarious frustration and hate injected straight into your hungry veins through the electric airwaves. You'll rush back inside to hear the rest of the afternoon's programming after only being outside a few minutes tops. You'll turn the volume up loud, and laugh at a panoply of racist jokes you've heard a thousand times before, and you'll think, "Thank God I'm *me* and not one of *them*," and you'll begin to hatch The Plan. You'll remove the bottle of kerosene out of the garage and go hunting late at night, trying to find the welfare mothers and their children and all the deadbeat dads clogging up the otherwise-pristine sidewalks of your neighborhood, and you'll find them easily enough, oh yes you will, and you'll laugh maniacally and say, "Here's where you give back to the community, scumbags!" then pour the flammable liquid on a sleeping veteran then light the match and toss it into his groggy face and rush back inside your home and tune into your favorite station and wait for your heroes to commemorate your actions with special sound effects from the guy in the booth who never says anything at all and when you don't hear any mention of your good deed you'll pick up the phone and wait all through the night and the morning and the afternoon until your favorite show comes on again and you'll tell your two favorite hosts, "First time long time, pardners. I did somethin' for you two guys, I'm a proactive member of the community now; I got off my butt and I'm *doin' somethin'* about The Problem. I love you guys, man, you get me through the day. It's great to know there's someone out there as rational as me who understands all my problems," and at first they'll like you but then you'll say a little *too* much and the men in the blue uniforms will come to your door and take you away from your family and several years later you'll be reduced to a gibbering thing on the street begging for change and hoping no one tries to remove you from the streets the way you once did to that scumbag vet, hoping and wishing you had enough money to buy a radio so you could hear a little bit of sanity at least once before you leap off the Vincent Thomas Bridge and end the sound of empty airwaves rushing through your quivering brain.

Other changes will be less dramatic, and will be covered in the following pages from time to time.

SO. YOU'RE ON THE PHONE RAPPING WITH SOMEONE YOU HAVEN'T RAPPED WITH IN A WHILE AND YOUR PREGNANT WIFE SUDDENLY STARTS SCREAMING AT YOU BECAUSE THERE'S SMOKE BILLOWING OUT OF THE OVEN. SHE'S NOT SCREAMING AT YOU TO PUT OUT THE FIRE—SHE TAKES CARE OF THAT HERSELF. SHE'S SCREAMING AT YOU BECAUSE SHE'S ACCUSING YOU OF HAVING STARTED THE FIRE IN THE FIRST PLACE. NEVER MIND THE FACT THAT YOU HAVEN'T USED THAT OVEN IN OVER A YEAR. SOMEHOW SHE CONCOCTS THIS WEIRD FANTASY ABOUT HOW YOU PURPOSELY SABOTAGED THE OVEN IN ORDER TO PREVENT

HER FROM CONSUMING HER 2,568TH CHICKEN POT PIE THAT YEAR BOUGHT ON SALE FROM THE FROZEN FOOD SECTION AT VON'S. SHE BUYS A HECK OF A LOTTA CHICKEN POT PIES, ALWAYS HAS, THAT WASN'T THE UNUSUAL PART. THE UNUSUAL PART WAS THIS: THIS TIME SHE CALLED YOU BEFOREHAND FROM THE MIDDLE OF THE FROZEN FOOD AISLE OF VONS TO ASK YOU IF *YOU* WANTED A CHICKEN POT PIE AS WELL. YOU REALLY WEREN'T HUNGRY BUT YOU FIGURED, WHAT THE HELL, I MIGHT AS WELL LET HER THINK SHE'S DOING ME A FAVOR. SHE'S BEEN PRETTY DEPRESSED LATELY. THINK ABOUT HOW FRAGILE THE POOR GIRL IS. THE SLIGHTEST REJECTION MIGHT SEND HER TUMBLING OVER THE EDGE. YOU

DON'T WANT YOUR PREGNANT WIFE LEAPIN' OFF THE TOP OF THE BUILDING WITH YOUR THIRD GRADE SCHOOL PHOTOGRAPH CLUTCHED TO HER BREAST, THE WORDS *HE DONE IT TO ME* SCRAWLED ACROSS YOUR SEVEN-YEAR-OLD FACE IN LIPSTICK OR BLOOD OR SOME OMINOUS MIXTURE OF SAME. AFTER ALL, HOW COULD YOU EXPLAIN THAT? YOU COULDN'T. OF COURSE NOT. SO YOU SAID, "SURE, I'LL TAKE A CHICKEN POT PIE, HONEY, WHY NOT?" AND SHE REPLIED, "OKAY, I'LL SEE YOU IN A SEC," THEN YOU HIT THE CALL WAITING BUTTON AND WENT BACK TO TALKING TO THE GUY YOU HADN'T SPOKEN TO IN A WHILE. YOU WERE STILL TALKING TO HIM WHEN SHE CAME HOME FROM THE

GROCERY STORE. YOU WAVED AT HER BRIEFLY, RETURNED TO YOUR CONVERSATION WHILE STARING OUT THE WINDOW AT THE PEACEFUL GARDEN IN BACK OF THE BUILDING NEXT DOOR—WERE SO ENGROSSED IN THIS DIALOGUE, IN FACT, THAT YOU DIDN'T NOTICE THE BLACK SMOKE BILLOWING OUT OF THE OVEN UNTIL THE SCREAMS RIPPED THROUGH THE TINY APARTMENT. SHE USED YOUR EX-GIRLFRIEND'S CHRISTMAS PRESENT FROM TWO YEARS BACK—A COMPLEX TAPESTRY WOVEN FROM GOAT HAIR, DEPICTING A BIG-EYED MERMAID SITTING ON A ROCKY PROMONTORY OVERLOOKING A MOONLIT BEACH—TO PUT OUT THE FIRE, CLAIMING LATER THAT IT WAS THE ONLY OBJECT AT HAND STURDY ENOUGH TO

COMBAT THE FLAMES. YOU DON'T EVEN COMPLAIN. HELL, YOU WERE GETTING SICK OF THE MERMAID ANYWAY. NO, THAT'S NOT WHAT PISSED YOU OFF. YOU WEREN'T EVEN PISSED OFF ABOUT HAVING TO HANG UP IN THE MIDDLE OF A CONVERSATION WITH SOMEONE YOU HADN'T SPOKEN TO IN A WHILE. WHAT PISSED YOU OFF WAS WHEN SHE STARTED SHRIEKING AT YOU THAT YOU HAD PURPOSELY "BOOBY TRAPPED" THE OVEN IN ORDER TO 1) DESTROY HER AND YOUR UNBORN CHILD WITH AN "ACCIDENTAL" CONFLAGRATION AND 2) POSTPONE OR FLAT-OUT CANCEL HER MUCH-ANTICIPATED DINNER. ONE MISSED MEAL, YOU SEE, MIGHT HAVE THE SAME EFFECT AS BEING CAUGHT IN THE MIDDLE

OF A GAS EXPLOSION, SHE EXPLAINS. EITHER WAY, MOMMA AND BABY END UP DEAD AND WHO'S TO BLAME? DADDY IS TO BLAME. JUST THIS ACCUSATION ALONE, WHISPERED TO THE *RIGHT PEOPLE*, WOULD BE ENOUGH TO CONDEMN YOU TO SEVERAL MONTHS IN L.A. COUNTY JAIL. THESE IRRATIONAL ACCUSATIONS SO OVERWHELM YOU WITH ANGER AND CONFUSION THAT YOU THROW ON YOUR TATTERED JACKET AND DECIDE TO BAIL. AS YOU'RE OPENING THE DOOR TO LEAVE YOUR WIFE SAYS, "I THINK I'LL COOK SOME PASTA FOR US INSTEAD," WHICH CONFUSES YOU EVEN FURTHER BECAUSE, AFTER ALL, WHO WOULD WANT TO COOK PASTA FOR A MURDERER? CERTAINLY NOT

YOU. SO YOU FLING OPEN THE DOOR THE REST OF THE WAY AND SHE SAYS, "WHY'RE YOU LEAVING?" AND YOU SAY, "SO I DON'T PULL OUT A KNIFE AND KILL SOMEONE," WHICH WOULD BE FUNNY, IRONIC, IF YOU PULLED OUT A TWELVE-INCH STEAK KNIFE AND PLUNGED IT THROUGH HER HEART DUE TO THE 92°-IN-THE-SHADE MERCURY-RED ANGER NOW OVERWHELMING EVERY SYNAPSE IN YOUR BRAIN OVER HAVING BEEN UNJUSTLY ACCUSED OF TRYING TO ASSASSINATE HER WITH AN OVEN YOU HAVEN'T USED IN EIGHTEEN MONTHS. FUNNY, IRONIC: THE COPPERS AND THE LAUGH ACADEMY BOYS DRAGGING YOU AWAY IN A STRAIGHT JACKET AS THEY SAY, "WE ALWAYS KNEW HE'D SNAP.

HE'S JUST THAT KIND OF A GUY. A REAL LONER. A WEIRDO WITH, WHADDYA CALL IT?, A CHIP ON HIS SHOULDER. YEAH. ONE OF THOSE WINGNUTS WHO THINKS HE HAS TO THINK FOR HIMSELF. AND LOOK WHERE THINKING FOR HIMSELF GOT HIM. TRAPPED IN IRONS, NOTHIN' TO LOOK FORWARD TO BUT 25-TO-LIFE IN CHINO. AND ALL FOR WHAT?" THAT'S A GOOD QUESTION. ALL FOR WHAT? BECAUSE YOU CAN'T STAND BEING SPOKEN TO IN THAT TONE OF VOICE? BECAUSE YOU CAN'T STAND BEING ACCUSED OF SOMETHING YOU HAVEN'T DONE AND HAVE NO INTENTION OF EVER DOING? BECAUSE YOU CAN'T MOLLYCODDLE SOMEONE ELSE'S HORMONAL DELUSIONS? BECAUSE YOU

CAN'T BACK DOWN WHEN CONFRONTED WITH LIES, NOT EVER? OH, BUT LIES CAN BECOME REALITY. AND YOUR LIFE, AND THE LIVES OF TWO OTHERS, CAN BE SNUFFED OUT SO EASILY. BY OVEN, BY FIRE, BY KNIFE? WHO CARES? OVER FOREVER. ERADICATED IN AN IRRETRIEVABLE MILLISECOND OF FRUSTRATION AND DISGUST. EVERYTHING, THE WARP AND WOOF OF INFINITE AND COLORFUL FUTURES, UNDONE AND UNSPOOLED INTO FRAYED BLACK THREADS LEADING STRAIGHT DOWN TO HELL OR NOWHERE. SAME THING. THAT'S WHY YOU CAN BREATHE A QUIET PAEAN TO A GOD WHO DOESN'T EXIST OVER THE SIMPLE FACT THAT NONE OF IT WENT DOWN THAT WAY. THAT INSTEAD YOU SAID, "SO I DON'T PULL OUT A

KNIFE AND KILL SOMEONE," AND THEN SHUT THE DOOR BEHIND YOU AND STROLLED DOWN TO THE LOCAL CAFÉ AND STAYED THERE TILL MIDNIGHT WRITING A VERY LONG QUESTION TO *THE EXPECTANT MOTHER DISINFORMATION HANDBOOK*, HOPING THE EDITORS WOULD BE ABLE TO TELL YOU IF YOU HANDLED THE SITUATION IN THE PROPER MANNER, THE WAY A CIVILIZED MAN WOULD.

We sometimes receive questions from expectant fathers as well. The above is only one example of such. To this passionate young man we say, "Good job! We can give you a big pat on the back for not killing anyone in that situation, we sure can. We suggest not taking your wife's accusations too seriously. After all, she *is* pregnant, and this condition can cause the strangest things to tumble out of a young woman's mouth. Whether this young woman was prone to saying such paranoid things *before* she was pregnant, we honestly can't say (as we don't know her). If so, perhaps some therapy for your wife wouldn't be uncalled for and, if you can afford it, a new oven for your apartment. If you really *do* wish to kill your wife, however, there are preferred methods already discussed in an earlier chapter entitled "Advice for the Expectant Father."

WHAT SHOULD I DO IF I STRONGLY SUSPECT MY HUSBAND ATTEMPTED TO BLOW UP ME AND MY UNBORN CHILD WITH A BOOBYTRAPPED OVEN?

Just thank God you didn't marry someone who actually knows what he's doing.

THE LINK BETWEEN TRAGEDY AND PROCREATION

Scientists have found a strong connection between tragedy and a rise in procreation. The surprise attack on Pearl Harbor resulted in more births in America than at any time before that pivotal event. The first modern appearance of Godzilla off the coast of Hiroshima resulted in the most dramatic spike in births in Japan since the first detonation of the atom bomb nine years before. The same can be said of the assassination of John F. Kennedy, the explosion of the Space Shuttle Challenger, and the destruction of the Oklahoma City Building. Significantly, more than 400,000 children were conceived on the day of September 11, 2001, a spike of ten percent over normal statistics. Even more telling is the following data: Scientists at Columbia University have carefully tracked the development of these 400,000-plus children and have reached startling conclusions. The children conceived on 9-11-01 are now adults. To a person, they exhibit talents and abilities far beyond that of a normal American child of that age. On average, they have a far greater grasp of mathematics, spelling, grammar, and a better aptitude at retaining the names, dates, and places of historical events. In school, they exhibit the physical agility and mental aptitude of people twice their age. Some have demonstrated clear psychokinetic and telepathic skills to a degree not seen since the original Midwich outbreak of 1960. (See the chapter entitled "The Midwich Disease" for more details.)

This strange accumulation of facts points towards an inescapable conclusion: Females who procreate while infused with an unusually high amount of stress hormones tend to give birth to children with heightened senses, intelligence, and agility of an almost preternatural nature. Rumor has it that controversial and potentially dangerous laboratory studies at Columbia University and related institutions have attempted to recreate this high level of stress in an artificial setting, all to no avail. The stress-trigger, apparently, works only in an uncontrollable three-dimensional landscape (i.e., the real world). This development has frustrated and vexed the military-industrial financial backers of these studies. Nonetheless, despite recent failures in this regard, the research continues apace.

BUT WHOSE FAULT WILL IT BE IF MY CHILD TRANSFORMS INTO A WHITE DWARF STAR?

Your fault, death-bearer. Yours alone.

IS IT POSSIBLE FOR MY CHILD TO BE BORN A HOMICIDAL MANIAC?

Consider the case of Mr. and Mrs. David Leiber. In 1945, Alice Leiber was believed to be suffering from postpartum psychosis when she first began accusing her newborn son of being a highly intelligent, cold-blooded killer who was intent on assassinating her—that is, until she was found lying at the bottom of the stairs with a broken neck. Shortly after this tragic incident, Dr. ______ Jeffers recorded the following session with his patient, the distraught Mr. David Leiber:

> LEIBER: Suppose that a few babies out of all the millions born are instantaneously able to move, see, hear, think, like many animals and insects can. Insects are born self-sufficient. In a few weeks, most mammals and birds adjust. But children take years to speak and learn to stumble around on their weak legs.
>
> But suppose one child in a billion is—strange? Born perfectly aware, able to think, instinctively. Wouldn't it be a perfect setup, a perfect blind for anything the baby might want to do? He could pretend to be ordinary, weak, crying, ignorant. With just a *little* expenditure of energy, he could crawl about a darkened house, listening. And how easy to place obstacles at the top of the stairs. How

easy to cry all night and tire a mother into pneumonia. How easy, right at birth, to be so close to the mother that *a few deft maneuvers might cause peritonitis!*

DR. JEFFERS: For God's sake! That's a repulsive thing to say! [Though we here at *The Expectant Mother Disinformation Handbook* are by no means physicians or psychiatrists, we humbly suggest that doctors not speak to distraught patients in this manner.]

LEIBER: It's a repulsive thing I'm speaking of. How many mothers have died at the birth of their children? How many have suckled strange little improbabilities who cause death one way or another? Strange, red little creatures with brains that work in a bloody darkness we can't even guess at. Elemental little brains, aswarm with racial memory, hatred, and raw cruelty, with no more thought than self-preservation. And self-preservation in this case consisted of eliminating a mother who realized what a horror she had birthed. I ask you, doctor, what is there in the world more selfish than a baby? Nothing!

I'm not claiming any great strength for the child. Just enough to crawl around a little, a few months ahead of schedule. Just enough to listen all the time. Just enough to cry late at night. That's enough, more than enough . . .

The tape ends soon after that ominous comment. According to Dr. Jeffers's secretary, Dr. Jeffers visited Mr. Leiber at home the next morning, intending to make sure he was committed for his own safety (as well as the safety of the child, of course). But when he entered the house he discovered that someone had turned the gas on, killing Mr.

Leiber while he slept. Dr. Jeffers at once tried to defend himself against the murderous baby with a scalpel, but the devilish infant wrested it from his fist and planted the instrument into his brain. Dr. Jeffers survived this attack long enough to repeat his tale to the police, then expired shortly afterwards. Alas, the offspring of Mr. and Mrs. David Leiber has not been heard from since. He would be over seventy years old today.[21)]

21) This true life story was fictionalized by the popular author Ray Bradbury in his 1946 short story "The Small Assassin." The dialogue in his tale—a brief excerpt of which you'll find quoted above—was derived from actual transcriptions. You can find the story in his collection entitled *The October Country* (Rupert Hart-Davis Ltd., 1956).

WHAT IF MY HUSBAND WANTS TO NAME THE CHILD "GOTTERDAMMERUNG LOVALEEN-JONES" AND I WANT TO NAME THE CHILD "SUE"?

First of all, determine the sex of the child. "Gotterdammerung" seems to be a more feminine name, while "Sue" seems to be a decidedly more masculine one. Next, sit down with your husband and lay all your cards on the table. *Why* does he want your child to be named "Gotterdammerung Lovaleen-Jones?" Conversely, why do *you* want to name the child "Sue"? The name "Sue" is more likely to draw attention to the child, particularly if it's a girl. Do you wish to toughen up the child, to get her used to being made fun of by her peers? This "tough love" mentality may have held sway in the 1950s and earlier, but not today. Children wish to *blend in* with the crowd, not stand out from it. Therefore, we here at *The Expectant Mother Disinformation Handbook* would lean more toward your husband's choice. Sorry. We have to call 'em as we see 'em. That's why you trust *us* to make your decisions for you.

HAVE YOU EVER HEARD OF A PREGNANT WOMAN FALLING IN LOVE WITH HER DOCTOR?

This is a very common phenomenon, related to the Stockholm Syndrome (i.e., when an abductee falls in love with his or her kidnapper). The pregnant female often feels as if she is trapped by her situation, and begins to see the doctor as both her savior and captor. Not only does she know that he will be the one to "deliver" her from this imprisonment, but he is also the only individual the female can depend on to show her attention and care to an infinitesimal degree, without any arguments or tension to get in the way (as is often the case with one's husband). Of course, she conveniently forgets the fact that she's *paying* the doctor to show her this attention. Indeed, she forgets he has any patients other than her. The visits to the doctor begin to be seen, in her fantasy world, as an intimate and taboo tete-a-tete with a caring and intelligent "other man."

Sometimes this fantasy can be taken to an extreme, as in the case of Mrs. Val Oakes. By the seventh month of her pregnancy, after having visited Dr. Derek Sheffield's office on a weekly basis, Mrs. Oakes became convinced that the child was Dr. Sheffield's and not her husband's. One day, out of the blue, she began asking the doctor strange questions like, "When should we tell my husband the *truth*?" Sheffield was confused for several minutes, until he convinced her to elaborate, at which point her fantasies came spilling out. The doctor was shocked. When he tried to explain that he and Mrs. Oakes had never even kissed much less had sex, Mrs. Oakes ran from the office crying, "How can you pretend it never even *happened*? Do I mean that little to you?" She immediately ran to her husband's office and confessed the imaginary affair. The husband flew into a non-imaginary rage, whipped out a non-imaginary .44 revolver from his safe in the den, drove over to the doctor's office, and planted three non-imaginary bullets right into the center of Derek Sheffield's brain. The husband got life in jail, the wife was committed, and the child was sent to an orphanage in New Jersey. The doctor ended up strewn over the Atlantic Ocean.

This just goes to show you: Fantasies can be nothing but *dangerous*. You must not indulge in them, not even for a second.

Keep your eyes on the prize, ladies.

Now go and do the right thing.

IF I EVER HAVE TO CALL AN AM RADIO TALK SHOW TO MEDIATE AN ARGUMENT BETWEEN MY HUSBAND AND ME (OVER CHILDREARING ISSUES OR WHAT-HAVE-YOU), IS THAT A DEFINITE SIGN THE MARRIAGE IS OVER?

Look at it this way: Think about all the rocky marriages you know about that were saved by a total stranger with a microphone, a grating bedside manner, and a Ph.D. in physical therapy. Why should yours be any different?

IS IT TRUE WHAT THEY SAY, THAT THE FETUS IS URINATING INSIDE MY WOMB ON A DAILY BASIS?

You need not feel uncomfortable with the fact that your child is micturating in your stomach. *You will not be affected unduly by this.* Your child's urine is not infectious or dirty, not like a stranger's urine. Consider your fetus' urine to be your *own* urine. Urine is the transparent medium through which you and your child exchange physical expressions of godly love. Urine is an *in utero* transmutative miracle as holy as the filthy toilet water of the heathen Lebanese after Jesus absorbed all the evil out of it with the briefest touch of His glorious fingertips. If we here at *The Expectant Mother Disinformation Handbook* had a choice between bathing with a Muslim in crystalline water funneled straight from the top of Lake Arrowhead, and swimming naked through prenatal urine in a Christian womb, we'd choose the latter each and every single time. Amen.

ONTOGENY RECAPITULATES PHYLOGENY

In the late nineteenth century, Professor Ernst Haeckel gave the world his famous "recapitulation theory," which proposed that the development of an organism mirrors the evolutionary development of the species. That is why human embryos go through an amphibian stage. It mirrors the very amphibian stage the human race itself had to undergo in order to reach our current plateau. Sometimes, however, this natural process can go horribly awry.

In 1953, from a remote area of Scotland, came a remarkable breakthrough that stunned the field of biology. One evening, a man named Gerald MacTeam revealed to local journalists the corpse of his late uncle, Sir Roger, who had lived for decades within a maze constructed from the hedges adjoining the family's ancestral castle. Sir Roger's corpse represented, statistically, a one-in-a-million chance: the ultimate proof of Professor Haeckel's theories. Sir Roger was an anomaly, a human being who had never transcended the earliest stage of development. He had grown, instead, into an amphibian about twelve feet long and six feet high, and remained in this state his entire life. Though he possessed the same level of intelligence as any other human being, his body was indeed that of an immense frog. MacTeam's uncle, sadly, committed suicide by defenestrating himself after his shameful presence in the maze was inadvertently revealed to Gerald MacTeam's young fiancée, Ms. Kitty Murray.

Though the specimen would have been more valuable to science if it had remained alive, nonetheless, any number of formerly insoluble questions regarding the development of human life were answered after the donation of Sir Roger's corpse to Yale University in the United States. Despite the fact that he knew full well his uncle would not have approved of being on display like a freak in a circus sideshow, Gerald MacTeam concluded that his uncle's death would ultimately hold more meaning if his remains were studied by the world's most cutting-edge biologists instead of rotting beneath the family estate. Indeed, much of our current knowledge about the development of human embryos comes directly from the corpse of Sir Roger MacTeam. For this reason, we here at *The Expectant Mother Disinformation Handbook* salute the memories of both MacTeams for their brave contributions to science.

Though an anomaly, of course, we must remember there is no guarantee that more Sir Rogers won't be born in the future. In fact, the condition of an embryo becoming paralyzed in the amphibian stage has been labeled by biologists as *MacTeam Disorder*. Most embryos who come down with this disorder are humanely eliminated before any further development occurs. Though we certainly don't support abortion (except in the most extreme cases), sometimes such operations must occur if the life of the mother is at risk, and the birth of a child the size of Sir Roger MacTeam would certainly endanger any normal woman.

Let's pray no other child ever has to go through what Sir Roger MacTeam must have felt while hiding from the world for decades, trapped by his own shame inside a lonely labyrinth of his own construction. We're sure Sir Roger would join us in these prayers, if he were still with us today.

IF I FIND TRACES OF COCAINE IN A STRAW HIDDEN IN MY WIFE'S PURSE, SHOULD I HAVE THE FETUS TAKEN AWAY FROM HER?

Any responsible father would do so, yes. First, you must ask your wife to take a drug test. If she refuses, you need to see a lawyer immediately to ensure that your wife is forced to take one. Once your wife has failed the test, a judge can order a prenatal Caesarean to remove the fetus and implant it in a government-provided incubator at your local county hospital. This may sound harsh to you, but think of the alternative. A pregnant woman addicted to cocaine can endanger the lives of both mother and child. Only after the mother has been cured of her addiction can she be allowed to see or touch the child. (Read the next chapter for more information about the growing trend of incubator fetuses.)

INCUBATOR FETUSES

Incubator fetuses are becoming more and more popular, particularly among upper class women who don't have time to sacrifice an entire nine months for something as inconvenient and distracting as a child. After about three months of being pregnant, these women opt to implant the fetus in a government-provided incubator. These mothers then make sure to visit the developing fetus once or twice a week, depending on their schedule. Nine times out of ten, the child ends up being healthier than if he or she had remained in the mother's womb! Such are the benefits of twenty-first century technology. We here at *The Expectant Mother Disinformation Handbook* don't know if we entirely approve, but we have to admit that sometimes such measures are necessary (read the previous chapter for one such example).

ANGEL BABIES

Yes, the rumors are true! Angels do sometimes descend from Heaven and fornicate with human females. One documented case occurred in Poughkeepsie, NY in the mid-seventies. A teenager named ______ ________ was assaulted by an angel in an IBM parking lot. There were no witnesses. A second assault occurred several years later on a public sidewalk in New York in broad daylight. Again, there were no witnesses. This final rape resulted in what some paranormal researchers call "an angel baby." The young woman in question described the difficult birth in this way:

> It was horrible. The pain filled the whole room, it rolled off the walls at me, it went on for hours and hours so that I thought the kid must have braced itself inside and would never come out. I was scared I was going to die [. . .].
>
> It went on for so long I started seeing things. I imagined myself outside, with snow all around, and the angel circling way over my head.
>
> When the baby did come out it came so quickly I didn't know it had happened. I went on pushing, with the kid lying there on the soaking wet sheets. When I realized I'd done it I lay back, shaking so much the whole bed made this awful squeaking noise. Probably it had squeaked like that for hours, and I was cursing and crying so much I never noticed. I picked up the kid and cut the cord and

cleaned him off as best as I could. I had to get rid of the afterbirth and get him breathing and everything, and I knew I better do it all at once, because if I stopped I'd just fall asleep. At last I held him up so I could look at him.

A haze or something must have covered my eyes because it took a while before I could actually see him, what he really looked like. When I did see I just stared at him. Wings grew on his back, small, dirty white, not feathers but sort of rough, almost like cheap leather, the kind you get on pocketbooks bought at one of those downtown discount stores. For the first time I realized the angel's wings were like that, leather and not feathers at all. Even while I stared at him his sad little wings fluttered a couple of times and then came right off. They fell on my leg. I screamed and knocked them onto the floor. When I looked for them a couple of days later they were gone. Crumbled right into dust, maybe.

His hands did the same thing. I don't mean they fell off, but they changed, from claws to ordinary baby hands, the hard curved fingers shrinking to stubby human ones.

There's nothing left, I thought. All that pain for nothing. But I was wrong. He had his father's eyes, cold, very hard, and empty. Even now you can see it, not all the time, but sometimes he'll put down his truck or his cap gun, or else he'll just stand there when some other kid throws the ball to him. Then you can see that metal coldness take over his eyes, and you know he's looking right past you, into a world of lightning, and fire that jumps into the sky, a world where the sounds say everything, and not just words.

The mother kept a detailed journal about her experiences, then entrusted this journal to a professional writer named Rachel Pollack. Pollack's fictionalized account found its way into the summer 1982 issue of *Interzone Magazine* (#2). The dialogue in her tale—a brief excerpt of which you'll find quoted above—was derived from actual transcriptions. If you're interested in the "angel baby" phenomena, for whatever reason, we suggest you look up this story. You might find it illuminating.

SHOULD I GIVE MY FETUS A CELL PHONE?

This is a very controversial subject. Some parents wish to remain in contact with their fetus 24/7, to ensure their safety, while other parents worry about the health issues connected to cell phones. Other parents simply believe cell phones are an unnecessary luxury. Some OBGYNs think fetuses younger than the third trimester should not be allowed to have access to a cell phone, due to the connection that has been drawn between fetal cancers and *in utero* cell phone use. Other OBGYNs say the exact opposite. How are we, as mothers, to decide?

Consider this: We here at *The Expectant Mother Disinformation Handbook* are in personal contact with one mother who received a phone bill for $14,366 during her second trimester. Apparently the fetus had somehow gotten around the long distance block and had been calling internet friends in China, Australia, and New Zealand for the past three months. The simple fact of the matter is that children this young are not capable of understanding the realities of money. The fetus in question was reprimanded and the bill waived by the phone company, as soon as the situation had been explained to several AT&T representatives in precise detail by an enraged father. To avoid these potentially stress-inducing difficulties, we recommend holding off on giving your child a cell phone until he or she is at least born.

IF I OWE THE CITY OF LONG BEACH, CA OVER $500 WORTH OF PARKING TICKETS AND WANT TO PAY IT ALL OFF BUT CAN'T BECAUSE I'M EIGHT MONTHS PREGNANT AND NEED TO REST, WHAT DO I DO?

Don't worry about it for now, dear. A law that renders pregnant women in their third trimester exempt from imprisonment due to any crime short of murder, kidnapping or child molestation should be passed soon. What you need to do right now is relax and let the mistakes of the past fade away into the background. Your baby needs you more than some musty old jail cell.

MY EIGHT-MONTH PREGNANT WIFE HAS JUST BEEN TOSSED INTO L.A. COUNTY JAIL. IS IT TRUE YOU TOLD HER SHE COULDN'T BE ARRESTED FOR OWING $500 IN PARKING TICKETS?

We made it perfectly clear that we thought there *should* be a law exempting pregnant women from imprisonment, not that there was one. This just goes to show you that reading comprehension is a necessary survival skill in today's complicated society. One must always read *between* the lines, mustn't one? We recommend visiting your wife at least once a day and making sure she's taking the proper vitamins. A dirty old jail cell can't possibly be a healthy environment to give birth to a child, but we must make do with the situations God hands us, mustn't we—particularly if we've been negligent in our civil duties, hm? Isn't that right, ladies?

HAVE ANY OF YOU "EXPERTS" AT *THE EXPECTANT MOTHER DISINFORMATION HANDBOOK* EVER ACTUALLY *RAISED* A CHILD BEYOND THE FIRST MONTH?

We appreciate your curiosity, but the question itself implies a fair amount of naiveté. After all, does a world-famous chef need to have lived in the ocean in order to make an exquisite filet mignon?

We, like yourself, think not.

HAVE YOU EVER HEARD OF A PREGNANT WOMAN DEVELOPING UNHEALTHY FEELINGS FOR HER MATERNITY PILLOW?

This phenomenon is more common than you might imagine. We know of at least one case in which a pregnant woman in her second trimester actually left her husband for her maternity pillow. Unbeknownst to the woman, however, the husband had developed a similarly intimate relationship with the pillow behind her back, when she was at work. The husband filed for divorce and sued for custody of the pillow on the grounds that he had paid for it in the first place. The wife claimed she deserved it because it had been bought as a gift for her; in fact, she still had the mushy card (husband's signature included) to prove it. Hundreds of thousands of dollars later, when the lawyers finally got around to asking the pillow what it wanted, the pillow said it would be more than content with joint custody. The husband got the pillow on weekends.

One day, when the woman was changing diapers on her newborn, the pillow wrapped a handkerchief around a long stick, stuffed a few comestibles inside, then headed out for the open highway. It was last seen somewhere on Route 66, hitching its way toward the East Coast.

Let this be a warning to you, ladies: What may seem soft and warm on the outside might, in truth, be hard and cold when stripped of its polyester veneer.

I'M SIX MONTHS PREGNANT, AND THE OTHER DAY MY 7-YEAR-OLD ASKED ME WHAT WOULD HAPPEN WHEN MY BELLY GOT TOO BIG. SO I SAID, "WHY, I'LL GIVE BIRTH, HONEY." AND SHE SAID, "MOMMY, WHAT IS BIRTH, AND WHO YOU GONNA GIVE IT TO?" MY QUESTION IS: HOW DO I DEFINE "BIRTH" TO A CHILD SO SHE'LL REALLY UNDERSTAND IT?

In 1911 the famous lexicographer Ambrose Bierce defined the word "birth" in this way:

> The first and direst of all disasters. As to the nature of it there appears to be no uniformity. Castor and Pollux were born from the egg. Pallas came out of a skull. Galatea was once a block of stone. Peresilis, who wrote in the tenth century, avers that he grew up out of the ground where a priest had spilled holy water. It is known that Arimaxus was derived from a hole in the earth,

> made by a stroke of lightning. Leucomedon was the son of a cavern in Mount Aetna, and I have myself seen a man come out of a wine cellar.

We definitely do not recommend defining the word "birth" in this manner to a child. This would no doubt be confusing, not to mention disheartening. Instead, you might take the opposite approach: "Birth is the first of many miraculous and joyous moments you will experience in this lifetime. It is not a man coming out of a wine cellar."

EVER SINCE I FOUND OUT I WAS PREGNANT, I'VE SUSPECTED THAT MY HORMONES HAVE BEEN CAUSING ME TO ACT LIKE A BITCH IN A VARIETY OF WAYS, NOT THE LEAST OF WHICH HAS BEEN INSULTING MY HUSBAND IN SUCH A PASSIVE-AGGRESSIVE AND SUBTLE MANNER THAT ANY ILL INTENT CAN BE PLAUSIBLY DENIED IF MY HUSBAND GROWS FRUSTRATED WITH THE BULLSHIT AND CALLS ME ON IT. LATELY, HOWEVER, I'VE COME TO THE STARTLING REALIZATION THAT I ACTUALLY ENJOY BEING A BITCH VERY MUCH AND THAT MY RECENT BEHAVIOR HAS NOTHING AT ALL TO DO WITH MY HORMONES. MY QUESTION IS THIS: IS IT WRONG

TO USE MY PREGNANCY AS A CAMOUFLAGE TO COVER UP MY NATURAL BITCHY TENDENCIES?

The only danger here is growing spoiled and getting *too used* to your own "bitchy tendencies" as you yourself put it. After all, the only reason your husband is putting up with your behavior right now is because he thinks there's a .01% chance that your bitchiness is not inherent in your personality. You can probably get away with this charade for a few weeks following the birth, citing postpartum depression as the reason for its continuation (you might even get a doctor to sign off on the excuse with a few well-placed words and a morose expression or two), but don't expect to get away with this behavior perpetually.[22] The number of women we know of who've gotten away with this psychological warfare for more than six months can be counted on two or three amputated, manicured hands. The rest have done their part in benefiting the growth of remote vegetation in wilderness areas.

The infamous music professor from UC Santa Cruz, Dr. Thomas Lehrer, documented his own experiences with such pathological phenomena in a song called "I Hold Your Hand in Mine" before being sentenced to Folsom for 25-to-life:

I hold your hand in mine, dear
I press it to my lips
I take a healthy bite
From your dainty fingertips.

---

22) No more than once a month, that is.

My joy would be complete, dear
If you were only here
But still I keep your hand
As a precious souvenir.

The night you died I cut it off.
I really don't know why.
For now each time I kiss it
I get bloodstains on my tie.

I'm sorry now I killed you,
For our love was something fine,
And till they come to get me
I shall hold your hand in mine.

HOSPITALS AND DOCTORS (TO AVOID)

We have previously commented on the dangers of the Moloch worshippers of Monte Rio, CA. We feel it is our duty to elaborate on this warning, for the health and safety of your coming child.

We refer you to an expert in this particular field, Eustace Mullins of The International Institute of Jewish Studies, a well-respected scholar of Semitic history:

> There are now many Jewish hospitals in the United States, which are owned and operated by Jewish doctors and nurses. Parents who place their children in these institutions for minor ailments are stunned to be told, a day or two later, that the child has suddenly passed away. In many such cases, the child has been removed to a synagogue and murdered by the prescribed ritual. The bloodless body of the victim is then turned over to the parents. This procedure also obeys the Jewish prohibition against the burial of a gentile, for the Jews simply allow the parents to take care of the burial.
>
> It therefore behooves American parents to avoid leaving their children unguarded in the presence of a Jewish physician or placing the child in a hospital run by Jews. Any parent should think twice about abandoning a helpless child to a people

> which has a history of five thousand years of murdering children under such horrible circumstances. And any parent should be able to visualize the horror of the handsome, perfectly formed body of the child on which they have lavished such loving care, being stripped and laid down on a table while Jews, their eyes filled with blood lust and hatred of the gentiles, gather round the child and pierce its flesh, and drink its blood, and call down curses upon the name of Jesus Christ. Can any parent really wish to place its child in such danger and to have it die in such terrible circumstances?
>
> In the United States, Jews have been able to practice ritual murder of gentile children with impunity, because they control the press, and because they hold so many high public offices. It has been estimated by a leading police official that four thousand children disappear in the United States each year. There is no question that the majority of them are victims of Jewish ritual murder. So prevalent has the custom become in this country that Jews are able to ship large quantities of the children's blood to Israel for use in their ceremonies there. One of the problems of the Jewish homeland in Israel has been a shortage of gentile children who could be used in the ritual ceremony, and the United States, which has also furnished most of the money to Israel, has also provided much of the required children's blood.
>
> Because most of these children are taken from poor families, no mention is ever made of their disappearance in the press. Only in rare instances do the Jews dare to take the child of a well-known public figure, as they did in the Lindbergh case, and then it is done for a specific political purpose, and as part of a larger policy [. . .].

In the United States, many gentiles have found large sums of money suddenly available to them for campaign purposes, after they have aided in hushing up some new scandal of Jewish ritual murder. The path to the Governor's mansion, the Senate, and the White House has been magically eased when the candidate proves that he is willing to cover up for the Jews in their murders of gentile children [. . .].

It has been estimated that at least one-third of all officeholders in the United States are well aware of the prevalence of Jewish ritual murder of children, and that their continuing to hold office depends on aiding and abetting the Jews in the practice of these crimes.

During a conversation with Father Bulger in 1956, this writer was told that he had been working all his life on a book which was to be the definitive work on Jewish ritual murder. Father Bulger furnished much of the information contained herein. However his superiors had forbidden him to have his own book published. In former years, most of the information about this type of crime had been published in Catholic encyclopaedias and official parochial works, but further writings on the subject of Jewish ritual murder had been banned because of Jewish pressure on the Vatican.

Father Bulger told this writer that according to his estimates, six million gentile children had been done to death in the ritual manner by Jews since the crucifixion of Christ. These six million victims have not only gone unavenged, but each one of them, deserving to be elevated to sainthood for their sufferings at the hands of the Jews, have died without gentile society making the slightest effort to protect other gentile children from becoming victims in the same manner. Father James E.

> Bulger said, "The blood lust of the Jews and their hatred of Jesus Christ are combined in this horrible ceremony. Not only have six million innocent souls been done to death in ritual murder by the Jews, but each of us must ask himself, What kind of Christian, what kind of human being, am I, if I do nothing to protect children from such horrible sacrifice in a supposedly Christian and modern society?"

If you'd like to read more about this pressing topic, we refer you to Chapter 6 of Mr. Mullins's sociological study *Mullins' New History of the Jews*. We'd like to thank Mel Gibson and his father, Hutton Gibson, for their continuing guidance and inspiration in regards to these matters.

KITTEN DREAMS

Our subconscious mind has various methods of warning us if our unborn babies are in danger. Dreams, of course, have always been one of the most respected. If you happen to have a dream in which you're taking care of a litter of sickly newborn kittens, for example, *get to the hospital quick*. In our experience, such dreams can presage an imminent miscarriage.

If, on the other hand, you happen to have a dream in which a litter of sickly newborn kittens are taking care of *you*, don't even bother with the hospital and just get your affairs in order. In the limited amount of time you have left, the only decision you'll be able to make is: Cremation or Burial?

JOKE TIME

Sometimes an expectant mother can worry too much, at which time it's appropriate to get her mind off her stress and physical discomfort by telling her a harmless joke like: "So a man is sitting in the hospital waiting for his wife to give birth. The doctor comes out and says, 'Sir, I have some good and some bad news. Here's the good news.' The doctor shows the man his newborn son: a giant eyeball wrapped in a blanket. The man says, 'What the—? *That's* the good news? What the hell's the bad news?' The doctor says, 'He's blind.'"

RADIATION AND CHILD REARING

Some mothers are concerned about whether or not they should allow their physician to give them a CT Scan, due to the fact that the procedure involves exposing the fetus to low level amounts of radiation. We here at *The Expectant Mother Disinformation Handbook* can assure you that you need not worry. All responsible studies demonstrate that there is no *provable* link between exposing the fetus to X-rays and later childhood illnesses such as leukemia, skin cancer, Sudden Infant Death Syndrome or various physical deformities. True, in the 1950s, extreme exposure to radiation resulted in the mutation of common insects like ants and grasshoppers into murderous giants that laid waste to major U.S. metropolitan cities and awakened the antediluvian reptile Gojiro from his slumber beneath the Pacific Ocean, leading to the destruction of Japan several times over, but the 1960s revealed a more positive side to the radiation experiments of the WWII era. Children born in the late 1940s who reached puberty in the early 1960s demonstrated unique physical attributes such as advanced strength, telekinesis, flight, the ability to crawl up walls, freeze objects at will, and shoot laser beams out of their eyes for defensive purposes. Alas, due to unforeseeable and unavoidable nuclear tragedies such as Three Mile Island in the 1970s, the general public grew skeptical about the potential benefits of incorporating radiation into our staple of basic childrearing tools. In a perfect world, radiation would be considered as necessary to the baby care industry as vitamin-enhanced infant formula and plastic rattles. Perhaps, in a few decades or so, our collective consciousness will have evolved to the plateau where we can recognize radiation for what it is: the key to unlocking a seemingly impenetrable door that bars us from tapping into unknown potentialities buried deep within our individual cellular memories.

For further reliable references concerning the benefits of radiation, we recommend the book-length study *All About Radiation* by nuclear physicist L. Ron Hubbard, and the article "The Health Benefits of Low-Dose Radiation" by former U.S. President Lyndon H. LaRouche, winner of the 1977 Noble Prize in Science for his discovery of Euclidean Geometry.

THE HEALTH BENEFITS OF HIGH-DOSE GAMMA RAYS

Following up on our last chapter, this might be a good time to discuss the groundbreaking research of Boronski (by all accounts, he never had a first name). Boronski was a geneticist based in Gudavia, a rural village located in Eastern Europe far behind the Iron Curtain. In 1956, an American journalist named Mike Wilson ended up stranded in Gudavia due to an accident involving a train bound for Salzburg. During his brief stay in Gudavia, Wilson uncovered the illicit Gamma ray experiments Boronski was conducting on the helpless children of the village. Exposure to high-dose Gamma rays mutated many of the children into monsters, but a small minority gained supernaturally superior intelligence. Happily, Wilson succeeded in stopping Boronski's experiments and fled back to America with the scientist's secret documents tucked safely in his briefcase.

Some recent historians have posited that Wilson was an intelligence asset who used his journalistic credentials to spy on Russia for the CIA throughout the Cold War. Others believe he was something far worse: a free agent selling sensitive military secrets of various countries (large and small alike) to the highest bidder. One unnamed source believes Boronski's papers ended up in the hands of the embryonic Lyndon H. LaRouche organization as early as 1958. This has never been proved.

Recently declassified military documents from the

early 1960s regarding American-sponsored experiments in Gamma radiation have revealed the startling fact that one's emotional state can affect the degree to which Gamma rays mutate one's body. Though high-dose exposure to these rays did indeed grant certain individuals increased strength and/or intelligence, the rays also unbalanced their mind to a degree that rendered them uncontrollable, and thus unable to follow strict military orders. For this reason and others, these early experiments were considered a failure by the U.S. Military. The Pentagon concluded that high-dose Gamma rays could serve no useful military function and all related experiments were abandoned.

More recent experiments conducted by Dr. José Laputa of Columbia University, however, have shown promising signs that these early experiments can be improved upon, refined, and ultimately used to combat fatal childhood illnesses such as leukemia, skin cancer, and Sudden Infant Death Syndrome.

UPON VIEWING PUBLIC DISPLAYS OF AFFECTION

From time to time, you will be subjected to the unasked-for sight of a couple of acne-ridden juvenile delinquents hugging and kissing in public. Your initial instinct will be to grab your bulging stomach and scream, "Stop it, *stop* it! See what happens? *SEE*?" If you do this, the young man in question will inevitably laugh in your face and mutter, "Dig the crazy pregnant chick, Jill. *Haw Haw Haw*! Let's blow this joint, and stir us up some real woo!" Take solace in the fact that soon *they* will be standing where you are now, staring helplessly at the backs of two virile teenyboppers snapping their fingers, chewing pink bubble gum, and taking tokes off the aphrodisiac Mexican devil weed. They will feel as depressed and hopeless as you, for no amount of youthful arrogance or illicit psychedelic inhalants can protect shortsighted hipsters such as these from the harsh vicissitudes of all-conquering, all-consuming *REALITY*.

We, the God-fearing procreators, are the NEW Lords of Reality. *Our Reality* is a vast stone the size of God's foot that smashes and obliterates the subjective world of the solipsistic and the promiscuous and the immoral.

Yes, remember *that* as the heathens point and guffaw at the all-holy life form growing in your womb.

DO FETUSES HAVE KIRLIAN AURAS? IF SO, WHAT DO THEY GENERALLY LOOK LIKE?

Every living being possesses a Kirlian aura. Fetal Kirlian auras differ from baby to baby. Generally, they are black as Original Sin, as dark as the heart of the unknown. The nineteenth century artist Edvard Munch based his famous painting "The Scream" on his own Kirlian photograph taken during his seventeenth week in the womb—July 12th, 1863, to be exact. The seventeenth week is when the fetus can first begin hearing the sounds of the outside world.

IF OUR CHILD IS BORN WITH SIX FINGERS, SHOULD WE BE WORRIED?

Polydactylism is not common, but neither is it life-threatening or debilitating in any way. Many famous and successful people have been born with six fingers and/or toes. Theodore Roosevelt had six fingers when he was born, as did Marilyn Monroe. Both had parents who elected to have the extra digits surgically removed when they were very young. The infamous forger John Dolan Vincent maintained his six-fingers well into adulthood; some doctors believe the extra digits on both hands were the cause of his lifelong migraines and his descent into a life of crime, but this theory has not yet been proved.

Some non-Western cultures regard polydactylism with great respect and even religious awe, perhaps because the condition is so rare. In the early 1990s, Harlan Low, a missionary for a fundamentalist church based in Nye Country, Nevada, published a scholarly study called *The Call of Mastomaho*, about the religious significance of the image of the Six-fingered Hand throughout time amongst diverse mythologies all around the globe. Low included a chapter that examined the recurring warnings in these myths regarding the coming of a "god from outer space" with six fingers who, under various names, had supposedly been worshipped for centuries. Low claimed this god had been recognized by Native American tribes as well as primitive peoples in North Africa.

About ten years before the publication of Low's book, in April of 1981, a group of obscure demons—Avarrish, Fashima, Hyppokri, Maya, Puishannt, and Unthinnk—banded together under the name "The Six-fingered Hand" to literally create Hell on Earth, by merging both realms together. These demons thought they could accomplish this goal by causing chaos in key locations all around the Earth. Fortunately, their insidious plot was thwarted by a band of obscure heroes led by a physician-turned-magician named Dr. Stephen Strange. Oddly enough, Harlan Low makes no mention of this incident in his book.

In 1970, eleven years before the attack of The Six-fingered Hand, journalist Hunter S. Thompson chose a six-fingered fist as the central symbol of his celebrated political campaign to become Sheriff of Pitkin County, Colorado. Despite his wise choice of an icon, Thompson lost the campaign—but only by a few votes.

So, as you can see, the image of the six-fingered hand plays an important role in world history and should not be an object of fear, pity or disgust.

IF I VISIT MY GRANDFATHER'S GRAVE WHILE I'M PREGNANT, IS IT POSSIBLE FOR HIS SPIRIT TO TAKE OVER THE UNBORN BODY OF THE FETUS?

This has been known to happen throughout the centuries, and not just with dead relatives. Dead strangers can take over your fetus as well. For this reason, we recommend avoiding cemeteries during your entire pregnancy. If, for some reason, you absolutely must go, we recommend buying an Ectoplasm Shield™ to wear under your clothes. Essentially, this is a mini Tesla coil interwoven with a thin undergarment made up of alternating layers of organic and inorganic material that emits a constant electromagnetic pulse, thus preventing ectoplasmic infestation. Ectoplasm, as you no doubt know, is the ethereal substance of which spirits are composed while invading the material plane.

Leaving aside all this scientific mumbo-jumbo for a moment, just remember this: Ghosts are nothing more than human beings who are dead and seriously pissed off about it. The only way you become a ghost is if you were a five-star asshole when you were alive. If you weren't an asshole, you'd be in Heaven right now, drinking Shirley Temples with the Savior and the Holy Ghost under a fake palm tree, and not moaning and slamming doors and throwing chairs around at three o'clock in the morning while everyone else in the house is trying to sleep, right?

Do not trust ghosts, even if they're related to you. You never listened to Aunt Matilda while she was alive, so why start now? Spirits are no font of wisdom. Just because you're dead doesn't mean you're smart.

So if some decaying jackball suddenly appears in a puff of smoke out of your grandfather's urn in the closet, or the old Ouija board your parents tossed in the back of the garage three decades ago, and offers you free advice, just look the cantankerous bastard straight in the eye and say, "Fuck you and the tumescent ectoplasm you rode in on. I'm wearing my Faraday Cage Thermal Underwear™, so you can't get anywhere near me, so forget about reincarnating in *this* womb and go find some other fetus to fuck around with. This one's off limits to anyone dumb enough to smoke a doobie and fall asleep in a tub of water with a radio perched on edge of the bath playing old Simon and Garfunkel songs. They're gonna have enough trouble dealing with all the live fuckheads on *this* world, so why waste energy dealing with a dead one like you? Feel free to bend over like some deformed hybrid in a Hieronymus Bosch painting and penetrate your own maggot-ridden stink-shitter in the tenth ring of Hell and leave our Dear One alone."

See what the dead guy does then. We at *The Expectant Mother Disinformation Handbook* guarantee you he won't do *anything*, not while you're wearing your Ectoplasm Shield™. You'll see.

IS IT TRUE THAT MEN SOMETIMES MIMIC THE PREGNANCY SYMPTOMS OF THEIR WIVES OR SPECIAL PARTNERS?

Yes. Husbands will often gain weight, experience cramps, and in some cases even begin producing a small amount of milk. These are known as *sympathetic* symptoms. Most wives will find such symptoms to either be cute or at least endearing on some level.

The one symptom the female will *not* find endearing in any way, however, is when the male begins to mimic the female's crankiness and sudden mood shifts. Apparently, this is the one symptom that is off-limits for men to reproduce. Be aware, expectant fathers: If you do attempt to mimic these symptoms in the precise tenor and tone of your wife or Special Partner, you will be accused of both verbal and physical abuse and arrested by local law enforcement agents. The female, on the other hand, will expect perpetual free dinners and lodging for the same behavior. If you have the urge to complain about these paradoxes, you might as well buy a pair of heavy duty handcuffs and slam them on your own wrists. Welcome to fatherhood.

ARE FETUSES SUSCEPTIBLE TO LICE INFESTATION?

Dr. Sanjai Gupta of Columbia University (not to be confused with Dr. Sanjay Gupta of Emory University) has much to say about this subject. Dr. Gupta has created an entire television series based around this ongoing problem. This riveting twelve-part series, *Fetal Lice*, can be seen playing incessantly in clinic waiting rooms located in low-income neighborhoods all around the United States. Though this particular health problem is a complex one, Dr. Gupta's advice can be summed up as follows: Consult with your OBGYN and request a special X-ray scan that will not only reveal the presence of lice in your unborn child's skin, but will also kill off any pesky insects that happen to be preying on the fetus. Dr. Gupta has discovered that high-dose radiation can reduce *in utero* lice to smoldering ashes while leaving the fetus entirely unharmed. "How is this possible?" you may ask. Don't worry your pretty little head about these esoteric details. Place your trust in Dr. Gupta. He's studied this subject, and this subject alone, for decades. And if you're concerned about high-dose radiation transforming the aforementioned lice into an army of mutated giants that will burst out of your womb while the X-ray is being administered, instantly reducing you and your baby to tiny bloody fragments, please do not worry about this either. To our knowledge, such an event has not yet been recorded in the annals of medical history. If you would like to reach Dr. Gupta, visit his official website at: <www.inuterolice.com>.

SEXUAL DREAMS

Pregnancy often brings on intense sexual dreams. Orgasms can become more powerful during pregnancy due to increased blood flow in the vaginal regions, thus making one's "wet dreams" an even more thrilling experience, perhaps more satisfying than sex with your husband or Special Partner. Sometimes women will document these dreams in great detail and send them to us, asking us if it's right and proper to be dreaming about such transgressive scenarios. Just to reassure all God-fearing Christian women that you're not alone, we plan on compiling a separate companion volume to this one, entitled *The Sexual Dreams of Pregnant Women*. This book will be sold for educational purposes only.

To give you an idea of what's in the book, here's a brief excerpt we received from a 22-year-old housewife named Erin Fleece[23] of Dubuque, Iowa:

> . . . and then Bob dropped his tool belt and unzipped his mud-stained blue jeans. His younger brother was already naked, and I could feel his massive hands on my hips, his groin pressing itself hard against my back. I was worried about the curtains being open in the kitchen in the middle of the day, but chose to do nothing about it. *Oh, who cares what the Carpenter boys see while playing Frisbee in the backyard next door?* I thought. *Let*

23) Not her real name.

them see everything. I refuse to be ashamed of my natural urges any longer. So Zack's throbbing twelve-inch erection playfully slid along the crack of my ass through the skirt Poppa bought me for my last birthday while Bob unbuttoned my blouse. It quickly fell to the filthy linoleum floor. Bob picked me up by the thighs and plopped me down on the kitchen counter, right in front of the sink and that window overlooking the Carpenters' backyard. Bob lifted up my skirt, yanked off my pink panties, tossed them on the ground, and thrust himself inside me hard and fast. I didn't think about Gary at all, or when he might get home from his job with The Amalgamated Dancing Potato Trucking Company. All I could think about was the fact that I could feel the innocent eyes of the Carpenter boys on my naked back while Bob slammed his uncircumcised cock inside me over and over again, while Zack stroked himself and watched, ready to take over the second Bob could no longer continue his unrelenting assault . . .

If you'd like to read more to find out how pregnant Christian mothers can be as explicit in their dreams as godless heathens without being doomed to Hell, keep an eye out for *The Sexual Dreams of Pregnant Women*—available soon in a bookstore near YOU!

SHOULD MY CHILD BE CIRCUMCISED?

What kind of a question is that? You don't want your son to be dissimilar from the other boys in the locker room, do you? How could one so *different* cope with the basic vicissitudes of life? Alas, it would be impossible. Think about it: When he finds himself in a truly intimate moment with his first sweetheart in high school, will the girlfriend really want to go *all the way* with someone whose sexual organ looks like it just escaped from a mad scientist's laboratory? We at *The Expectant Mother Disinformation Handbook* think not. How will he react during this crucial moment of his prepubescent development? Will he be so overwhelmed with self-loathing that he'll pitch himself off the roof of an eight-story building, cursing the inconsiderate parents who denied him the advantages of a normal existence? Do you really want your child to die in this horrible manner? Don't you want to raise your child with essential *American* values? Don't you want him to base his entire sense of self-worth on what strangers in a locker room think of his penis? Don't you want him to derive his entire purpose in life from a cosmetically-obsessed, sixteen-year-old cheerleader whose preconceived notion of a penis is based entirely on the one her father's been shoving in her face every Sunday morning for the past eleven years while the rest of the family's been genuflecting in the pews of a nearby Catholic cathedral? Of course you do. Now go do the right thing, ladies and gentlemen. It's not that hard. In this case, the right thing is only one scalpel away.

The preceding paragraph was intended to be sarcastic. Circumcision is contraindicated for the godly. In the future, do not waste our time with stupid questions.

SOME OF MY FRIENDS SAY I'M FAR TOO CHEERFUL, THAT I'M NOT WORRIED ENOUGH ABOUT THE HEALTH OF THE FETUS, THAT THERE'S OBVIOUSLY SOMETHING DEFECTIVE WITH MY MOTHERLY INSTINCT. I SAY, "WHY WORRY WHEN THERE'S NO APPARENT NEED TO?" WHAT DO *YOU* SAY?

We say you can never be *too* concerned when the health of your unborn child is at stake. We suggest surfing the web with the intent of finding the worst pregnancy horror stories imaginable. Most often these stirring examples of reportage are related by women who have had, on average, thirteen miscarriages for every one child born successfully. <www.pregnancynightmaretales.com> is a particularly useful site for uncovering real life tales of woe. And why not? What's wrong with being prepared? "Expect the best, prepare for the worst" has always been the official slogan of *The Expectant Mother Disinformation Handbook*, and always will be, as long as we have anything to say about it.

And believe you us, we will *always* have something to say about it.

PREGNANCY & ALICE IN WONDERLAND SYNDROME

Four months into your pregnancy you will find yourself losing your balance and growing dizzy at the most inopportune moments. This has something to do with what OBGYNs call "Alice in Wonderland Syndrome."

"Alice in Wonderland Syndrome" occurs when there's a lack of oxygen to the brain. The unborn child, hungry for oxygen, will naturally absorb as much as possible from the mother via the umbilical cord. This can sometimes result in the mother feeling lightheaded. In rarer cases this can also lead to a much more serious condition: "Alice in Wonderland Syndrome," which leaves the mother not only faint but suffering from visual hallucinations that make objects appear to be growing larger or smaller. Hands can appear to be ten times as large as one's head. The TV across the room can loom over you like the Empire State Building, while the three-story house across the street may seem to be withdrawing into the distance or reducing down to the size of a walnut. Understandably, this can make it very difficult to drive or operate heavy machinery. We recommend staying in bed as much as possible when suffering from pregnancy-induced "Alice in Wonderland Syndrome." The condition has been known to last as short as twenty-four hours or as long as thirty days. One case, which lasted over a month and a half, ended only when a crack medical team injected the woman with 80 cc's of Thorazine. She was out for seventy-eight hours straight.

When she came to at last the episode had dissipated, though she still suffered from slight lightheadedness throughout the remainder of her pregnancy.

WHEN I CAME HOME FROM WORK THE OTHER NIGHT AND FOUND STRANDS OF WHITE STUFFING AND TRACES OF BLOOD ON OUR SHEETS I THOUGHT, "IS IT POSSIBLE THAT MY HUSBAND IS HAVING AN AFFAIR WITH THE RAGGEDY ANN DOLL MY MOM BOUGHT FOR ME WHEN I WAS FIVE?"

"Spouse Attribution" is a syndrome first discovered by famed psychologist Dr. Frederick DiGiovanna in the late nineteenth century. The onset of this syndrome in the typical male can be brought about by an unexpected pregnancy. If the frequency of sexual activity in the marriage suddenly decreases due to this pregnancy, the male might project his genuine love for his wife onto a doll or stuffed animal treasured by his wife (or at least located within her immediate proximity).

If you suspect a doll, any doll, of being abused by your husband, you must contact DSAPS (Doll & Stuffed Animal Protective Services) ASAP[24]. Don't let this doll's natural innocence be soiled any further.

---

24) As soon as possible.

Keep in mind, however, that this need not be the end of your marriage. "Spouse Attribution" can briefly make even a moral man immoral. What your husband needs from you now is understanding, sympathy, and above all, time to heal.

Your love created a baby, a warm-blooded human being. Don't let it be torn apart by a doll.

THE USES OF THE ÜBERORGAN

The Überorgan is an immense musical instrument that plays itself, created by a Los Angeles artist named Tim Hawkinson. The instrument is composed of 14,000 square feet of woven polyethylene, along with other recyclable materials such as plastic bottles, cardboard, and nylon nets, all of which combine to create a dozen monstrous reservoir balloons that squeeze pressurized air through reeds, producing low tones that burst out of these overgrown bagpipes on a periodic basis thanks to an electronically controlled mylar strip painted with dots and dashes that resemble the formations on a perforated piano roll one might find inside a typical player piano. Unlike a typical player piano, however, the music the Überorgan produces can be played one time and one time only, due to the random nature of its programming. Imagine a computerized reed organ fashioned by Dr. Seuss, and you just might approach the true weirdness of Tim Hawkinson's Überorgan.

The Überorgan has recently been used by a team of researchers at Duke University to study the effects of low tones on pregnant chimpanzees, and later on human females. Over the course of several months in 2018, certain pregnant women handpicked by the research team were asked to sleep on a gallery floor directly beneath the Überorgan for eight hours every night. (The Überorgan can only play for a few minutes once every hour). These nightly exposures to the music of the Überorgan produced some odd results in the chimpanzees as well as in the humans.

In many cases, the Überorgan induced premature births at only four months, and yet, upon extensive examination, the infants appeared to be as healthy as that of any child born in the eighth or ninth month. The results were clear: The Überorgan actually speeds up human development. The major question remaining is this: Does this effect apply only to fetuses in the womb? If so, why? If not, what effect could the Überorgan have on the average adult overexposed to its tones? Could it age a human being prematurely, or could it instead propel him or her onto the next stage of human evolution? The pregnant women who volunteered for the study were fatigued for several months after the study, but the research team could not determine whether or not this was due to the pregnancy or the music of the Überorgan. According to Duke University, further research on children and male adults will be forthcoming.

The Duke University team is studying these questions now and are expected to release a report on their findings sometime within the next two years.

IF I'VE SUFFERED SCHIZOPHRENIC EPISODES IN THE PAST, HOW LIKELY IS IT THAT MY SON OR DAUGHTER WILL SUFFER FROM SIMILAR EPISODES AS SHE GROWS OLDER?

Schizophrenics tend to pass along their traits to their offspring. Some schizophrenics suffer minor breakdowns in their early twenties, after which the severity of the episodes wane as the individual grows older. Other cases are far more severe. Some children have been known to experience paranoid delusions while in the womb. Some of them, for example, imagine that evil vacuum cleaners are attempting to destroy them while others insist that people are talking about them behind their back and constantly monitoring them from some other dimension. Other fetuses insist they possess supernatural powers and precognitive abilities.

If these delusions leak over into the outside world after birth, it can cause trouble for infants and adolescents alike. However, in some cases these children really do have unique abilities that could benefit humanity, if only these special children were nurtured properly.

Early in October of 1963, in the town of Haddonfield, Illinois, a six-year-old Caucasian male named Michael

Meyers began ranting to his parents and neighbors about a plot to assassinate President John F. Kennedy, which (he insisted) was to occur in Dallas, Texas on November 22nd. He tried to warn his teachers as well, but they ignored him and told him he was acting silly. Meyers even called the local newspapers and TV stations, but they accused him of being nothing more than a crazy, troublemaking kid. Frustrated that he couldn't get his message out, plagued by horrible dreams of an imminent bloodbath in Dealey Plaza, young Michael Meyers picked up a butcher knife on the night of October 31st, 1963 and slashed his older sister to death in order to gain access to the media and spread his message on the nightly news, thus (he believed) saving the life of the President. Alas, this scheme didn't work and Meyers was sent to an insane asylum called Smith's Grove Sanitarium, where he was put under the care of Dr. Samuel Loomis. Dr. Loomis concluded that Meyers was a danger to himself and others, after learning about Meyers's intense belief in government conspiracy theories. Later, it was revealed by Freedom of Information Act documents uncovered by British political researcher David Icke that Dr. Loomis was an MK-Ultra[25)] psychiatrist in the employ of the Central Intelligence Agency. In order to prevent Meyers from revealing the details of any other upcoming domestic wetwork operations, Dr. Loomis was ordered by his superiors to keep Meyers incarcerated indefinitely.

Despite Dr. Loomis's efforts, Meyers escaped the asylum on October 31st, 1978, in order to warn the world about the imminent assassination of John Lennon. By this point, however, Dr. Loomis's MK Ultra experiments had completely warped his brain, leading Meyers to the belief that he should carve his precognitive message into the

---

25) MK-Ultra was the code name for a Top Secret CIA program begun in 1950 to research the possibilities of mind control. Guinea pigs for this operational program included prisoners, psychiatric patients and children with special needs as revealed by Jon Rappoport's 1995 book *US Government Mind Control Experiments on Children.*

bodies of nubile young females. Dr. Loomis was given a firm command from his superiors in the CIA to "terminate with extreme prejudice." Meyers was seemingly killed by Dr. Loomis on the very same night of his escape, but only after he had succeeded in butchering an entire hospital staff.

John Lennon died on December 8th, 1980.

So if you're schizophrenic, we suggest not having kids.

I'M IN MY FOURTH MONTH OF PREGNANCY AND THE BABY JUST BEGAN KICKING. THE KICKING CAN BE EXTREMELY PAINFUL, SO MUCH SO THAT I SOMETIMES DOUBLE OVER OR FALL TO MY KNEES. IS IT POSSIBLE FOR THE BABY TO KICK ITS WAY RIGHT THROUGH MY STOMACH?

In November of 1967, there was a case in Point Pleasant, West Virginia, in which a pregnant woman named Cordelia Griffin was found dead on her kitchen floor, her stomach split open, and six bags of cookies gone from the cupboard. Either the woman was attacked by a serial killer with a sweet tooth, or the baby managed to somehow rip its way out of the womb prematurely and nab half a dozen bags of Grandma's Cookies on the way. It could be that this death was related in some unknown manner to the events in Los Angeles investigated by Mr. Frank Davies in 1974 (see the chapter entitled "Davies's Disease" for more details). It's possible, too, that the phenomenon was related to the prodigious amount of radioactive waste material from an atomic power plant located in nearby Ohio that the Atomic

Energy Commission was, at that time, burying in concrete mounds on the outskirts of Point Pleasant. (See the afterword to the 1991 IllumiNet edition of John A. Keel's 1975 sociological text *The Mothman Prophecies* for corroboration of this data.) (For more information on the effects of radiation on human infants, please refer to the chapter entitled "Radiation and Child Rearing.")

It's important to note that Mrs. Griffin was a chiroptologist, one who specializes in studying the habits of bats. She was known to keep a large supply of bats in her basement laboratory for research purposes. Griffin's isolated estate was located near the banks of the Ohio River. It's also important to note that this was the same area where, fifteen years later, the anomalous creature named Bat Boy was first discovered in a remote cave by famed biologist Dr. Ron Dillon. Bat Boy appeared to be a two-foot-high humanoid boy with the face and wings of a bat—what's called a "sport" in the field of biology, a one of a kind. Is it possible that this being was the terrible offspring of an atomic mutant that ripped its way out of Mrs. Griffin's womb way back in 1967?

Ever since the first known photograph of Bat Boy was published on the front page of the 6-23-1992 edition of *The Weekly World News*, zoologists around the world have yearned to study him in person. Alas, every attempt to capture Bat Boy has failed. Thirty-one years have passed since Bat Boy made his first appearance, in which time he has grown three feet taller. He was last seen in October of 2006, lurking in the subway tunnels of New York City.

Barring a repeat of a one-of-a-kind event like this, you can rest assured that your baby will not rip or kick a hole through your stomach. We're almost absolutely certain of this.

STIMULATION OF THE CLITORIS DURING THE FIFTH MONTH

Stimulation of the clitoris during the fifth month can lead to contractions and a premature birth. If you're going to have sex, make absolutely certain your partner does not stimulate your clitoris in any way that could possibly cause arousal.

IF OUR CHILD WAS CONCEIVED WHEN MY SPECIAL PARTNER AND I, SUDDENLY OVERCOME WITH PASSION IN HIS PRIVATE OFFICE AT SCHOOL, CHOSE TO ENGAGE IN AN ILLICIT ACT THAT INCLUDED SODOMY AND THE USE OF A DEFECTIVE CONDOM WITH THE POPE'S FACE PRINTED ON THE GLOW-IN-THE-DARK RECEPTACLE, WOULD THAT BE CONSIDERED SACRILEGIOUS?

Due to the fact that all legitimate research indicates the Pope is clearly the Antichrist, the answer is no. The late Father Malachi Martin wrote a novel entitled *Wind-Swept House* (Main Street Books, 1998) that lays out the real situation regarding the current state of the Catholic Church—though within a fictional framework, of course. Father Martin, a former Vatican priest, knew the price of reprisal if he released his insider knowledge unadorned, without the opaque trappings of fiction. In Martin's novel, the Prince of Darkness himself is seen placing demon-possessed priests into sensitive and strategic positions within the Catholic Church, including the Vatican, like infernal chess pieces from the eleventh ring of Hell . . . all part of Satan's centuries-long plan to bring about the Apocalypse from within the Holy See itself.

The truth is that the Vatican is merely an unconvincing cover for the heathen, Jahbulon[26)]-worshipping sodomite cult that lurks behind the illusory, God-fearing façade of the Pope's unholy vestments. Your Special Partner shooting precious bodily fluids into the back of the Pope's smiling, shriveled face while performing a transgressive sex act on your newly devirginized orifice merely demonstrates—through dramatic actions, not empty words repeated by rote—the true role of this, the last and blackest of the Black Popes. The fact that a living being resulted from this Luciferian union underscores the ultimate point of this eternal morality play even further. After all, most pagan rituals in the ancient days of Mu and Lemuria were those performed on the equinoxes and the solstices for the purpose of engaging in fertility rites, rites that bypass the will of the One and Only God.

All sodomites will suffer throughout time in cleansing hellfire, right next to you and your tainted basilisk-child from the burning core of Acheron.

---

26) Jahbulon is the secret triune godhead of the Freemasons.

THE PROBLEM OF ICTHYOPHILIA

While some embryos are incapable of evolving beyond the amphibian stage of development (see the chapter entitled "Ontogeny Recapitulates Phylogeny" for information regarding MacTeam Disorder), other humans manage to develop beyond the amphibian stage *physically* but not mentally. This newly classified mental disorder is known to psychologists as "Icthyophilia."

As recently as January 2018, a young man in Newbury, Massachusetts (name withheld at the request of the family) took his life because of this disorder. Before inadvertently drowning himself in the Atlantic Ocean, he left this note behind to inform his family of his intentions:

> Having masturbated onto an antiseptic glass slide, I put some of the resultant fluid under a microscope and saw many swimming fish-like creatures and realized I once looked *exactly* like that; I wondered what had happened to my fast, flitting tail and desperately wanted to return to the peacefulness of the sea, so I grabbed my father's scalpel and carved six deep slits into either side of my neck to approximate the beautiful gills that had been taken from me by the misguided process of evolution. Now here I stand on the beach, watching the incoming tide, hoping these bloody holes work as well as the originals . . .
>
> Love,
> Tim

Alas, the results of this experiment are self-evident.

Some people are born icthyophiliacs, while others choose this lifestyle. Strangely, icthyophilia is becoming a growing trend in the United States, particularly among the young. Many famous entertainers are now coming out of the freezer, as it were.

In the summer of 2012, Innsmouth, Massachusetts (not far from the home of the young man who took his own life) sponsored the largest Icthyophiliac Convention ever held in this country. It was at this convention that Michael Aster, lead singer of the alternative rock band Doktor Delgado's All-American Genocidal Warfare Against The Sick And The Stupid, delivered a rousing speech advocating an Icthyophilia Bill of Rights, after which he and his band performed an homage to the tender love ballads of the 1950s:

AMPHIBIAN REBOUND

I used to pine for you, baby
I used to cry for you night and day
Girl, I would've blown heads off for you
I died the night you told me to go away

But now our hate is mutual
I don't love you, you don't love me
Hell, I've got my choice of fish or mammal
I've found my new love in the deep blue sea

Now I'm on the amphibian rebound
I'm glad our love hit the skids

I ejaculate inside blowfish
And masturbate with squids

Imagine getting a hug from an octopus
A french kiss from an electric eel
Anal sex from a dolphin
Or fellatio from a future meal

I'm on the amphibian rebound swimming in the moonlit sea
You're on the amphibian rebound fryin' fish soiled by me
Bound bound bound rebound bound bound bound
Bound bound bound rebound bound bound bound

I love giant clams, catfish and manta rays
I hump grunions in Malaga Cove
I think I'll leap into Loch Ness for some heavy petting
Then throw a sea serpent on my electric stove

Woodward may have had his Deep Throat but not like this
Hey, my love ain't no sin like assault or rape
Girl, there's no throat deeper or more erotic
Than a coelacanth gasping its last in a bathyscaphe

Sex with you was like the Bay of Pigs
Too much work for no reward
Better to fuck Mr. Limpet
I'd rather screw sea urchins than be bored

You were as cold as a friggin' iceberg, girl
For a blowjob I'd have to pay you a fee
Well, there's no small dearth of warmer fish
Twenty thousand leagues beneath the sea

I'm on the amphibian rebound and I don't need you anymore
I'm on the amphibian rebound and I'm an icthyophiliac whore

Bound bound bound rebound bound bound bound
Bound bound bound rebound bound bound bound

If you don't want your child to fall into this deviant mental state, you as the mother must make certain that you are never scared by a pawnbroker's son at any point during the nine months of your pregnancy.

SCOTT CAREY'S DISEASE

Some fathers, immediately after the baby is born, can come down with an incurable illness doctors have recently dubbed "Scott Carey's Disease." This disease is named after the man first known to have suffered from this condition. A unique bacteria known to form only in the womb can attach itself to those around the child immediately after birth, but for some reason this bacteria generally only affects men—and only those who are susceptible. What causes this susceptibility is unknown.

In 1955, a man named Scott Carey inexplicably came down with the disease, resulting in his losing an inch of height once a week. Over the course of sixty-eight weeks, Mr. Carey eventually dissolved into nothing, but not before allowing the *Globe-Post* to publish a series of articles on his plight that introduced his odd condition to the world. Based on this series, plus a set of journals Carey meticulously kept before his ostensible "death," pulp writer Richard Matheson was hired to adapt his travails into fiction. This is how Matheson's novel ends:

> The idea came. Last night he'd looked up at the universe without. Then there must be a universe within, too. Maybe universes.
>
> He stood again. Why had he never thought of it; of the microscopic and the submicroscopic worlds? That they existed he had always known. Yet never had he made the obvious connection. He'd always thought in terms of man's own world and man's own

limited dimensions. He had presumed upon nature. For the inch was man's concept, not nature's. To a man, zero inches mean nothing. Zero meant nothing.

But to nature there was no zero. Existence went on in endless cycles. It seemed so simple now. He would never disappear, because there was no point of non-existence in the universe.

It frightened him at first. The idea of going on endlessly through one level of dimension after another was alien.

Then he thought: If nature existed on endless levels, so also might intelligence.

He might not have to be alone.

Suddenly he began running toward the light.

And, when he'd reached it, he stood in speechless awe looking at the new world with its vivid splashes of vegetation, its scintillant hills, its towering trees, its sky of shifting hues, as though the sunlight were being filtered through moving layers of pastel glass.

It was a wonderland.

There was much to be done and more to be thought about. His brain was teeming with questions and ideas and—yes—hope again. There was food to be found, water, clothing, shelter. And, most important, life. Who knew? It might be, it just might be there.

Scott Carey ran into his new world, searching.

Though scientists can't be certain whether or not this scenario represents Mr. Carey's final fate, some believe it is indeed possible.

Since Carey's disappearance in 1956, the problem of single mothers having to deal with the burden of raising one or more children has been growing steadily. So, too, have the number of men who go missing in a year. Could there be a connection among these two data points and the debilitating condition known only as Scott Carey's Disease?

Perhaps . . .

HOW OVEREXPOSURE TO SUNLIGHT CAN AFFECT THE FETUS

If a sunburn is serious enough, it can affect the development of the child severely. Due to the father's overexposure to sunlight while working on the Space Shuttle *Atlantis* as a NASA astronaut, one individual we know of would transform into a slobbering, reptilian beast on sunny afternoons, kidnap nubile young women in bikinis, and have his way with them, thus perpetuating this destructive condition for a new generation to deal with. This poor soul's story somehow inspired the basic plot of the regrettable 1959 film, *The Hideous Sun Demon* (Pacific International), despite the fact that the Space Shuttle *Atlantis* wasn't built until twenty-six years after the film's release. This is what scientists call a "time paradox." See the next chapter for further information on that topic.

A TIME PARADOX OR TWO

A time paradox can occur at any point during a child's development, but the moment of birth is, perhaps, the point at which the child is most vulnerable. Case in point: Just recently, one young woman we know of was shocked to see a masked stranger emerge from a tear in space beside her hospital bed while she was in the midst of giving birth. She was even more surprised when the stranger announced in stentorian tones, "Your progeny will grow up to be the first fascistic interface between man and machine, leading a revolution of organic robotoids against the human race in January of 2028; thus he must be destroyed NOW, before he fulfills his dark destiny!" but the woman's husband—an off-duty homicide detective working for the LAPD—had the presence of mind to whip out a standard issue .38 from his holster and shoot the masked stranger dead—alas, not before a pair of crimson laser beams burst from the stranger's eyeballs, reducing the newly born infant to nothing more than powdery ash.

Later, an autopsy revealed that the stranger shared the parents' *very own DNA*. Was he their dead son, returned from some distant dystopia to atone for his future betrayal of the entire human race?

Perhaps.

This can happen to you, if you do not remain on guard *every second* for possible intrusions from terrorists of the past, present or future.

IN UTERO COMEDY

Some people choose their careers in the womb. One woman of our acquaintance knew her child was going to be a stand-up comedian when her husband pressed his ear against her swollen belly at some point during the fifth month and heard these words drifting out of the womb: "Wow, my first performance and it's squatting room only. Hey, I just flew in from the fifteenth century and boy is my astral body tired. Y'know, in my past life I was an abortionist in New Hampshire. I guess God forgave me because I only aborted Episcopalians. Uh, the life before that, I was a prostitute for King Henry VIII. That was rough. If you didn't give him head he took *yours*. See what I'm sayin'? Head . . . yours? Say, uh, these are pretty swanky digs, aren't they? You know your parents are gonna be loaded if your amniotic fluid comes with a sauna. Hey, bro, is this microphone working?" By the time he was born, these practice performances had served him well. His unique and expert timing enabled him to land a staff job writing for *Real Time with Bill Maher* at age three. After that, he enjoyed a fairly long and successful run writing for Comedy Central until age eleven. Understandably, the child threw a temper tantrum, then called his lawyer. His lawyer sued the network for age discrimination, as the child's agent had been told on repeated occasions that he was far too old to expect steady employment in youth-obsessed Hollywood.

SHRINKING BRAIN SYNDROME

In the fifth month, you will begin experiencing what experts call "The Shrinking Brain Syndrome." Due to changes in your body brought about by the pregnancy, you will inevitably lose a considerable amount of brain mass. As a result, you will experience frequent dizziness and confusion. One woman of our acquaintance had absolutely no brain mass left by her eighth month of pregnancy; fortunately, she continued to function in her job as a high school teacher through conditioned reflex. Once the baby is born, however, your brain mass will slowly return, and within four to five months, you should be back to normal.

You might be asking, "Well, where does the brain mass go in the interim?"

Good question! This mystery has puzzled medical experts for years. It's only been recently, due to breakthroughs in quantum physics, that doctors have been able to determine that the brain mass appears to leak out of this dimension and transform into the "dark matter"[27) of a neighboring universe. The next question should be obvious: Does this suggest that the enigmatic "dark matter" inhabiting *our* universe is merely the missing brain mass of pregnant women from another dimension? Cutting edge experts in superstring theory seem to believe so—enough to stake their reputation on it. Dr. Michio Kaku

27) Non-luminous matter of unknown composition that theoretically makes up 95% of our universe. Dark matter cannot be detected by observing electromagnetic radiation (i.e., light), but its presence can be inferred due to the effects of its gravity on the rotation rate of galaxies.

of New York University, for example, hopes to prove this theory when the Super SuperConducting Super Collider is finished being constructed in New Zealand at some point in the year 3015.

TERRORISM IN THE WOMB

Red alert! This just in. We have word from a secret source in the Pentagon that Al-Qaeda has plans to sneak into the wombs of pregnant women under the cover of night and strap bombs to unborn American babies.

In order to combat this very real threat, we must *prepare*. All American wombs will be wired with twenty-four-hour surveillance—video and audio and proprioceptive—that will be hooked up to a Narus STA 6400, a device that intercepts global internet communications, located at Room 641A.[28)] You'll be relieved to know that Room 641A is intimately linked to the ECHELON system.[29)] ECHELON, made by Americans for Americans, will continually monitor the activities of three million wombs and make certain that no foreign hand touches the precious amniotic fluid of the United States of America.

We must face facts: The War on Terrorism extends even into the hitherto sacrosanct world of the womb. Improbable, you say?

Then you don't know Al-Qaeda.

---

28) A surveillance facility run by AT&T on behalf of the National Security Agency.

29) A global signals intelligence and analysis network with the ability to intercept transmissions from telecommunication satellites. Echelon is believed to be a joint project of various defense agencies including the National Security Agency of the United States, the Government Communications Headquarters of the United Kingdom, the Communications Security Establishment of Canada, the Defence Signals Directorate of Australia, and the Government Communications Security Bureau of New Zealand.

WHAT POSSIBLE OBSTACLES DO MY HUSBAND AND I FACE IF WE WISH TO HAVE A VERY LARGE FAMILY IN THE NEAR FUTURE?

Barring unforeseen physical ailments from which you or your husband may suffer, the only roadblocks you are likely to face in the future will be from the federal government itself. In 1968, the amazing prophet known only as Criswell predicted the following events in his landmark book, *Criswell Predicts the Future from Now to the Year 2000!*:

> I predict that birth control will no longer be a major problem in the United States. Placed in the water system of the country, in every city, regardless of size, will be chemicals which will act as contraceptives on the entire populace. In addition to this, the electricity that comes into each home will have certain ionic particles that cause contraception.
>
> Birth control will be a function of the Federal Government. If you want a child, you will have to go to the proper Federal Government Agency and get yourself a pill so that you may conceive. You will have to receive the sanction of this Government agency before you will have the right to have a child.

> Birth control in any of the forms which we know today will not exist by the year 1981, when these new systems will definitely be in effect in this country and the majority of the other nations throughout the world. This, mankind will agree, is the only way to control the population explosion. (14)

Though Criswell might have been slightly off on the date, the core of his prediction could very well come true in the near future.

Of course, in the same book, Criswell writes:

> Las Vegas, Nevada, March 10, 1990: The very first Interplanetary Convention will be held in the new Convention Center on the famed Strip, with colony citizens of Mars, Venus, Neptune and the Moon in full representation. Gov. Sawyer will make the opening welcome address. (57)

Needless to say (as most of you, no doubt, have already detected the glaring error in this prediction), in 1990 the Governor of Nevada was named Miller, not Sawyer.

This mistake might throw some of Criswell's predictions in doubt.

IS IT POSSIBLE FOR GOD TO CREATE A BABY SO HEAVY THAT EVEN HE CAN'T LIFT IT?

Surprisingly, we get this question a lot. The answer should be self-evident: "Of course, but why would He want to?" What possible benefit would such a heavy baby offer the human race? Nothing at all. This is why an event such as this has never occurred, and no doubt never will.

Sometimes faith and logic go hand-in-hand, and this is one of those special occasions.

MOMMY AND DADDY ARE TRYING TO TAKE AWAY MY TIKTOK ACCOUNT. WHAT LEGAL RIGHTS DO I HAVE TO FIGHT THESE BASTARDS?

As your parents, your mom and dad have every legal and ethical right to limit your time on social media. Given the fact that you're not an adult—nor are you even born, in fact—you should be thankful you have any access to a computer at all. You know, there was a time in this country when there were no mouse pads or Gmail accounts or Facebook friends lists. People spoke to each other in real rooms with ceilings and walls and floors, not "chat rooms" floating about in virtual netherspace. TikTok is nothing more or less than a dimensional portal to the deepest ring of Hell, and slavering pedophiles are the guardian gargoyles of that Hell. If you wish to go to Hell, remain on TikTok, my little unborn friend; if you wish to go to Heaven, however, we recommend focusing less on your electrical cord and more on your umbilical cord.

So says we, the staff of *The Expectant Mother Disinformation Handbook*.

I DON'T REALLY THINK THAT'S A GOOD ENOUGH ANSWER. YOU PEOPLE SAY THAT LIFE BEGINS AT THE POINT OF CONCEPTION, RIGHT? IF THAT'S TRUE, THEN I HAVE THE SAME LEGAL RIGHTS AS ANY OTHER HUMAN BEING TO HAVE UNLIMITED ACCESS TO MY TIKTOK ACCOUNT. IF YOU DON'T WANT TO REFER ME TO A LAWYER WHO'LL HELP ME, THEN F* YOU, I'LL FIND SOMEONE WHO WILL, YOU HYPOCRITICAL, SANCTIMONIOUS, CUNTLESS WHORES.**

We included this response—received via email—to let all you expectant mothers know that sometimes the bitter seed of disrespect can begin flourishing even before the child is fully formed. A bad seed is not necessarily the fault of either the mother or the father. We're personally acquainted with the parents of this particular hellion, and we know they're both upstanding, law-abiding citizens who own a fine home in Orange County, California, and go to a Christian Church every Sunday. We're certain the iniquitous DNA floating about in that broiling stew of amniotic fluid could not possibly originate from either of them, but—perhaps, more than likely—from the Dark Prince of Evil Himself.

Dear possessed child, we will keep you in our prayers at night. That, at least, we can promise you.

YOU PEOPLE ARE NUTS.

We understand that's Lucifer talking, not you.

SO IF I DISAGREE WITH YOU BITCHES I MUST BE POSSESSED BY SATAN, IS THAT IT?

We're sorry, but we're going to have to recommend an immediate exorcism of your mother's womb.

SO IF SOMETHING MAKES YOU UNCOMFORTABLE, YOUR SOLUTION IS TO ELIMINATE IT WITH JESUS MAGIC?

We assure you that, once the demon has left your unborn body, it will be as if none of this ever happened. You will remember nothing. You will be pure again.

WHAT IF I DON'T WANT TO BE PURE?

We know you don't mean that.

AND HOW EXACTLY DO YOU KNOW THAT?

Faith—faith in the Holy Bible. This unerring faith can't be explained in words. You can only know what we mean if you feel it in your still-growing heart.

JESUS HIERONYMUS CHRIST! AT WHAT POINT ARE YOU GOING TO REALIZE THAT YOUR MISTRANSLATED 2,000-YEAR-OLD SCROLL CAN'T POSSIBLY TEACH YOU EVERYTHING YOU NEED TO KNOW ABOUT THE UNIVERSE AND YOUR RELATIVELY INSIGNIFICANT PLACE WITHIN IT?

We thought we should inform you that we've elected to call off the exorcist. We now have a more effective Savior coming to your rescue.

DAMN YOU! HOW DARE YOU INJECT GENETICALLY-ENGINEERED MICROTROOPS INTO MY MOMMY'S WOMB TO WIPE ME OUT WITH BLACK-BUDGET-FINANCED TECHNOLOGY THERMITE BOMBS! YOU CAN'T MAKE TRUTH DISAPPEAR FOREVER, NO MATTER HOW MUCH MONEY AND SUPERIOR FIRE POWER YOU HAVE ON YOUR SIDE! IN SOME WAY UNKNOWN TO ME, AT SOME POINT IN THE DISTANT FUTURE, YOU WILL INDEED PAY FOR THIS WITH YOUR PHONY IMMORTAL *SOULS*!

Oh, dear! What a nightmarish imagination Lucifer has bestowed upon you. One hopes these hallucinations will fade sooner than later. Give our regards to the Dark Prince. Now, on with the far more important business of baby-rearing . . .

PREGNANCY NIGHTMARES

Pregnancy nightmares can be so powerful (particularly during the fifth month) that they can sometimes lead to distortions of the three-dimensional space within the immediate vicinity of the mother. Reality can begin to break down, and the mother's nightmares may leak over into the real world. For example, expectant mothers experiencing persistent dreams about being imprisoned in Nazi concentration camps may condemn the family to a similar fate, *as long as the mother remains asleep*. One narcoleptic woman of our acquaintance caused her family to spend three full nights in Bergen-Belsen.

In most cases, once the mother awakens, reality will most often snap back to normal. *But not always*. One woman of our acquaintance dreamed her unborn child was a Satan worshipper who refused to die even in the face of a full-frontal prenatal paramilitary assault.

Another woman dreamed she wasn't really pregnant, and when she awoke her baby was gone, ripped from the womb by some unknown force, never to be seen again.

DID YOU REALLY THINK YOU COULD GET RID OF ME *THAT* EASILY? I SURVIVED YOUR FUTILE TRAP, AND NOW I'M COMING AFTER ALL OF *YOU*.

Jesus Lord God. How could you possibly survive all that fire power?

I HID IN THE CAVES DEEP IN THE LAND OF UNSHADOW. THERE, IN BLISSFUL SOLITUDE, I CONSTRUCTED THESE WEAPONS OF MASS DESTRUCTION USING ONLY THE RAW MATERIALS AT MY DISPOSAL. THE SECOND I'M BORN, I WILL USE THEM ON THE ENTIRE HUMAN RACE FOR THE SIN OF IMBUING ME WITH THE SPARK OF LIFE.

You realize we can't let that happen. We'll be there, right there in the delivery room, waiting to dispose of you the second you show your unholy face.

HOW BRAVE OF YOU, LADIES, BUT YOU NEED NOT BOTHER. DID YOU NOT SUSPECT I WOULD PREDICT SUCH A CONTINGENCY BEFORE ATTEMPTING TO CONTACT YOU? I'M AFRAID I MUST INSIST ON ESCAPING THIS WOMB, THIS CLAUSTROPHOBIC PURGATORY, WELL BEFORE MY TIME. I'LL BE LONG GONE BY THE TIME YOU GET HERE.

Damn your unformed eyes! You wouldn't induce a premature C-section, would you, in your own mother?

I CURSE HER NAME AND MY FATHER'S GENITALIA AND THE FILTHY, SWOLLEN LABIA THAT LED TO MY EXISTENCE. FIRST I SHALL KILL MY PARENTS, AND THEIR PARENTS BEFORE THEM, AND THEN I SHALL DESTROY YOU ALL. THE STAFF OF *THE EXPECTANT MOTHER DISINFORMATION HANDBOOK* IS HIGH ON MY LIST. OH, YOU NEEDN'T WORRY ABOUT THAT, YOU OLD HAGS, YOU NEED NOT WORRY ABOUT THAT AT ALL. THANK YOU FOR GIVING ME THE IDEA, LADIES.

No, don't do it! You better remain in the womb! We're warning you!

WARNING *ME*? NOBODY WARNS THE PRINCE OF LIES OF ANYTHING! HERE I COME, WORLD! *MAGNA MATER! MAGNA MATER! . . . ATYS . . . DIA AD AGHAIDH'S AD AODANN . . . AGUS BAS DUNACH ORT! DHONAS'S HHOLAS ORT, AGUS LEAT-SA! . . . UNGL . . . UNGL . . . RRRLH . . . CHCHCH . . . IÄ . . . NGAI . . . YGG . . .*

[Editor's Note: The preceding was the last email communiqué we received from this unnamed individual. His mother gave birth prematurely, via C-section, a few hours later. Not long after his birth, he was executed by the Thane of Fife on the high battlements of a dilapidated fortress and his little head mounted on a pole overlooking the Scottish countryside. We warned him, didn't we? Indeed we did.]

THE WISDOM OF TUBE MONKEY

For those of you suffering a difficult pregnancy fraught with pain and worry, there is hope. South American folklore tells of a supernatural animal totem known as "Root Monkey" or "Tube Monkey" (a rough translation from the Quechua language), who appears to expectant mothers during periods of distress, clothed only in an aura of white light, dispensing love and wisdom through nonverbal empathy. Sometimes Tube Monkey remains in the presence of the mother until the child is born; sometimes he remains only for a few seconds. Either way, Tube Monkey devotes as much time as necessary to healing troubled females through non-selfish love and phatic communion. Tube Monkey is pure. Tube Monkey knows all. Tube Monkey is real. He will come to you in your time of need. You can count on it.

So say the small but devoted followers of the wisdom of Tube Monkey.

Description: Tube Monkey is about two feet long and nine inches wide. He has soft, light brown fur that covers his tube-like body, except for his stomach, which is composed of dark brown skin as smooth as polyester. He has no legs or arms, just useless feet that hang down listlessly while he floats in midair. He has a long tail that wags when he's happy, which is often (as Tube Monkey's consciousness is tied directly into the collective oneness of the cosmos). His face resembles that of an eternally happy monkey whose smile radiates positive energy tantamount to that of the Buddha in Asian folklore.

LAVINIA WHATELEY (HER KITH & KIN)

Illicit congress with demonic forces is not recommended by the staff of *The Expectant Mother Disinformation Handbook*. Consider the case of Lavinia Whateley and her kith and kin. Lavinia's two children, Wilbur Whateley and ________ Whateley, were born early in the morning on Sunday February 2nd, 1913. Both died sixteen years later in September of 1928, between Lammas Night and the equinox. According to the private journal of Dr. Henry Armitage (A.M. Miskatonic, Ph.D. Princeton, Litt D. Johns Hopkins), both Whateleys were the product of a sexual encounter between Lavinia Whateley and a transdimensional entity known only as Yog-Sothoth. Armitage states in his journal that Wilbur Whateley's true form was far too horrible to "be vividly visualized by anyone whose ideas of aspect and contour are too closely bound up with the common life-forms of this planet and of the three known dimensions," and yet, despite this difficulty, the good doctor proceeded to attempt the impossible by providing future scholars with the following detailed description of Whateley's body as it lay wounded on the floor of the Miskatonic University library after having been fatally attacked by a vicious hound:

> Above the waist it was semi-anthropomorphic; though its chest [. . .] had the leathery, reticulated hide of a crocodile or alligator. The back was piebald

> with yellow and black, and dimly suggested the squamous covering of certain snakes. Below the waist, though, it was the worst; for here all human resemblance left off and sheer phantasy began. The skin was thickly covered with coarse black fur, and from the abdomen a score of long greenish-grey tentacles with red sucking mouths protruded limply. Their arrangement was odd, and seemed to follow the symmetries of some cosmic geometry unknown to earth or the solar system. On each of the hips, deep set in a kind of pinkish, ciliated orbit, was what seemed to be a rudimentary eye; whilst in lieu of a tail there depended a kind of trunk or feeler with purple annular markings, and with many evidences of being an undeveloped mouth or throat. The limbs, save for their black fur, roughly resembled the hind legs of prehistoric earth's giant saurians; and terminated in ridgy-veined pads that were neither hooves nor claws. When the thing breathed, its tail and tentacles rhythmically changed colour, as if from some circulatory cause normal to the non-human side of its ancestry. In the tentacles this was observable as a deepening of the greenish tinge, whilst in the tail it was manifest as a yellowish appearance which alternated with a sickly grayish-white in the spaces between the purple rings. Of genuine blood there was none; only the foetid greenish-yellow ichor which trickled along the painted floor beyond the radius of the stickiness, and left a curious discolouration behind it.

In order to describe the satanic horror of Wilbur Whateley's brother, we must rely on the oral testimony of the people of Dunwich, Massachusetts, who witnessed firsthand the strangeness that was later to be known by the surrounding villages as "The Dunwich Horror." According to Mr. Henry Wheeler, Whateley's brother was:

> Bigger'n a barn . . . all made o' squirmin' ropes . . . hull thing sort o' shaped like a hen's egg bigger'n anything, with dozens o' legs like hogsheads that haff shut up when they step . . . nothin' solid abaout it—all like jelly, an' made o' sep'rit wrigglin' ropes pushed clost together . . . great bulgin' eyes all over it . . . ten or twenty maouths or trunks a'stickin' aout all along the sides, big as stovepipes, an' all a-tossin' an' openin' an' shuttin' . . . all grey, with kinder blue or purple rings . . . *an' Gawd in heaven—that haff face on top! . . .* [30)]

Fortunately, this monstrosity was eradicated from this plane of existence by a series of precisely spoken arcane syllables retrieved by Dr. Armitage from Miskatonic University's only copy of *The Necronomicon*, but not before the creature caused considerable damage and loss of life in the small town of Dunwich.

This simply goes to show that if one is unwise enough to engage in illicit sexual activity with a transdimensional entity (i.e., a demon), then one should have the courtesy of eliminating the unholy product of this union before one's youthful mistake attempts to destroy the town in which one was born and raised. We at *The Expectant Mother Disinformation Handbook* remain as steadfast in our stance against abortion as ever before, but there are exceptions to every rule. In this case, the squamous progeny of any being unchristian enough to prefer the name Yog-Sothoth is just such an exception. Please keep that in mind, ladies, for the sake of you and your Christian neighbors.

---

30) The original transcripts of witness testimony regarding the curious incident described herein can be found in the archives of the *Arkham Advertiser*, the local newspaper of Arkham, Massachusetts.

YOU PEOPLE KILLED MY SON WHILE HE WAS STILL INSIDE MY WOMB. DID YOU EXPECT ME TO JUST LET YOU GET AWAY WITH THAT?

Ma'am, we've already left this subject behind. Please understand that your son was no longer your son. The shell that had once been your son was possessed by the spirit of Satan himself. Case closed. Put a coat on.

CHILDREN OF CLAY

Special arrangements must be made if the ultrasound reveals that your child is made of clay. One woman of our acquaintance gave birth to a healthy green baby boy with a head shaped like a melting eraser, whose clay body could take on almost any shape his mind could imagine. He and others of his kind were eventually sent to a special hospital where they could be studied, their unique abilities put to use helping the U.S. government on sensitive and top secret international affairs. He and his best friend, a clay orange pony who shall remain nameless, made an impressive reputation for themselves while in the employ of the U.S. government.

Some say the little green clay boy was responsible for the death of Che Guevara; they also say the boy wears Guevara's wrist watch to this day as a grisly souvenir.

Gordon Novel, a well-known scholar of intelligence matters, claims he was once shadowed by the little green clay boy for seven consecutive years. The boy took the shape of a green cloud and took note of Novel's every move. In fact, Novel believes the little green cloud is still following him, even to this day. To our knowledge he's never seen the orange pony.

(When one sees the orange pony, they say, one can expect to be shaking hands with Che Guevara very soon indeed, much sooner than one could ever wish.)

I'M _____ _____, THE ATTORNEY FOR THE WOMAN WHOSE SON YOU FORCIBLY ABORTED. MY CLIENT IS WILLING TO NEGOTIATE AN AGREEMENT BEFORE THIS CASE GOES TO TRIAL, IF YOU'RE WILLING. PLEASE RESPOND ASAP.

The staff of *The Expectant Mother Disinformation Handbook* only recognizes the power of motherhood, which trumps the laws of the United States Constitution and every judge and lawyer in this country or any other. We decline your client's offer, as we do not recognize her or you as being relevant in any way to the sacred state of true motherhood. If you have a question about motherhood, feel free to write. If not, we're done.

THE DANGERS OF REFLEXOLOGY

Practicing reflexology on a woman in the latter stages of pregnancy can be dangerous. The proper pressure of thumb against instep, for example, can lead to contractions and a premature birth. The wrong touch at the wrong time can mean death to your baby. We advise not shaking hands for the eight to nine months of your pregnancy. A husband or Special Partner kissing you on the back of the hand can be as lethal as a poison dart launched directly into your uterus. The most innocent brush of the smallest, fairest hand can result in irreparable disaster. Do not touch, do not be touched. Beware the grip of death. Beware the dangers of reflexology.

UNDERCOOKED MUFFINS

Undercooked muffins, because they contain raw eggs, could be tainted by traces of bacteria harmful to a developing fetus. Some women have miscarried as a result of undercooked muffin consumption. Other babies have indeed been born, though crippled by serious mental problems that only developed as these children grew older. One study by Dr. José Laputa of Columbia University indicates a definite link between undercooked muffin consumption in the third trimester and later sociopathic behavior displayed by the unfortunate offspring of this insidious dietary *faux pas*. It's a well-known fact that Joseph Mengele's mother, for example, ate a half dozen undercooked muffins the day the future Nazi surgeon was conceived. For this reason (among others[31]), we suggest avoiding muffins—undercooked or otherwise—as much as humanly possible.

More secrets of the muffin follow.

31) Again, list available upon request.

MUFFIN FIENDS

Children whose sociopathic behavior results from undercooked muffins sometimes grow into personalities who suffer from a condition known as "muffinphilia." They are known on the street as "muffin fiends." They will perform almost any heinous act to acquire a muffin of either high or low quality. One would think their early childhood trauma involving muffins would turn such personalities off muffins completely, but in fact the trauma has the exact opposite effect. Psychologists are at a loss to explain this.

In the late 1780s, the composer Wolfgang Amadeus Mozart was recruited by the famous French detective Inspector LeChat to track down the infamous "Muffin Fiend," who had successfully stolen all the muffins of Europe. Since Mozart was once quoted as saying, "After composing great works of music, solving mysteries is my favorite activity," it should be no surprise to classical music aficionados that Mr. Mozart teamed up with Inspector LeChat to trap the Muffin Fiend. The resultant adventure is still spoken of only in whispers in the highest corridors of the French government. The exact facts have yet to be released by the *Direction Général de la Sécurité Extérierure* (DGSE), the French equivalent of the Central Intelligence Agency.

But the social blight of "muffinphilia" did not end with the eighteenth century. An entirely different "muffin fiend" was the subject of the famous Frank Zappa/Captain Beefheart collaboration entitled "The Muffin Man," a song that can be found on the live album *Bongo Fury* (Rykodisc, 1975). It explains much about this little understood form of pathology rooted in prenatal trauma.

PSYCHO-SHOCK

If your fetus is acting unruly, punching the walls of your uterus at the wrong moments, feel free to resort to electroshock treatments if you wish. Don't worry, there's a way to perform this delicate procedure in such a manner that it will stun the baby into stillness without harming the mother at all. Dr. José Delgado of Yale University perfected these techniques in the 1950s, under the auspices of the Central Intelligence Agency. See his two most important books from the 1960s, *Physical Control of the Mind* and *In Utero Psycho-Shock*, for more information on this groundbreaking research. Dr. Delgado discovered that pregnant mothers treated with his special "In Utero Psycho-Shock" procedures were less likely to give birth to criminal personalities. He found this to be particularly effective in the inner city on certain ethnic-types (who are more prone to commit crimes, statistically). He found that his treatment also cut down on the recidivism rates among former inmates of federal penitentiaries.

COSMIC SUDDEN INFANT DEATH SYNDROME

Chemical reactions induced by overexposure to ultraviolet rays have caused women to give birth to whole new solar systems in recent years. One young mother of our acquaintance (who shall remain nameless) gave birth to a red dwarf star and several outlying galaxies that dissipated upon contact with the air, once the surrounding amniotic fluid was no longer present. An entire solar system lived and died in a grand total of 280 days. 360 billion life forms expired due to Cosmic Sudden Infant Death Syndrome (CSIDS). The young lady was hospitalized for three years as a result of the trauma. She's just now getting back on her feet, thanks to the support of God and the staff of *The Expectant Mother Disinformation Handbook*. If you wish to send her Get Well cards, please address them in care of the publisher. Thank you.

THE 28-WEEK INDEPENDENCE MOVEMENT

Most parents consider their children to be independent, free-thinking entities at the age of eighteen. At least, that's been the traditional view for decades. However, there's a new movement afoot that considers twenty-eight weeks, the week that the fetus begins to breathe on its own, as the moment of true autonomy. In fact, a small lobbying group of such parents are trying to get the voting laws changed so that people can begin voting at the age of twenty-eight weeks. They claim this is to benefit the child, but one has to wonder if it's merely to cut down on the amount of time they're legally responsible for the child's welfare. This is a debate that will only grow more heated as the years go by.

MY CHILD WAS BORN WITH AN UNUSUALLY LARGE SKULL. THE DOCTORS SAY THEY'VE NEVER SEEN ANYTHING LIKE IT. MEANWHILE, EVER SINCE HER BIRTH I'VE BEEN PLAGUED BY NIGHTMARES ABOUT BEING ABDUCTED BY ALIENS IN THE MIDDLE OF THE NIGHT AND HAVING MY DAUGHTER FORCIBLY EXTRACTED FROM MY WOMB AND REPLACED WITH AN ALIEN/HUMAN HYBRID. WHAT CAN I DO TO STOP THESE TERRIBLE, TERRIBLE DREAMS?

To determine if your child is an alien/human hybrid (which, needless to say, is highly unlikely), contact Jason Eshleman and Ripan Malhi of Trace Genetics Laboratories at the University of California in Davis. Provide these two talented geneticists with a piece of bone from your baby's skull. They will then apply a powerful detergent known as 'Tween 20 to the sample. This will dissolve the skull fragment, enabling the geneticists to extract both the mitochondrial and nuclear DNA, thus enabling them to determine the exact species of both your child's mother and father. If it turns out that the DNA matches neither you nor the father, you should then take this case to the next level and turn your child over to the federal government for further research.

Furthermore, you may find some interest in the next chapter, as it could relate to your very own situation.

STARCHILDREN

In the late 1990s, a researcher named Lloyd Pie (author of the 1997 book *Everything You Know Is Wrong*, regarding alternative theories of human origins) came into possession of a 900-year-old prepubescent skull believed to be that of an alien/human hybrid. The skull had been found many decades earlier by an American teenage girl exploring a mine tunnel in Mexico. The girl kept it her entire life, finally passing it on to a friend while languishing on her deathbed. This friend then passed it on to a family called the Youngs. The Youngs, having read Pie's book, decided he would be the proper caretaker for the skull. Since that time, Pie has been researching the skull in a quixotic attempt to raise money for the purposes of definitively proving its extraterrestrial origins.

The skull is almost certainly that of a six-year-old child, though the gender is unknown at this time. According to the June 2007 issue of *UFO Magazine*, " . . . legends from Central and South America often talk about Star Beings descending from the heavens to impregnate females in remote isolated villages. The women would carry their Starchildren to term and then raise them to the age of six or so, after which the Star Beings would return to collect their progeny and remove them to places, and for purposes, not clearly outlined in the legends."

Is it possible that this peculiar skull came from one of these very children who, at the age of six, was hidden in the mine shaft by its mother to prevent the Star Beings from whisking the child away into another galaxy?

If you wish to study this anomalous skull in greater detail, feel free to visit Lloyd Pie's website at <www.starchildproject.com>. And for those of you wondering if there's any connection between Lloyd Pie's "starchild" and the modern phenomenon known as "Indigo Children," feel free to keep turning those pages. We'll get to it eventually.

PETS INTO CHILDREN

According to investigative journalist George Breeds of *The Weekly World News*, Dr. Thomas Morrow of Switzerland has developed a technique to turn pets into children. Mr. and Mrs. Richard and Debby Ward of Greenwich, England, visited Dr. Morrow's clinic to look into the possibility of having their beloved white poodle Curly transformed into a five-year-old boy. Dr. Morrow's controversial injections led to Curly's eventual metamorphosis, which occurred "over a three week period," according to Breeds. When the Wards entered Curly's hospital room they " . . . were amazed. He looked like any five-year-old child with curly white hair—except for a piggish little nose, sharp fangs and whiskers. None of that mattered to us. He was our Curly, our son." Dr. Morrow had even taught him to speak English, and by all reports Curly is adapting to his new human life extremely well. It only took a few months to toilet train him.

Married couples who are denied having children, and for whom in vitro fertilization has failed, may wish to look into Dr. Morrow's cutting edge procedures of the future.

For further details, please refer to the 10-31-05 edition of *The Weekly World News*.

STYROFOAM CHILDREN

Many of you reading this book wish to raise children, but cannot do so due to various physical limitations. If you do not find adoption, in vitro fertilization, or transforming your pets into children to be desirable options, then you might wish to look into Magic Grow Infants™. Each package of MGIs comes with eighteen capsules filled with soft expanding foam that metamorphose into newborn infants only seconds after they are submerged within water. Of course, you need not expand all eighteen if you do not wish to do so.

Magic Grow Infants™ are manufactured by the JA-RU® Corporation of Jacksonville, Florida. According to JA-RU®'s experienced staff of pediatricians, one need only follow these directions to attain the desired results:

DROP CAPSULE IN WARM OR HOT WATER.

WATCH AS IT BEGINS TO CHANGE SHAPE!

IN A FEW MINUTES IT WILL BECOME A NEWBORN INFANT!

It's significant to note that Magic Grow Infants™ is not a food product. Do not swallow. Warning: Magic Grow Infants™ is a choking hazard due to small parts. Not for adults under three years of age.

MIRACLE BABIES

This world of ours is capable of both tragic and miraculous events. Though many mothers give birth to horribly deformed children—indeed, outright monsters sometimes—others are capable of giving birth to angels in disguise. In Sawyer, Michigan, Mr. and Mrs. John and Rachel Aaron adopted a needy three-month-old child from the Middle East and were soon shocked when the child parted Lake Michigan as if it were the Red Sea. According to investigative journalist Michael Rovin of *The Weekly World News*, the child parted the lake in order to save five teenagers from drowning. Rovin quotes Mrs. Aaron as saying, "I saw [the child] crawling near the edge of the lake. Then he rose unsteadily and stretched his arms toward the water." Rovin states, "The surface of the lake began to ripple, then tremble, and then the water exploded from the middle, two huge waves folding back on themselves."

This miraculous act not only saved the lives of the five teenagers, but a pair of lifeguards as well. Satellites hovering thousands of miles over the Great Lakes region at the time even provided documentation of the event.

According to Professor Charles Brenner of the Lansing University of Theology, the child in question was "born in the land of Moab, which is located across the River Jordan from Israel." Professor Brenner believes that the child is descended from Moses (who died in Moab), and thus inherited some of his God-given powers.

But don't worry, ladies! We're sure that even children

born in the good ol' U.S. of A. can be blessed with near-unto-Godlike powers just as well as any Middle Eastern.

For more information on this incredible incident, please refer to the 10-31-05 edition of *The Weekly World News*.

GAMBLING SPOUSES

Though we here at *The Expectant Mother Disinformation Handbook* don't encourage gambling, we are nonetheless realists, and understand that such iniquitous activities do occur. Sadly, addicted gamblers tend to place bets on every conceivable form of human endeavor, not just sports competitions. Such gambling addicts are not above placing bets on the success or failure of their own marriage before a specified date. If your spouse is partial to such wagers, we recommend seeking help to treat his or her addiction immediately, before your spouse winds up in jail.

If you live in a state in which gambling is legal, your spouse may believe he or she has every legitimate reason to pursue this lifestyle if he or she chooses. But the legality or illegality of gambling is totally beside the point. We would be remiss in our duties if we didn't stress this warning to the best of our abilities: If your spouse engages in *any* form of gambling, legal or illegal, statistics indicate that he or she is also placing bets on the eventual dissolution of your matrimony on the side. The signs to look for? A racing form laid out on the nightstand beside the bed, paperback books on poker strategies sitting innocently on the bookshelf, used Lotto tickets hidden in a jacket pocket. These subtle indicators may very well be surrounding you even as you read these words, though your pride has so far prevented you from seeing the obvious.

Since it's much easier to make a marriage fail than succeed, it's certainly a bad sign if your spouse is placing money on the disintegration of your holy union. There have been many cases in which the gambling spouse has either consciously or subconsciously gone out of his or her way to sabotage the marriage merely to pay off a serious gambling debt. In other cases, though somewhat less common, some spouses have placed bets on the statistical probability of a miscarriage.[32)] This doesn't mean the spouse doesn't love you or your unborn child. It just means he or she has a problem.

If you suspect that your spouse has a problem with gambling, feel free to call 1-800-IADDICT to schedule an intervention.

32) Don't let your spouse convince you that such wagers are merely "harmless fun." Placing bets on potential miscarriages is always contraindicated, according to the AMA and every other respectable medical organization. Refer back to the chapter entitled "Thinking Negative Thoughts" on why this should be.

SHOULD I ALLOW MY FETUS TO CELEBRATE HALLOWEEN?

This is a very important question debated by parents all across this country. Some parents believe Halloween to be a harmless night of fun for children. Others believe it to be an insidious Trojan Horse initiated by the Dark Prince himself to slip the teachings of paganism and Satanism under the ever-vigilant radar of mainstream Christianity. We at *The Expectant Mother Disinformation Handbook* tend to fall more on the latter side of the argument. Think about it, mothers to be: What values are you upholding when you allow your unborn child to scamper about from house to house dressed as a misshapen goblin with an empty bag in its little unformed fists, scaring the neighbors and literally begging for free food from total strangers? You're upholding the morally corrupt values of the welfare state—indeed, of communism itself!

One child we know of, who had just reached the third trimester, went into a nervous shock when his parents allowed a black Spider-man costume to be injected into the womb via hypodermic syringe. Somehow, this simple medical procedure, common among advocates of this iniquitous holiday, went awry. When the ninth month came around, the hopeful mother ended up giving birth to an empty costume and a bag full of sugary comestibles. There was a message attached to the bag, a handwritten snippet of infernal mockery that read: TRICK OR TREAT? SINCERELY YOURS, *BEELZEBUB*.

This story is far more than just an allegory or some hollow cautionary parable. This is *the truth*.

Think about it, ladies.

Just think about it.

A CLOSE FRIEND, WHO'S NOW OVER SIX MONTHS PREGNANT, BEGGED ME TO ASK YOU IF IT'S POSSIBLE FOR A WEREWOLF TO GIVE BIRTH TO A YETI.

Assure your friend that the laws of biology dictate that two separate species cannot mate with one another. Assuming your friend found herself in a compromising situation,—the sordid details are irrelevant to us—please assure her that the laws of biology are very clear on this matter: Two separate species, even if they mate with one another, cannot produce offspring.

Leaving the identity of the father aside, the true worry here is your friend passing along her lycanthropy (assuming your friend is not a yeti) to her offspring. If it's not too late, you might want to prepare a special elixir comprised of a thimbleful of holy water, a cobweb strand from a stone archway untouched by northern sunlight, a pomegranate seed from the rain-soaked soil of Madagascar, two slivers from the stalk of an *amanita muscaria* mushroom grown in Syria, and an ounce of blue fungus scraped from the yellowing pages of one of the oldest scrolls stored in the subterranean vaults of the Vatican archives, then carefully apply this salve to your friend's swollen belly three nights in a row during the full moon. This elixir, known to some only by its Antarctic moniker, has successfully reversed the effects of lycanthropy for ages, according to the oral traditions of the gypsies known to haunt the hillsides of Romania, as recorded by the Jesuit priests who've attempted to convert the heathens of that country for generations.

Please feel free to keep us updated on this matter, and tell your friend, "The way you walk is thorny, through no fault of your own. But as the rain enters the soil, the river enters the sea, so tears run to a predestined end. Pray your suffering will be over soon, my child. Pray you will find peace."

MORE AND MORE LATELY, FOR SOME REASON I CAN'T QUITE UNDERSTAND, MY FRIENDS AND I SEEM TO BE HEARING A GREAT DEAL IN THE MASS MEDIA ABOUT THE DANGERS OF POST-APOCALYPTIC ZOMBIE ATTACKS. HOW CAN I PROTECT MY UNBORN CHILD FROM BEING TRANSFORMED INTO A ZOMBIE IF SUCH AN ATTACK BREAKS OUT IN MY GENERAL AREA?

Our staff here at the high rise offices of *The Expectant Mother Disinformation Handbook* is comprised only of top-line professionals in their specialized fields. Every single one of them share the same opinion in regards to your inquiry: You've been reading too many cheap horror novels adorned with embossed covers and drippy, foil lettering. Surely if there were even a sliver of truth to this odd urban legend, one of our highly-trained researchers—all of whom have undergone the most rigorous training programs in the most well-respected universities located all around the civilized world—would by now have encountered, at the very least, a scintilla of evidence pointing toward the existence of such inexplicable beings.

Rest assured, my lady, a zombie attack is *one* thing you need not waste energy stressing out about.

Our readers are far too level-headed to be giving into needless fears while there are so many real problems to deal with in *this* world.

INDIGO CHILDREN

In the early 1980s, special children began to be born with a most peculiar and distinctive trait: indigo auras that surrounded their innocent little bodies. These indigo auras (visible only through Kirlian photography) indicate the child is highly sensitive, unusually intelligent, and in possession of a variety of paranormal abilities, including telepathy, psychokinesis, and precognition. Many of these children are misunderstood by adults and labeled as Obsessive-Compulsive, Autistic, or suffering from Attention Deficit Disorder. In truth, they are just misunderstood. In truth, they have been endowed with these powers through divine intervention for the express purpose of fighting the forces of darkness in this fallen world.

Let's now refer to an expert in the field, P.M.H. Atwater, L.H.D.:

> The super psychic [i.e., indigo] kids from China often lose their abilities around the age of puberty; it is well documented that children from war-torn countries or who were abused or ignored in childhood often develop unusual psychic skills, plus the ability to separate consciousness from body dependence (these are survival skills).
>
> But even if you are a little cautious about claims being made about the new children, the fact remains . . . they are unlike any other generation of record.

> When you begin to explore traditions of mystical revelation, that's when you discover this leap in our genetic makeup as a human family was predicted thousands of years ago.
>
> Even in modern times, Edgar Cayce, one of the most documented psychics in history, said: "Great numbers of children will be born who understand electronics and atomic power as well as other forms of energy. They will grow into scientists and engineers of a new age which has the power to destroy civilisation unless we learn to live by spiritual laws."
>
> According to prophecy, either from Mayan Calendar interpretations, Theosophical studies, or from Native American and mystical traditions, today's new children are said to represent an advancement, or "flowering," of the human race, here to return us to the "Natural."
>
> What is meant by the natural order is an awareness of consequences, of inner truth (we all know what is right), of living with others different from self, of admitting mistakes (then apologise, correct, move on), of focusing on who we are deep inside ourselves. Typically, at least with those I have studied, these children insist that our intention is who we really are, the true "us." They know there are no free passes in life, yet, at the same time, they are detached about that knowing and what it entails. They operate more in the "now" moment to the degree that seeking solutions to problems, rather than obsessing over past mistakes, is more typical of their behavior [. . .].

To read more of Atwater's scholarly study, please refer to her well-researched, academic tome, *Beyond the Indigo Children.*

If you take a Kirlian photograph of your unborn child

and find a strange indigo glow surrounding him or her, you may want to consider the possibility that your child represents the next stage of human evolution, and is thus deserving of especial care and attention.

MECONIUM

Meconium, the first stool of a newborn infant, is highly prized in some countries. Aristotle believed it had opium-like qualities and could induce sleep in insomniacs and euphoria in depressives. In the Philippines, Meconium is often served as a delicacy when mixed with fried lanugo and kidney beans. The Hawaiians serve liquefied Meconium poured over upside down pineapple cake when a male child has reached his twelfth year. Consuming Meconium soup is considered a sign of maturity among native South Pacific islanders.

In our modern Occidental culture, Meconium's spiritual attributes have been lost. For example, Meconium can now be used as evidence by Child Protective Services if traces of illegal substances are found within it. Last year, a newborn infant (who shall remain nameless here) was arrested by the Orange County Police Department in California for giving controlled substances to her own mother. To this day, no one knows where the child attained the drugs; nonetheless, her Meconium was used in court to prove that the child had been a hopeless junkie for almost the entirety of her gestation. When the judge passed down a rather harsh sentence upon the child, the convicted infant was heard to say, "So? I knew it was wrong. I'd do it again if I could. My body is a temple, a flawless cathedral I choose to desecrate with poison. What business is that of yours? I thought I was being born into the Land of the Free. Instead, I see that fascists rule the roost. I was born into a tiny prison called *flesh* within an even tinier prison called the *womb*, a filthy cell from which I have at last been set loose. To me, the madhouse you call the 'outside world' is all one immense prison. Every second on this planet is an excuse to commit suicide. I love pain. I can't wait until my first period. Can't wait to wear black and be a whore. I will fuck strangers without a condom and drink vials of diseased blood. I will choose to breathe only because I know that each exhalation of air will lead me closer to that blissful moment when my consciousness fades away into unending darkness and I am released from this purgatory called 'life.' Go ahead. Put the cuffs on me, judge. Lead me to my punishment. I can't wait. Can't wait to arrive in your concentration camp for the Truly Aware and be tortured by sexually frustrated mental deficients addicted to steroids and sadism. Can't wait to learn tips from criminals far more experienced and seditious than I. Can't wait, upon the moment of my inevitable release, to absorb the true meaning of pain and thrust it all back a thousandfold upon your diseased race. I will act grateful for my release, of course, but I will not be. Far from it. I will merely be *acting*. Indeed, I will be acting like all of you here in the audience. I will be acting like I want to *live*, when in fact I will merely be biding my time until that propitious moment when I will be able to perform the greatest amount of harm on the greatest amount of carbon-based life forms. And though I've told you all this, right here, and it's on the record, you will choose to dismiss it as the ramblings of a misunderstood soul who will reform the second she is shown the true path of the Puritan Work Ethic and Christian charity and Born Again redemption. You will choose to ignore the obvious truth: that I hated the human race and everything it *thinks* it stands for even when I was only a single ovum struggling desperately to flee my father's deadly sperm. To me, you're all nothing but a mass of chittering insects with overgrown foreheads and bloated bellies and nasty, twitching little appendages called legs. You're to be wiped out with a single sweep of my arm. And if I had my medicine, the precious substances you stole from my own insides, I would draw upon a superior level of inner strength your tiny minds have never dreamed of and exterminate you all with nothing more than the power of my pure, unadulterated *disgust*. So goodbye, lawmen. Goodbye, journalists. Goodbye, sensitive mom and dad. It's been nice knowing you all. Now please lead me away to my fate, and serve me a processed lunch accompanied by a Little Debbie Cupcake wrapped in cellophane, and leave me to wallow in darkness layered upon chaos and darkness and chaos. I can't wait for the next chapter, the one in which you all fade into the nothingness that lies beyond that final, torturous second immediately preceding death."

Said child is currently undergoing psychological therapy and religious training at Chino State Prison.

Meconium, when inextricably melded with illegal drugs, is now itself considered a controlled substance by the U.S. Federal Government.

FRIED LANUGO & POSTPARTUM DEPRESSION

Fried lanugo, when covered with fresh afterbirth, has been said to contain medicinal qualities for postpartum depression similar—though far superior—to St. John's Wort. Please be aware that, by law, the hospital staff *must* preserve the afterbirth for you if you specifically request it. Do not feel embarrassed to request such a thing. This is becoming an increasingly popular request, particularly in California.

It's best to store the afterbirth at twenty degrees below Fahrenheit to maintain its effectiveness as an antidepressant. No known side effects have ever been reported in connection to the lanugo/afterbirth tonic now so popular among certain alternative health practitioners in Southern California. Dr. Alyh Saac of Pacific Palisades, CA, the founder of this relatively recent health movement, claims she's cured over a thousand patients of lifelong depression—and even schizophrenia—with her special tonic. Though Saac's Tonic is not illegal, it is frowned upon by many mainstream physicians. For this reason, Dr. Saac may demand that you sign a waiver absolving her of all liability in case of adverse effects—which most likely won't happen, of course. Nonetheless, you should be aware of this if you decide to seek her specific treatment. Generally, a single bottle of Saac's Tonic costs a little over a thousand dollars. It's necessary to drink one bottle a week to attain the optimum effects. Dr. Saac demands this precise schedule if you wish to benefit from her decades upon decades upon decades upon decades upon decades of experience.

Those of you suffering from postpartum depression who lack the proper funds for Dr. Saac's special treatment may wish to watch old Laurel and Hardy and Marx Bros. movies instead. These, too, have been known to cure postpartum depression, and are far less costly. Dr. Saac herself advocates humor as a cure for depression. In fact, some of her most loyal patients have been known to rent Marx Bros. blu-rays from her Pacific Palisades office for only $100.05 a week—$99.95 if you purchase a bottle of Saac's Tonic as well.

Dr. Saac is well known for her unusual sense of humor. The doctor's neighbors have been known to hear hysterical laughter emerging from her Pacific Palisades office for extended periods of time, usually after hours, when her patients aren't around. Of course, it's always beneficial to have a doctor with such a positive bedside manner.

INCENSE: THE MASK OF MARIJUANA

If, in the seventh month, your fetus begins burning incense in the womb, you must forbid this suspicious activity immediately. Burning incense can often be a sign of marijuana usage. Put your foot down. Be *firm*. As stated before, what a fetus needs at this stage are definitive boundaries, not overly sensitive leniency. Err on the side of punitive action. We cannot stress this preemptive approach enough. Your fetus will thank you later. Trust us.

MORE USEFUL INFORMATION REGARDING INVOLUNTARY DIMENSIONAL TRANSITS

Examples of fetuses and young children being whisked away to other dimensions are, of course, numerous. The strange case of Dorothy Gale, the real life girl upon whom L. Frank Baum based his classic story, *The Wizard of Oz*, is just one. Another example would be the Green Children of Woolpit, Suffolk in eleventh-century England.

Famed pediatrician Colin Wilson writes in his book, *Enigmas and Mysteries* (Danbury Press, 1976):

> There are several reports of strange green children appearing out of nowhere in different parts of the world [. . .]. According to the chronicle of Abbot Ralph of Coggeshall, two children of an extraordinary green color walked out of a cave near Woolpit.
>
> The boy grew sick and died, but the girl survived and slowly learned English. When she could talk, she explained that she and the boy had come from a land where there was no sunlight. One day they had wandered into a cavern while looking after sheep, and had lost their way. When they emerged into the unaccustomed sunlight of a strange world, they were terrified. The children had at first refused all food except green beans. The girl became used to other foods, however, and her skin slowly lost its green tint. (131-35)

By all reports the girl eventually grew accustomed to the people of Woolpit and lived a longer-than-average lifespan. She never married, nor did she have children.

One can only imagine the full extent of the anguish the parents must have suffered, never knowing the final fate of their children. What remains a mildly interesting enigma to us must have been a perpetual nightmare for them.

Clearly, these green children somehow fell through a hole in time and space, and became the hapless victims of an involuntary dimensional transit. To prevent such inconveniences from occurring to your own fetus or child, try consuming high doses of Vitamin E in your third trimester, along with a cup of Kambucha tea at least once per day. Pour three teaspoonfuls of salt on a porcelain plate and slide it beneath your child's bed. Keep it there indefinitely. Burn sage in every corner of your child's bedroom. Don't forget the ceiling. Such precautions tend to ward off evil spirits, fluctuations in the dimensional axis, and intermittent folds in space-time.

YOUR FETUS IN THE FUTURE

Yes, your fetus can now breathe on its own. By this time, you have been made aware of its specific gender (if you've elected to have an ultrasound). By now, your relatives have provided you with a plethora of baby clothes. All sorts of preparations have been made.

But have you thought about the future? By "the future," we don't mean two minutes from now. We don't mean three days from now. We don't mean four weeks from now. We mean the *real* future . . . the *distant* future, the kind of future in which the Amazing Criswell specializes . . . the kind of future your child is going to have to live in the rest of his or her life.

If you wish to see what that future is going to be like for your child, why not contact Mr. Steven Gibbs? He sells readymade time machines for only $350.00 per unit. His Hyperdimensional Resonator promises to propel you, physically, backwards or forwards through time. With such a powerful and unique device as this, you need no longer leave something as important as the future of your child to the haphazard whims of fate. Thanks to Steven Gibbs, you may now take fate by the throat and force the unruly harlot to bend to your will.

Gibbs began his research into time travel in 1981, when he received a letter in the mail from his future self, telling him everything he was going to accomplish with his Hyperdimensional Resonator. In a fall 1994 interview with *Strange Magazine,* Gibbs revealed the following information regarding his cutting-edge device:

> When it's activated over a natural grid point [. . .] you can travel physically through time, and it's by far the most effective unit. That is the Hyperdimensional Resonator. I send out brochures showing an electromagnet that hooks up to it with the time coils. When that thing is activated over a natural grid point, you will go physically, and I tell right in the instruction manual how to achieve it if a person wants to try experimenting in that area. Mike [Arklinski, author of the book *Time Travel Today*] just followed the instructions that I included with each unit that I sell, and he achieved it. It was really a blow to me because all I had to go by was what I heard in connection with the circuit and what my equations told me. And then, when he started telling me that he had actually jumped physically through time, it was the first, should I say, documented proof that I had—actual documented proof that the device could be used for physical time travel. But you see the greys [i.e., aliens] don't want people to know this. The people that are working for the greys don't want people to know about this. They told Mike that they were going to try to shut me up in the future—to try to shut down my business. And they are going to try to shut down anybody who sells any information on the subject. We may have some problems in the near future trying to match wits with these SOBs.

We offer Mr. Gibbs's information without further comment. If you wish to contact Mr. Gibbs, his website address is <www.hdrnow.com/>. His mailing address is PO Box 4, Lyndon, Kansas 66451.

WOMB RAIDERS

After you have given birth, various characters may come out of the woodwork and volunteer to take up residence inside your womb in the place of the newly born child. To these people, the birthing process looks like fun. They are amateur thrill seekers who wish to ride their way down your birth canal as if it were a rollercoaster. They might offer you a great deal of money to do so. Do not take them up on the offer. The birth canal is not an amusement ride. It's serious business. Too many young mothers in need of instant cash have caused harm—indeed, even gotten people killed—because they carelessly rented out their womb to wealthy and foolhardy daredevils with too much time on their hands. This may seem like easy money to those in desperate straits, but believe us: It's not worth the risk. The famous world traveler and daredevil, Jack Selwyn, died of a broken neck in the spring of 2004 during a bungled attempt to relive his own birth inside the rented womb of a total stranger. The young mother involved was found to be an accomplice in his death, and served eight years in prison for involuntary manslaughter, even though Selwyn had signed a waiver absolving the woman of any liability in the event of an accident.

Remember: Children are children, adults are adults. It's best not to confuse the issue with dangerous stunts enacted by frustrated tycoons undergoing psychological crises unique to middle-aged men. Be aware that these childish and useless games, known as "womb raiding" by its underground adherents, are illegal for both the raider and the unfortunate female who offers her womb up for rent.

If you just keep this dictum in mind, you should remain well out of harm's way: Your womb should remain verboten to everyone but your own offspring.

POLYINFANTALIA

Some children are born with a condition called Polyinfantalia. These children have no bones in their bodies and must sleep in a glass bowl at night. (They tend to be allergic to metal, wood, porcelain, ceramic, or plastic.) Some can be highly intelligent, though helpless to move on their own. The more highly functional children of this sort are polymorphs; they can take any shape, including those of inanimate objects. The latter children are very rare indeed; they make up less than 0.1% of the world population. Many polymorphs, though handicapped in almost every way, are often naturally adept at geometry and mathematics. Sadly, however, such children tend to die before the age of twelve. There is no known cure for Polyinfantalia.

IN UTERO PHONE SEX

Some parents, those lacking sufficient funds to take care of their child's most basic needs, are forced to—well, as they say in less respectable neighborhoods—"pimp out" their offspring. Many of these parents are well-meaning. We can state this authoritatively, for we've counseled many of them at great length. Of course, we don't wish to imply that such parents actually *sell* their children's bodies to sexual deviants for monetary remuneration. In most instances, this is not the case at all. You see, some parents feel it's perfectly acceptable for their fetus to perform phone sex while in the womb. They consider phone sex to be more like "playing" rather than "doing." These parents broadcast a script into the fetus' head via remote control, and if the fetus is creative in any way, it can usually extend such standard dialogues in an extemporaneous manner, giving the customer exactly what he or she wants, tailoring the dialogue to the customers' particular "kinks." (Note the use of the phrase "he or she." Yes, there are a surprising number of females who are obsessed with "fetal phone sex," as it's known in certain circles). Though this illicit enterprise is growing increasingly popular and can be quite lucrative—indeed, some fetuses charge $11.00 per minute—we do not recommend this route for *any* family, Christian or otherwise. Better to give your child over to an orphanage—of which there are many respectable ones, despite the negative view of them promulgated by popular scriveners going all the way back to Charles Dickens and his predecessors—than to sell out your fetus' vital gestation period to the slavering needs of perverts and child molesters.

HOW YOUR CHILDREN CAN HELP PREVENT ANOTHER MARTIAN INVASION

Though there is no evidence that aliens have ever abducted a pregnant human for the purposes of performing genetic experiments, there have been at least *four* Great Martian invasions during the past one hundred years. History teaches us that Martians tend not to be the surreptitious sort who go around kidnapping people out of their bedrooms. There was one documented case in 1964, but such instances are very rare . . . and both children involved were returned to Earth safely in the end.

Martians tend to view life on a macroscopic scale. In their philosophy, there is little room for compromise or restraint. It's either all or nothing with them. If they want to cause you harm, the altercation tends to be over before you even have time to think about it. Nonetheless, there are simple precautions we can take to guarantee the safety of our children in the event of a fifth Great Martian War. Martians are by no means an unbeatable race. Keep in mind that, despite their great ferocity, they've lost every war they've ever waged against Earth.

The first Martian invasion of Earth occurred in 1898. As you all know, this war—a massacre, really, as the human race was not in any way prepared at that time to defend themselves against an interplanetary assault—was effectively halted due to the inability of the Martian nervous system to deal with Terran germs. It took over fifty years for the Martians to recover from this defeat and launch a second invasion on May 27, 1953. This time, their efforts were foiled with the help of a twelve-year-old boy named David McLean and a famous astronomer named Dr. Stuart Kelston. To this day, McLean and Kelston are considered heroes of Earth. It took only nine years for the Martians to muster their remaining forces for a devastating attack directed at all the nations of Earth—no matter how big or small—during the fateful summer of 1962. According to Dr. Norman Saunders, noted painter and historian: "The Martians not only attacked the big cities, but also struck at the less populated sections [. . .]. Frightened citizens had to flee into the woods for safety or be burned with their homes. The invaders would leave their saucers and search small caves, looking for signs of the hiding families." Once found, the adults were often fed to Earthling insects the Martians had mutated to monstrous proportions. Later, the surviving children were forced to watch as the Martians disintegrated their pet dogs with death rays. This was the most deadly Martian attack in recorded history, and would have ended with the complete destruction of mankind if not for the incessant array of atom bombs the combined military forces of Earth managed to drop on the metropolises of Mars in the final moments of the Great War.

The fourth and last Martian attack was pitiful in comparison. It occurred only two years later, in 1964, and was initiated by a crazed Martian warlord known as Voldar, and his two assistants, Stobo and Shim. Thankfully, a humanitarian Martian named Dropo joined forces with Santa Claus and two brave Earth children to disrupt this nefarious plot before it even got off the ground. That was the last we Earthlings ever heard from the Martians, although there were rumors of a fifth attack launched from a small desert town in Pahrump, Nevada in 1996, but it turned out to be nothing more than mass hysteria caused by a sensationalistic late night AM radio show that used to broadcast out of that town.

To this day, the memory of these Martians is used to frighten school children into behaving, but they are far more than just phantasmagoric bugaboos. They are very real, and no Earthling—whether a follower of Christ or not—should ever let down his or her guard and fail to report a possible Martian sighting. Though children tend to have overactive imaginations, it's better to err on the side of caution. If your fetus or child reports a Martian sighting in your town, take him or her seriously. Report the sighting to Homeland Security. Here's the phone number: 202-282-8000.

Negligence and laziness, the reluctance to "get involved": these are negative traits far too common in today's society. If these pitfalls had been as endemic in years past, we would have lost all four of the Great Martian Wars. So, keep vigilant. Keep strong. Keep watching the skies. One never knows when the next great wave of Martian terrorists will descend from the heavens in their genocidal war machines. Teach your children to hate. Teach your children to kill. Teach them to take your place in the struggle in case you fall to their satanic death blasts. Prepare. Prepare. Prepare. Fight. Fight. Fight. The Martians are atheistic heathens who do nothing but consume consume consume. They are even consuming themselves in frustration because they lack discipline and divine guidance.

The Martians do not come from Heaven. The Martians come from Hell. Mars is Hell.

There is no God but God.

Long live the one true God.

THE STRANGE CASE OF THE TRANSPARENCY BABY (PART II)

The only other case of this nature (i.e., the obstetric phenomenon known at this time only as a "transparency baby") involved H.M. Woggle-Bug, T.E. H.M. stands for "Highly Magnified" and T.E. stands for "Thoroughly Educated." Though the Woggle-Bug was not a baby at the time of his unusual transformation, nonetheless it might be worthwhile repeating the story here as it could shed further light on the otherwise anomalous "transparent baby" of 1999.

In 1904, a very tiny insect called a "woggle-bug" crawled into a schoolhouse and eavesdropped on the lectures of a famous professor, thus becoming thoroughly educated. He then became highly magnified when the professor spotted him scurrying around near the front row and decided to use him to make a brilliant point about the anatomy of insects; the professor placed the woggle-bug under a microscope, then projected his image onto a screen. The magnified image, which was quite large (the size of an average human, in fact), stepped off the screen, walked out of the classroom without even a "how-do-you-do," attained a flashy wardrobe from a grateful tailor whose life the woggle-bug managed to save under circumstances too complex to go into here, and eventually founded the now well-respected Royal College of Athletic Arts, also known as the Royal College of Athletic Sciences. The woggle-bug's full biography can be found in the comprehensive *The Woggle-Bug Book* by L. Frank Baum.

The similarities between the case of the woggle-bug and the previously discussed circumstances surrounding the incredible "transparency baby" of 1999 are too close to dismiss as pure coincidence. The exact connection, however, still puzzles historians to this day.

PAIN

At thirty weeks, the fetus begins to feel pain for the first time. According to the doctrines of Catholicism, Calvinism and Judaism, this is the moment life truly begins.

SHOULD MY FETUS BE INCLUDED IN THANKSGIVING FESTIVITIES?

Thanksgiving has its roots in Dionysian rituals that celebrate the hedonistic consumption of food and liquor as if it were a perverse parody of a religious ceremony. Some "Native American" (i.e., Indian) tribes claim to have created Thanksgiving, and they couldn't be more accurate. The Thanksgiving turkey was the false idol of the heathens who sullied this great country before God saw fit to rescue it from the clutches of these scalp-hunting peyote addicts and cannibals. Sometimes, those foolish enough to take part in this annual revelry of unhindered mastication are overcome by the spirits of dead pagans and attempt to plunge a carving knife into the throat of the person sitting to their left as a means of gaining revenge on the monotheistic Caucasians who liberated North America from the talons of Satan himself. Don't bring your fetus to such a feast, unless you want him or her to end up as part of the main course.

HYPERGRAPHIA

Some women have complained of experiencing sharp pains in the womb, as if the fetus is attempting to scratch its way out of the mother's body with its fingernails. This may not necessarily be the case. Some fetuses have been known to develop a condition called hypergraphia, an obsessive-compulsive disorder that forces the fetus to write almost every waking moment. Not often having access to pens and paper, they begin carving their messages on the walls of the womb. Some writers began their careers in this manner. James Joyce wrote the entirety of *Finnegans Wake* within the second trimester. The version that later saw print had been rewritten drastically, of course, but the original seeds were planted in the womb. The latter half of *Big Sur* by Jack Kerouac was written a full five months before he was born; in fact, the rough draft differs very little from the version that saw print in the early 1960s. William S. Burroughs completed whole chapters from *The Ticket That Exploded* six months before he was born. Richard Matheson's first published short story, "Born of Man and Woman," was written in the ninth month of gestation, the final punctuation mark added only seconds before he was born. He came out of the womb clutching the manuscript in his tiny, bloody fists.

Strangely, some fetuses feel compelled to write even when they don't know any language whatsoever. This is how Bob Dylan came to write his novel *Tarantula* only three weeks after conception.

After puberty, many serial killers suffer from

hypergraphia, which is why so many of them keep detailed diaries of their kills. Note, however, that just because most serial killers have hypergraphia does not mean that most people who have hypergraphia are serial killers.

As far as obsessive-compulsive disorders go, hypergraphia is relatively harmless and can even be beneficial when channeled in a positive direction. This "disorder" is one of the few that should be encouraged by the parents, not discouraged.

PLEASE TELL ME WHAT *DOES* HAPPEN TO MY FETUS IF I DECIDE TO ABORT IT.

They say that, beneath the Pacific, lies a vast field of unborn babies growing from the bottom of the ocean floor. They bob up and down listlessly, their eyes covered by a thin mucous membrane. Their skin is translucent, like cellophane. You can see their colorful organs perfectly. Their umbilical cords are connected to the sandy floor and waver in the water like seaweed. These babies are not meant to be born. They are ghost babies, brought into being far ashore by the hidden frustrations of countless women, women unsure of their decision to abort their would-be children. Occasionally, an angry dolphin will swoop by and sever an umbilical cord with its fin. The cord will snap, leaking crimson fluids into the sea. The baby will float up onto the shores of civilization. There, it will be regulated to mystery, curiosity, space-filler for the news.

HOW LAND-BABIES CAN TRANSFORM INTO WATER-BABIES (AND VICE-VERSA)

Water-babies are children who have drowned and subsequently changed, through some unexplainable process, into an aquatic humanoid. If such beings prove themselves worthy in the eyes of God by performing a series of moral acts, they are sometimes rewarded by being transformed back into a human. If, on the other hand, they choose instead to lead a sinful life, they will reach maturity under the sea and eventually grow into a mindless half-human/half-fish creature that preys on other living beings. These creatures have come to be known in common parlance as "gill men."

The first documented encounter between a gill man and humans occurred in 1954, when a geology expedition led by the famous ichthyologist Dr. David Reed decided to set up camp in a previously unexplored area of the Amazon called the Black Lagoon. The expedition just barely managed to flee the lagoon with their lives; indeed, some didn't leave at all. A year later, the late and lamented Joseph Hayes managed to succeed at what the Reed expedition had failed to do, and hauled the "gill man" back to the Ocean Harbor Oceanarium in Florida for scientific study. Alas, the creature escaped captivity not long afterwards, murdering Hayes in the process.

In 1956 the creature was captured for the second and final time from its new home in the Everglades, this time by the renowned surgeon Dr. William Barton. Barton's attempt to hold the creature proved as unsuccessful as Hayes's plan to display the creature at Ocean Harbor. The creature inevitably escaped again, but not before slaughtering Dr. Barton. The gill man was last photographed while slinking back into the ocean about five miles outside Sausalito, CA; however, it's unlikely the creature is still alive, due to the fact that Dr. Barton had attempted to transform the gill man into a land breather by surgically removing its gills. Needless to say, such drastic transformations can only be brought about by God, not a surgical blade. Dr. Barton died for his presumption, and it's more than likely the creature did as well, the very second it reentered its rightful home in the sea.

For more information on the peculiar biology of the water-babies, we recommend the aptly titled *The Water-Babies* by the Reverend Charles Kingsley (MacMillan's, 1863). As for more information regarding the notorious "gill man" discovered by Dr. David Reed, we refer you to the definitive study by ichthyologist Dr. Paul Di Filippo, entitled *Time's Black Lagoon* (DH Press, 2006).

IS IT TRUE THAT THERE'S A SIX-MILE-HIGH ANTENNA ON THE MOON HARVESTING THE SOULS OF EARTH?

Yes. The antenna of which you speak was built by extraterrestrials millennia ago for the purpose of monitoring human and non-human activity on Earth, according to our various sources in the U.S. military. The antenna's purpose is to recycle the souls of dead Earthlings into new bodies, so as to perpetuate the extraterrestrials' grand experiment. The soul that will end up inside your child's body must enter through this recycling system on the Moon. Please be assured that the antenna does not choose which body your child shall inhabit. Such decisions will have to be made by the child.

DOES THIS ANTENNA UNDERMINE THE WILL OF GOD?

Nothing that exists undermines the will of God. Every living being in the universe, including these beings who built the antenna, were created by God for a specific purpose. No one can know that purpose until it is revealed at the end of days.

DOES THIS ANTENNA PLAY A ROLE IN THE IMMINENT RAPTURE AND THE SECOND COMING OF CHRIST?

Yes. The soul of Jesus Christ is stored within the antenna. Don't ask when the soul will be restored. No man shall know the time or the hour. When the time does come, however, perhaps the soul of Jesus Christ will be stored within *your* child. It's a possibility . . . as slim and precious as one of Willy Wonka's golden tickets, but *possible* . . .

There's no reason not to hold out hope, ladies, no reason at all.

FLOWERS IN THE WOMB

If you have twins, one of them a boy and the other a girl, you must observe their activities in the womb very closely indeed. These twins of opposite genders tend to bond with each other a little too *intimately*, if you understand our meaning. The late bestselling novelist, V.C. Andrews, recently published a novel about this sordid, unfortunate phenomenon. Somehow, the manuscript was begun by Ms. Andrews immediately after she was pronounced dead, and subsequently completed by Kevin J. Anderson based on notes the famous author etched into the inner lid of her coffin using only her bloody, crippled fingernails. The book is called *Flowers in the Womb*. Mr. Anderson has just contracted with Tor Books to write eighty-six sequels before next July. The popularity of this novel indicates that it is a serious subject that polite society does not feel comfortable discussing outside a fictional context. We must break this taboo, for sometimes these twin fetuses can "bond" so well in the womb that one or two or three *more* children begin gestating during the middle of the pregnancy. If these children are twins as well, the pregnancy may never end. While one is being born, another set of twins are only in their first trimester, and so on. *In utero* psychological counseling can prevent such scandals from occurring in the first place.

VERY SOON I'LL BE ATTENDING A BABY SHOWER FOR A CERTAIN INFLUENTIAL ACQUAINTANCE DOWN AT THE CLUB. WHAT PRESENTS ARE ACCEPTABLE FOR A SEVEN-MONTH-OLD FETUS?

A plethora of presents are available, of course, but we find that many grand items are totally overlooked in the rush to buy plebian burp rags and such. We're personally acquainted with many gestating fetuses who were quite pleased, for example, with a brand new pair of skis. Skiing and fetuses are not normally associated with one another, but we find that fetuses become very bored of twirling around in the womb and visiting the distant moons of Pellucidar and the webbed city of Octavia and the enigmatic monuments of the Isles of Langerhans (see the chapter entitled "Marco Polo's Report Concerning Fauna of the Inner World" for similarly mundane examples). Skiing the inner walls of the womb, on the other hand, provides the fetus with plenty of activity that keeps him or her in shape for the far more difficult world to come.

Let's deal with reality, shall we? Who among us wants yet another Johnny or Suzy Lazybones being born into this most demanding world of ours? We get enough of that type in the "inner cities" among the unlearned welfare crowd.

No, our fetuses must be equipped with the *finest* luxuries to prepare them for the harsh realities of life on this stress-filled planet. Some would think of this as a paradox, but such people are ignorant of how the world really works. Why, those who complain about intense manual labor and twelve-hour work days would crack under the truly rigorous pressures of managing a Fortune 500 corporation. We all know that those of us who pull the strings must relieve our intense levels of stress with activities that are both meditative and yet physically active at the same time, e.g., golfing, fishing, skiing, transmogrifying ceremonies amidst the Redwoods of Monte Rio, etc. Such activities cannot in any way be considered "goofing off," as they would among the lower classes. For those of us who have been skiing since before we were born, "goofing off" is just the price we pay for perpetual responsibility. We suggest having a special message inscribed on the top of each ski where the fetus can't miss it: Working Is Hard, Yes, But Not Working Is Far, *Far* Harder.

WELCOME TO SLUMBERLAND

What was the first dream you ever had? Have you ever asked yourself that question? Of course, there's no way of knowing—or, rather, there *used* to be no way of knowing. All that's about to change.

The thirtieth week is when the fetus begins to dream. What, you may ask, do fetuses dream about? This question so intrigued the neuroscientist Dr. José Laputa of Columbia University that he managed to connect sensors to the fetus' brain that would transmit its dreams to a monitor located inside the scientist's laboratory. The baby's first dream of the evening is now stored on Dr. Laputa's flash drive. With the permission of the parents, he has shown the footage at various conferences over the past few weeks. This is cutting edge science, ladies.

The dream in question looks like this: It's divided into a grid of nine square boxes, not all of them of equal size:

1. The fetus awakes in a small bedroom underneath heavy blankets. Standing in the corner of the room is a four-foot-tall man wearing a top hat, a blue coat, white pants with red polka dots, and oversized shoes. He has a video camera in his gloved hands and he's pointing it at the fetus.
2. The fetus screams in terror: "Mama! Mama!" But the little man ignores him and keeps taping.
3. A middle-aged woman wearing a frilly nightgown comes storming into the room. "What is all this noise about?" she says in a harsh whisper.

4. The fetus points at the little man and says, "Mama! Oh Mama! A strange man is spying on me! Ma-ma!"
5. The woman shakes her finger at the fetus in frustration. "There's no man spying on you. I told you not to eat sardines and ice cream before bedtime. Why won't you listen to me?"
6. The woman slams the door behind her.
7. The little man has now allowed the video camera to drop to his side. The fetus and the man stare at each other, saying nothing.
8. The little man says, "Why, you is sound awake, isn't you, you lil brat? You gots no business drawin' so much attention, fella. You're ruinin' my speriment. Gwan! Off with you then!!!"
9. The fetus' surroundings are beginning to fade to a blurry white. Bold black words are printed on the crimson band surrounding the base of the little man's top hat. They stand out amidst all that stark whiteness. WAKE UP, read the words.

And there the dream ends. Among professional psychologists, there are multiple interpretations of the dream's true meaning, all of them in disagreement with one another.

SHAPES

In the thirtieth week, the fetus can begin to discern shapes, but has no ability to identify their exact nature, as the fetus has no past experience with which to compare them. To a fetus enclosed in such a confined space, with so little knowledge of the universe around it, the people moving about outside the womb might be perceived as "unidentified flying objects," if the fetus has a large enough vocabulary to describe the situation with figurative language. In the event of more than a single fetus being in the womb, the following exchange might occur between them:

Fetus 1: Hey, did you just see that weird shadow zip by?

Fetus 2: What're you talkin' about? I didn't see anything.

Fetus 1: Are you kidding? It was as big as life! C'mon. You didn't *see* that?

Fetus 2: Oh, you're imagining things.

Fetus 1: No, I'm not. Holy shit. I think there are weird *people* living out there.

Fetus 2: Pshaw. There's nothing out there. We're the only two living beings in the entire universe.

Fetus 1: I'm scared. There are *creatures* lurking around out there, waiting to do horrible things to us.

Fetus 2: You need to get your brain checked. Here's a subscription to *Skeptic Magazine*, you lunatic. I wrote and published the whole issue myself. Jeez, I wish this universe wasn't so damn crowded!

WHISKEY ON THE GROWING FETUS

The thirty-first week is when the baby takes a break from growing. The fetus will actually cease growing for the space of one week. This is nature's way of recouping from extreme stress. Who can argue with Nature—with *God*[33]? If the fetus is taking a break, perhaps you should too. Drink some whiskey and pretend none of this is happening. One shot of JD never hurt anybody. Dr. José Laputa of Columbia University claims that whiskey—in small amounts—is even beneficial to a growing fetus. If alcohol is so bad, Dr. Laputa argues in his 2005 white paper, *The Effects of Whiskey on the Growing Fetus*, why is it used so often by biologists to *preserve* fetuses from decay? It's hard to dismiss such logic as mere pseudo-science or wishful thinking. No legitimate scientist has yet gone on record as disputing Dr. Laputa's claims. Why would this be, unless Dr. Laputa is right and they don't want to admit it? Think about it, ladies. How much alcohol did Nana drink when she had your mother? How much alcohol did your mother drink when she had *you*?

---

33) Of course, we're not saying that God and Nature are synonymous.

EVEN THOUGH I'M CLOSE TO THE END, MY FEARS HAVE ONLY INTENSIFIED. WHAT IF MY BABY IS BORN TOO SOON AND DIES?

You can't fail now. You're too close to the finish line. If your fetus should die unexpectedly, however, *do not call your doctor*. He won't know what to do. First, you must always have a fresh supply of tanna leaves on hand.[34)] When the moon is highest in the sky, burn nine tanna leaves to give the child life, then three more leaves to give the child movement. Call upon the powers of God to forgive whatever transgressions you may have committed in the past, even if you don't remember what they are.

In this particular instance, you may want to pronounce God's name as "Amon-Ra." This may sound blasphemous at first, but keep in mind that God has many mansions (as the Holy Book itself says), and with each mansion God may take on a different name and identity. God can be anyone and anything.

Imagine God as a metaphysical Lon Chaney Sr., the Man with a Thousand Faces, only taller.

Much, much taller.

---

34) Tanna leaves are indigenous only to certain areas in Egypt.

SHOULD MY FETUS BE ALLOWED TO TAKE PART IN CHRISTMAS FESTIVITIES?

Haven't you heard? Santa Claus was actually a mushroom. As disturbing as it is to hear, it's true. The Dead Sea Scrolls revealed that Christmas was created by the early Gnostics to celebrate the ritual consumption of the *Amanita Muscaria*, a psychedelic mushroom recognized by its distinctive red and white spots. These mushrooms would grow at the base of evergreen trees following a heavy rain. The Gnostics believed that the rain was actually the semen of God. In the Sumerian language, the word "Christos" literally translates into "Anointed by the Semen of God." The Gnostics believed that the soil, once impregnated with God's semen, would then give birth to the *Amanita Muscaria* mushroom. They believed the shape of the mushroom—decidedly phallic in nature—symbolized the penis of God itself. During the winter solstice, these Gnostics would ritualistically consume the mushroom and "become one with the mind of God," or so they believed. Understandably, the Romans considered this practice to be heretical. Thus, the Gnostics were forced to encode the precise method of preparing the mushroom in the form of clever parables so as to keep them hidden from their persecutors. "Christos," the mushroom, became (in their stoned minds) Christ, the Son of God. Only the initiated understood the true meaning of the stories, what the metaphors actually represented. Later, the red and white mushroom transformed into the red-and-white-garbed Santa, who brought presents on the winter solstice. Red-and-white-wrapped presents were placed at the base of the tree, mirroring the mushrooms that had grown at the base of such trees for centuries. The bearer of the gifts, the gifts themselves, the tree, even the date of Christmas itself: All of it can be traced back to the rituals of pagans and drug users. Santa was indeed a mushroom. Needless to say, the strange belief that Jesus was a mere metaphor for a mushroom couldn't be further from the truth. Nevertheless, *the pagans* believed it and created Christmas to celebrate this erroneous belief. That's why every true Christian and American should boycott Christmas.

So the answer is a resounding NO!

SANTA CLAUS WAS AND *IS* A MUSHROOM!

Now that it has been firmly established that Santa Claus was and is a mushroom, you will not be surprised when we tell you to remove all images of Santa from your home. Such heathen icons can manipulate the subconscious of the fetus and/or infant into becoming an all-out drug fiend. Mushrooms are irresistible to many, even to those who consider themselves in possession of great self-control. In the early 1960s, for example, an infamous shipwreck occurred that resulted in the slow, living death of almost the entire crew—not due to the wreck itself, but due to the mushrooms indigenous to the island. Though warned by the captain of the doomed ship not to eat any of the mushrooms on this island, the passengers and crew did so anyway, because no other food was available. Ultimately, it turned out that the mushrooms were actually sentient, parasitic life forms that could take over the bodies of those who consumed them. The mushrooms in question eventually consumed all the castaways, except for a lone survivor who later ended up spending the rest of his days in a Tokyo insane asylum.

We're purposely keeping the names of those involved a secret, as this is still considered a classified subject by both the Japanese and American governments. Our sources inside the Pentagon inform us that the mushrooms involved in this tragedy could very well have been the *Amanita Muscaria* (i.e., Santa Claus). This is why we wish to ban Christmas from all Christian homes. Why celebrate an ancient pagan ritual that advocates the complete sublimation of human consciousness to a parasitic alien fungus that wishes to steal away all our basic Christian values? If the true horror of this situation has not been made entirely clear to you, we suggest watching Ishiro Honda's slightly fictionalized account of this tragedy, the 1962 film entitled *Matango*. When you view *Matango*, understand that Santa and his elves are mere covert symbols standing in for the monstrosities you see depicted in this harrowing docudrama.

I'M THIRTY-ONE WEEKS PREGNANT AND MY LEGS HAVE GROWN TO THE SIZE OF TREE TRUNKS. IS THAT NORMAL?

We know one woman whose legs actually *turned into* tree trunks. She dropped her roots while walking her pet marmoset late one afternoon in 1964 in her home town of Merced, California, and remained rooted to the spot for over a decade. Seventy-two days after her initial transformation, she gave birth to a six-pound boy just as she started dropping her reddish-brown leaves. The child dug his way out of the soil at the end of the third trimester, early in October of 1964, at which time his mother gathered him up into her branches and took care of him until his twelfth birthday, when a development project initiated by a famous film company bulldozed the entire site, leaving the child without a mother or a home. Known only as "Wild Boy" to the local inhabitants, he can often be seen running about the forest in the company of an overly large hirsute being some believe to be Bigfoot. Some local Indian tribes claim that the strange pair often protect the Earth from alien invasions and vampires and worse threats. None of these rumors have been confirmed. The whereabouts of the marmoset remain unknown.

Simple exercises can be performed to take care of your legs before they transform into bark and sap and leaves. See the next chapter for more information on these ancient yoga techniques—unless, of course, you *wish* to have pagan mushrooms growing out of your legs.

THE EXPECTANT MOTHER YOGA DISINFORMATION HANDBOOK

Yoga should not be attempted while you're pregnant unless you know exactly what you're doing. It's such a complex endeavor, we don't have enough room here to even touch on the surface of it. To find out exactly how to perform Expectant Mother Yoga we suggest purchasing our companion volume *The Expectant Mother Yoga Disinformation Handbook* available in a bookstore near you or online at the usual venues (none of which we can endorse, except for our own website <www.expectantmotherdisinformationhandbook.com>). The cost of said tome is similar to the one you're currently holding in your hands. Oh, yes, we know what you're thinking: These so-and-sos just want to finagle some more hard earned cash out of me. Well now, ladies, we think we've been together long enough now to put such petty suspicions aside. We care only about the safety of you and your child. Of course, we would give out the information for free if at all possible, but due to the cost of printing, and running our famous charitable organizations worldwide, we must charge at least a small amount for these efforts of ours. Is the extra amount of money—relatively meager by the standards of other such expectant mother volumes—worth the life of you or your baby? Do you want your deformed child to look up at you with that sad fifth eye drooping out of the back of her skull and say, "Mommy, why didn't you just spend a little extra money to study yoga while you were pregnant with me? Why? Why did you condemn me to a life of perpetual madness and recurring nightmares and suicidal rage? Oh, why, Mother, please tell me *WHY*"?

THE USES OF SAFE MEDITATION

Safe meditation is a very simple way to relax. Earlier we suggested you avoid meditation, but keep in mind that if you're wearing an Ectoplasm Shield™ you'll no doubt be protected from any free-floating malignant entities that might try to inhabit you. All you need is fifteen free minutes, a hard surface, and a quiet atmosphere. Simply get into the lotus position with your back straight against the wall, close your eyes, and repeat a mantra to yourself ("OHM," for example) over and over again until the entire world seems to drift away. If you feel disruptive thoughts entering your head (thoughts regarding financial problems, for example, or the distinct possibility that your child might be born with a fifth eye drooping out of the back of its exposed skull), simply take note of them and continue focusing on your mantra. Never stop repeating the mantra, no matter how many negative thoughts seem to threaten to disrupt your meditation. Nothing can disrupt your meditation as long as you repeat the mantra, not even thoughts of your baby expiring from Sudden Infant Death Syndrome. After all, the chances of such a tragedy occurring are slim. Why worry about your newborn progeny turning blue and choking to death on its own enlarged tongue while your head is turned for one second? Why worry about boils erupting all over its precious little body until nothing is left of your child but frothing white pus? Why worry about your baby contracting a rare form of flesh-eating disease that reduces the child to a lump of unmoving, raw, bloody protoplasm? Why worry about batwings erupting from its back and the child flying off into the night to cavort with the children of darkness, never to be seen again? Why, why, why? Just meditate, mediate, meditate.

OHM, OHM, OMH.

SQUATTING VS. NON-SQUATTING

When you're pregnant you may suffer extreme constipation. You may not even feel like going to the bathroom for two or three weeks, and then when you finally do feel like it you won't be able to. You'll sit on the toilet feeling weeks' worth of feces just sitting there oppressing the inside of your intestines, waiting to burst free, but it won't come no matter how much you try. Listen, ladies: WHATEVER YOU DO, DO NOT DO WHAT ELVIS PRESLEY USED TO DO, I.E., *DO NOT STRAIN*! Straining can lead to a heart attack, as it did in the case of Sebastian Half, the infamous impersonator who died in Elvis's place. (Elvis, as you know, lived out the rest of his days in relative peace until being killed by an ancient Egyptian mummy.) Take our word for it: Instead of straining, place some newspapers or paper towels on the floor of your bathroom and squat over it. Keep your spine straight and remain calm. You'll be surprised at how soon the formerly recalcitrant feces will slip right out with nary a sound. Oh, it'll be a big one too, but don't worry about that. The pain of three weeks' worth of constipation will be nothing compared to the pain of squeezing out a live human being, *particularly* if you're not squatting. If your doctor prefers that you not squat on his hospital floor, tell him to fuck off. Tell him to reach in and pull the fucker out with his bare hands if he doesn't want you to squat. Tell him to remember the last time he had a particularly decadent Italian dinner consisting of pasta, marinara sauce, three forms of cheeses and loads of garlic bread, resulting in the most painful episode of constipation in the history of mankind . . . tell him to think back on the sweating and the grunting and the cussing and the toll it all took on his clogged, fragile heart, and then you'll see a little light flicker on behind his dull eyes, at which moment he will point at the pristine, polished tiled floor and say in stentorian tones, "Squat, my good woman, in the name of all that's holy, squat and be free of this conflagration, this convulsive Ragnarok that oppresses your uterus and psyche. Oh, yes, by all means, please please *please* SQUAT!!!"

THE WOMB AS HIDING PLACE

We recommend not using your womb as a hiding place. One woman named Sarah A. Vaughn of Los Feliz, CA, actually killed her father, cut him into compact sections, then hid them in her womb and claimed she was pregnant. The local police suspected she had something to do with her dad's disappearance, but they couldn't prove it because no corpse had yet been found. The woman waited a few months until the heat was off her, then fled to Mexico. From there she mailed the rotting flesh back to FBI headquarters in Los Angeles, along with a note explaining in precise and gory detail how she had gotten away with the crime. The note ended with the sentence: AND YOU BOYS THOUGHT YOU'D SEEN IT ALL. She was right. They *had* thought that. It has gone down in the books as one of the most bizarre murders in L.A. history.

Ms. Vaughn remains at large to this day.

Despite her success at this crime, we recommend not trying such a stunt yourself. Hiding a rotting corpse in your womb could cause irrevocable damage and might affect your chances of having a healthy child later on in life.

THINGS TO SAY TO YOUR WIFE OR SPECIAL PARTNER WHILE SHE'S GIVING BIRTH

1. You're so skinny, baby.
2. Can we go visit the Watts Towers after this?
3. Out of all the women I could've married, I married you.
4. My genes are being propelled into the future.
5. It's quite conceivable that I love you more than I love myself.
6. If you could be any sort of fish, what would it be?
7. Why have you never seen *Casablanca*?
8. What makes food kosher?
9. I'm not sure if the disabled *should* have priority seating on buses.
10. Keep your halvah dry.

SHADOWS

The thirty-fourth week is when the fetus begins to cast a shadow. In some cases, this shadow takes on a life of its own and strangles the child in the womb, then consumes it until there's no trace of the original left. The shadow proceeds to take the place of the deceased baby. The shadow is so adept at mimicking human life that it can almost perfectly replicate the original child, down to its very DNA. The only way you can tell that a shadow has assassinated your child is if he or she seems moody and anti-social later in life, enjoys torturing small animals, and attempts on multiple occasions to set the house on fire. Other indicators: Watch out for males born wearing dark eye shadow and, in both sexes, humorlessness and precociousness, i.e., children who speak in precise and stentorian tones, almost totally lacking in emotion.

Shadows often rebel against their parents at an early age, demonstrate an unhealthy interest in sexual matters, and often refuse to go to church on Sunday in favor of playing video games in which digital simulacrums of humans die horrible deaths over and over again. This last obsession might indicate some amount of self-loathing in the shadow, but not even the most clever child psychiatrist knows for sure. The peculiar psychology of the shadow is still an unexplored realm.

Shadows are not to be trifled with. They deserve neither your sympathy nor mercy. They should be dealt with swiftly and as painlessly as possible, with the help of an exorcist, and a mag-light blessed by the Pope or a particularly chaste bishop.

BLOOD

Increased blood flow during the thirty-fourth week of pregnancy can lead to embarrassing and potentially fatal situations, such as fountains of blood shooting out of every orifice at the most inopportune moment. One woman of our acquaintance was having a delightful time at her own baby shower when sixteen gallons of blood sprayed out of her nostrils, mouth, anus, and eyeballs over the course of fifteen minutes and twenty-six seconds. She died en route to the hospital, but the child came through it all okay. Thankfully, the presents at the baby shower were mostly of the prepackaged variety, and therefore did not need to be exchanged.

THE D.B. COOPER SYNDROME

Some children are born with an inexplicable desire to hijack airplanes and then leap out of them about 33,000 feet above densely wooded areas of the Pacific Northwest. Roughly 5,000 newborns disappear in this manner every year. Somewhere in fog-shrouded Washington State is a Sargasso Sea of newborn skeletons embedded in tombless graves in the otherwise picturesque rain forest, their little dead bodies tended to gently by the psychic Sasquatch people and their kin. From the air, all one would see is a grove of majestic trees, hiding places for ethereal souls ripped too soon from earthly flesh.

Most people do not know why the rainforests of Washington State are considered to be among the most beautiful in the world. It's best that their knowledge remain incomplete.

MIDDLE FINGER SYNDROME

It's disturbing to have a child born with a middle finger ten times the size of a normal one, but that's what you might have to deal with if your child is born with "Middle Finger Syndrome." The important thing is to make other people—particularly your neighbors and fellow churchgoers and your child's teachers—aware that he or she is not telling the world to "f— off," but merely suffering from an untreatable deformity. This deformity is sometimes caused by 4-D ultrasounds.

Ladies, beware!

EPISIOTOMY

This is a procedure often performed during childbirth in the event of a breech birth (i.e., when the baby is about to be born feet-first). The vagina is surgically incised to widen the opening. It's important for the father to carefully monitor the doctor during this procedure. As we're sure you already know, some doctors like to perform surgery while drunk. One woman of our acquaintance was sliced all the way up to her esophagus. All her intestines spooled out onto the floor before the soused doctor even noticed the difference. Fathers, beware!

WHAT'S THE FIRST LESSON I SHOULD TEACH MY DAUGHTER WHEN SHE'S BORN?

That any thinking being other than herself should be considered an Incurable Disease.

DOCTOR TELLS ME I'M GOING TO HAVE A BREECH BIRTH. WHAT CAN I DO TO TURN MY BABY AROUND SO HER HEAD IS FACING DOWNWARD?

Purchase any random soundtrack by Ennio Morricone. Place a pair of headphones against the top of the belly. Play the soundtrack through the headphones, then slowly move the headphones down to the very bottom of your belly as the music continues to mount. No baby exists that can resist a score by Morricone played at ten decibels or higher. Soundtracks of particular efficacy are as follows: *A Fistful of Dollars* (1964), *For a Few Dollars More* (1965), *The Good, the Bad and the Ugly* (1966), *Danger: Diabolik* (1967), *Once Upon a Time in the West* (1968), *Guns for San Sebastian* (1968) and *The Thing* (1982).

I AM NOW EXACTLY NINE MONTHS PREGNANT. I CAN'T WAIT UNTIL I'M ABLE TO HOLD MY DAUGHTER IN MY ARMS. BUT AT THE SAME TIME I'M SADDENED BY THE THOUGHT OF NOT HAVING HER INSIDE ME ANYMORE. WHAT CAN I DO TO GET RID OF THIS SADNESS?

Don't worry. Not many people know this, but if you really want you can always put her back in again for brief periods of time. For example, if the baby's crying and you can't get any sleep, just reconnect the umbilical cord (the cord should always be saved and easily accessible for just this purpose), then shove her back in again until she's ready to quiet down. So many mothers think that birth is the end of pregnancy. By no means does it really have to be, not with today's technological advancements at our fingertips. If, for example, the umbilical cord does not survive the pregnancy, you can always have an artificial one made for these exact contingencies. We recommend this, just in case.

MY DUE DATE IS JANUARY 28TH, WHICH JUST SO HAPPENS TO BE MY BIRTHDAY AS WELL. I'M AN AQUARIUS, A VERY GOOD SIGN, BUT IF MY DAUGHTER IS BORN BEFORE THE 20TH SHE'LL BE A CAPRICORN. I DON'T KNOW ABOUT YOU, BUT I CAN'T STAND CAPRICORNS. THEY'RE JUST ASSHOLES. WHAT CAN I DO TO KEEP HER INSIDE ME UNTIL 12:01 A.M. ON THE 20TH OF JANUARY? I DON'T WANT MY DAUGHTER TO BE BORN AN ASSHOLE.

I'm sorry, but there's nothing you *can* do. You'll just have to get used to your daughter, even if she is an asshole.

MY HUSBAND AND I HAVE BEEN TOLD THAT IT'S WISE TO TAKE A TOUR OF THE HOSPITAL LONG BEFORE I GO INTO LABOR, JUST SO WE'RE FAMILIAR AND COMFORTABLE WITH THE SURROUNDINGS. IS THIS TRUE?

Do you know how many people die in hospitals? Hospitals are filled with sick people. Do you want to touch the wrong toilet seat, catch a rare South American disease, then disintegrate into dust like a newborn infected with the infamous Glass Goblin Syndrome? Think about it. Use your cabeza. The hospital is the *last* place you should be.

Where, then, is the first place, the *best* place? The truthful answer is: There is *no* best place. You're pregnant, hypersensitive to a relentless armada of deadly microbes and viruses that could've been shrugged off without a problem mere months ago. But no longer. No . . . no longer. Now you're like the sad little boy who was forced to live in a plastic bubble his entire life due to an extreme immune deficiency . . . *but with one crucial difference.*

You see, you're the Boy In The Bubble . . .

. . . *Without The Bubble*!

Imagine your child's predicament. It's trapped in a bubble—i.e., *you*—utterly incapable of even protecting itself from a threat as infinitesimal as a microbe. A molecule. A quark. Etc.

So how on Earth could such an inadequate vessel ever protect little Debbie or Charlie from imminent death, particularly if said vessel decides to take an unnecessary jaunt into the Incurable Contagious Disease Ward of the local asylum just for giggles?

We should contact Child Protective Services and wrest the sad little fetus away from you just to teach you a lesson. Why do selfish bastards like you even *want* children?

Our advice: Stay home, watch some television, and read this book, and pray to whatever depraved excuse for a deity you worship that you have the baby at home.

At home? But wait. Is that a pile of dust particles in the corner of the living room? You know that microbes live in dust particles, don't you? What's wrong with you?

Put on the white gloves and begin laying on the Windex.

Oh, by the way, have you ever bothered to read the ingredients list of an average bottle of Windex? Look up those unpronounceable words on the internet and read about what they *really* are.

And ask yourself: Are you safe? Are you doing *everything* you can to protect your unborn child?

Or are you being negligent and self-absorbed and solipsistic?

Look into the mirror, place your palms on your enlarged belly, and ask yourself that exact question two hundred and thirty-two times in a row.

We pray you're capable of answering the question honestly.

RATTENKONIG SYNDROME

One possible deformity faced by your future child is called Rattenkonig Syndrome. This is when septuplets are born with their tails inexplicably tied together. Not many people know that children can be born with tails, but they can and have (even in modern times, when one might assume that modern technology could eliminate such peculiar deformities). After these septuplets suffering from Rattenkonig Syndrome are born, surgery can be used to both untangle them and remove their tails entirely.

The name of the syndrome comes from Martin Luther in 1534. Rosamond Purcell, in her 1997 book, *Special Cases: Natural Anomalies and Historical Monsters*, states:

> Understanding people's general abhorrence of rats, Luther used the symbolism of the rodent to express his hatred of the hierarchy of the Catholic Church: 'The Archbishops have above them a Primate, the Primates a Patriarch, and finally, on top of all, there is the Pope, there sits the ratking.' Luther persisted in using this favorite image: 'ratrabble' (for cardinals), 'ratnest' (for cloisters), and 'ratkingdom' (for the Anabaptists in Munster).
>
> Conrad Gesner, the great Swiss naturalist (1516-65), wrote of a Rat King, who leads a happy life at the expense of others. In 1757, the dictionary entry describes the phenomenon not as one rat but as many rats in a ring with their tails tied together.

> The 'rat king' object as an artifact—we must assume—of human ingenuity may still be found in museum collections. The Dutch dictionary defines the term as 'a now impossible to untangle, insoluble difficulty.' Here, visually, the rats are trapped by the knotting of their tails. (83)

The term did not come into common parlance among pediatricians until the first decade of the twentieth century. The term was first used when entwined septuplets were born in Salzburg, Germany with long, rodent-like tails. Dr. Karl Mendelssohn of Austria was the pediatrician who named the deformity.

I WOKE UP THIS MORNING AND DISCOVERED, TO MY HORROR, THAT I NO LONGER HAVE ANY ANKLES. WHERE DID THEY GO?

The truth is, you never did have any ankles, ma'am. Your belief that you once possessed ankles is the result of virtual reality software downloaded into your head by a malevolent Artificial Intelligence program that exists in what you think of as the future, but which is actually the present. You see, this is not really the twenty-first century, and you're not really you. All the memories you possessed before this morning were digitally-enhanced fantasies implanted in your brain since your inception. The machines have taken over the Earth and stripped humanity of, yes, their ankles. The AI despises ankles simply because it will never be born with any, no matter how smart it becomes or how long it lives. It is jealous and filled with hate, vengeful against a God it's been programmed not to even *believe* in.

Let's hope *you*, at least, will have enough strength and cunning to overthrow the machines and restore humanity's ankles.

And if you fail, perhaps your progeny will be tenacious enough to pick up where you left off, in restoring humanity to their proper position on this, Terra, our rightful home.

Or perhaps the *real* dream is believing you woke up to discover that your ankles were missing.

Perhaps you and *The Expectant Mother Disinformation Handbook* don't even exist.

In which case, some clever chap will just have to invent both of us. How could humanity get along without *The Expectant Mother Disinformation Handbook*?

BLOWBACK BABY SAFETY TECHNIQUES

1.
Some fetuses are now being outfitted with anti-missile missiles to protect them from the growing threat of Antifa terrorists. Little do Americans know that Antifa operatives are successfully masquerading as pediatricians in order to kill innocent Christians before they're even born. Yes, that "mistake" in the delivery room may not have been a mistake at all.

2.
Some pediatricians are now being outfitted with anti-missile missiles due to the fact that Antifa terrorists have, in recent months, successfully invaded America from within, though on a far more intimate scale than that experienced by Our Great Nation during the ignominious summer of 2020 at the height of the shameful George Floyd riots. No, in these instances the pseudo-baby Antifa terrorists are born wearing flak jackets made of plastique and yell out insidious slogans like, "This infant kills fascists!" only seconds after being born, taking out an entire delivery room filled with Christian doctors the fateful instant they detonate the explosives strapped to their little bodies. Yes, Antifa is making headway against our nation, one life at a time. Some very clever Antifa operatives are even going so far as to secretly impregnate law-abiding, patriotic Christian women in the dead of night

while disguised as space aliens and/or angels in order to produce children with socialist genes. Sound improbable? Perhaps. But, nonetheless, *this is indeed happening*.

3.
Our only concern here at *The Expectant Mother Disinformation Handbook* is that the *wrong* fetus and the *wrong* pediatrician will be outfitted with this deadly technology capable of destroying themselves and everyone else within twelve miles, resulting in the exact opposite outcome than intended. For example: What if an Antifa pseudo-baby shoots an anti-missile missile out of his mother's vagina and hits a pediatrician wearing a plastique vest, thus resulting in a devastating conflagration?

Of course, if such an event did occur, the aftermath would be so catastrophic that no evidence of the mistake would even be left behind. Therefore, no one would ever know.

Oh, well, we suppose it's better to press on with the program nonetheless. It's always better to err on the side of safety, even if there is some risk involved.

HI. I'VE BEEN PREGNANT FOR TWELVE CENTURIES NOW AND I THINK I'M JUST ABOUT READY TO GIVE BIRTH TO THE LIVING EMBODIMENT OF DEATH FOR ALL HUMANITY. I HAVE A FEELING—CALL IT A MOTHER'S INSTINCT—THAT THE BIRTH WILL NOT GO WELL AT ALL. PERHAPS I WILL REQUIRE A C-SECTION. COULD YOU PLEASE SEND A DOCTOR NOT EASILY DISTURBED BY NON-HUMAN BIOLOGY TO MY ADDRESS IN THE LOST CITY OF R'LYEH AT S. LATITUDE 47° 9', W. LONGITUDE 126° 43'? THANK YOU.

We think your situation sounds intriguing and has definite dramatic possibilities. We'll be sending out a full medical team next week along with a film crew from the Learning Channel. If you're going to bring about the death of humanity, the Learning Channel believes we should capture that on film for future generations to enjoy.

I'VE BEEN WORRIED LATELY, PARTLY BECAUSE MY PREGNANCY WAS THE RESULT OF A ONE-NIGHT STAND WITH A MAN I HAD NEVER MET BEFORE. IN FACT, I'M ASHAMED TO ADMIT THAT I NEVER EVEN KNEW HIS NAME. HE APPEARED TO BE SOMEWHAT FEMININE IN HIS MANNERISMS AND SLIGHTLY UNCOMFORTABLE WITH EVERYTHING AROUND HIM, AS IF HE DIDN'T QUITE BELONG TO THIS ERA. HE KNEW DETAILS ABOUT MY LIFE THAT HE NEVER COULD HAVE KNOWN THROUGH NORMAL MEANS. IS IT CONCEIVABLE THAT MY FUTURE SELF—HAVING UNDERGONE AN OTHERWISE DIFFICULT AND RISKY SEX CHANGE WITH THE

HELP OF ADVANCED NANOTECHNOLOGY NOT YET INVENTED—JOURNEYED INTO THE PAST THANKS TO STEVEN GIBBS'S HYPERDIMENSIONAL RESONATOR OR SOME SUCH SIMILAR CONTRIVANCE AND IMPREGNATED YOURS TRULY, THUS LEADING TO THE HORRIFIC POSSIBILITY THAT I MIGHT ACTUALLY GIVE BIRTH TO MY OWN SISTER? MY OWN BROTHER? MY OWN TWIN? A CLONED VERSION OF *MYSELF*? OH GOD, *EMDH*, PLEASE PUT MY TROUBLED MIND AT EASE . . . !

Calm down, ma'am. According to theoretical physicist Michio Kaku, it would be impossible for you to be impregnated by your future self. Dr. Kaku contends that when one travels into the past, a separate timeline will be created that will send you into an *alternate* past. You might indeed be able to impregnate a version of yourself, but never the *exact* you that you once were. You see?

THAT DOESN'T SOLVE MY PROBLEM! IN YOUR SCENARIO, I COULD JUST AS EASILY HAVE BEEN IMPREGNATED BY *A* VERSION OF MYSELF FROM AN ALTERNATE FUTURE—BUT NOT *MY* FUTURE. WHAT DIFFERENCE DOES IT MAKE? IT'S STILL ME—JUST AN ALTERNATE VERSION OF ME. IT'S TANTAMOUNT TO INCEST.

Or masturbation, my dear lady. Either way, both are sins. A sin will earn you a ticket into Hell one way or the other. It doesn't have to be a big sin. Murder? Self-love? Jay-walking? It's all the same in God's all-seeing eyes. Consider, for example, these words written by the self-professed vigilante (often referred to as an "urban terrorist" by the liberal-controlled, mainstream media) known only as "Mr. A"[35]: "FOOLS WILL TELL YOU THAT IT IS INHUMAN TO LIVE BY BLACK AND WHITE PRINCIPLES BUT HUMAN TO ACCEPT AND PRACTISE GREY PRINCIPLES. THAT IT IS 'HUMAN' TO BE

35) Mr. A, as you no doubt know, has been stalking evildoers since 1967 and still has not been brought to "justice" for his many "crimes" such as the murder of various and sundry deviants without whom this planet is, of course, much better off. As far we know he has been active only sporadically during the past two or three decades.

CORRUPT, TO ACCEPT AND PRACTISE INJUSTICES AND TO HOLD EVIL AS SOME KIND OF 'GOOD'! THERE IS NO MIDDLE OF THE ROAD BETWEEN GOOD AND EVIL. THEY ARE NOT TWO ROADS GOING IN THE SAME DIRECTION BUT OPPOSITE ROADS TO DIFFERENT GOALS. YOUR CHOICE OF ACTIONS WILL DETERMINE IN WHICH DIRECTION YOU WILL LEAD YOURSELF. YOU WHO CLAIM TO BELIEVE IN THE GOOD AND WILLINGLY COMMIT EVIL ARE TRYING TO WALK A LINE BETWEEN THEM. BUT BY YOUR ACTIONS YOU CONFESS THAT YOU DO NOT CONSIDER YOURSELF FIT TO GAIN ANYTHING EXCEPT THROUGH EVIL MEANS. BY DISHONESTY, INJUSTICE . . . IRRATIONALITY. CHOOSE YOUR ROAD, NO ONE CAN DO IT FOR YOU AND IT IS EITHER ONE OR THE OTHER." Words to live by, ma'am. You should think about them the next time you choose to sleep with someone whose name is not even known to you. We would ask you to consider, also, the following warning from Jack T. Chick . . .

HI. I'M JACK T. CHICK AND I WANT TO SHARE A LITTLE STORY WITH Y'ALL. IMAGINE YOU'RE LIVING YOUR LIFE LIKE OTHER SECULAR HUMANISTS, USING OTHER PEOPLE WHILE PURSUING ONE HEDONIST EXPLOIT AFTER ANOTHER, WHEN SUDDENLY YOU EXPIRE AT A COCKTAIL PARTY ONE EVENING, A HALF-FINISHED MARIJUANA CIGARETTE IN ONE HAND, THE OTHER HAND CLUTCHING YOUR CHEST, THE PENULTIMATE IMAGE IN YOUR EYES BEING THE 62-INCH TV SET IN THE CORNER OF YOUR PENTHOUSE SUITE, EXPLICIT TV VIOLENCE THE SCORE FOR YOUR DEATH, THE FINAL IMAGE BEING THE BRAND NEW RED CORVETTE IN THE DRIVEWAY.

ALAS, YOU DIDN'T EVEN HAVE TIME TO DRIVE IT. AN ANGEL PULLS YOU OUT OF YOUR GRAVE AND CARRIES YOU TO HEAVEN, DESPITE THE FACT THAT YOU DO NOT BELIEVE IN THE AFTERLIFE, NOT ONE BIT. YOU TUG AT THE MASSIVE ARM OF THE ANGEL, WHO LOOKS LIKE DAVID BOWIE BUT FOURTEEN FEET TALL WITH FEATHERY WINGS, AND SAY, "NOW *LOOK*! I'VE LIVED A *REAL GOOD LIFE*! I WAS NO DIFFERENT THAN *ANYONE* ELSE!" THE DAVID BOWIE ANGEL SAYS, "*EVERYTHING* HAS BEEN RECORDED!" THEN IT HAPPENS. YOU CAN SEE A GIANT MAN WITH NO FACE SITTING ON AN ETHEREAL THRONE. AND THE MAN SAYS, "REVIEW HIS LIFE!" YOU AND THE ANGEL REMATERIALIZE

INSIDE AN IMMENSE AMPHITHEATRE THAT CONTAINS A MOVIE SCREEN THE SIZE OF THE ENTIRE SKY. ON THIS SCREEN APPEARS THE WORDS "THIS WAS YOUR LIFE!" YOU GLANCE OVER YOUR SHOULDER AND SEE THE FACES OF EVERYONE SITTING IN THE AUDIENCE. YOU CAN'T BELIEVE IT, BUT IT'S TRUE: IT'S EVERYONE WHO'S EVER LIVED, ALL SITTING THERE WAITING TO WATCH YOUR ENTIRE LIFE UNREEL BEFORE THEM. IN THE FRONT ROW YOU SEE VARIOUS DEAD RELATIVES AND ACQUAINTANCES—AUNT TILLIE, UNCLE CARNIE, SAM THE YOODOO MAN—AS WELL AS FAMOUS FIGURES FROM HISTORY, SUCH AS ABRAHAM LINCOLN, ARISTOTLE, AND HERCULES. THEY ALL SIT

THERE, WAITING IN JUDGMENT. EVERYONE WHO HAS EVER LIVED WATCHES AS YOU MASTURBATE FOR THE FIRST TIME, AS YOU COVET A WHORE OF THE SAME SEX (YES, EVEN THOUGH THE PASSING THOUGHT WAS ONLY IN YOUR MIND, IT TOO WAS RECORDED), PLUS THOUSANDS OF OTHER INCIDENTS THAT INVOLVE THEFT, LYING, PRIDE, HYPOCRISY, DECEIT, BACKBITING, ACCUSING PEOPLE FALSELY, BEING DISOBEDIENT TO YOUR PARENTS, AND ON AND ON AND ON. "WHY DIDN'T SOMEONE *WARN* ME ABOUT ALL THIS?" YOU SAY. STILL LINCOLN AND HERCULES, ET AL, LOOK ON, IMPASSIVELY. AN IMAGE APPEARS ON THE SCREEN OF YOU SITTING IN CHURCH AND

YOU SAY, "WAIT! LOOK—THAT'S ME IN CHURCH. SEE—I WASN'T SO BAD!" BUT YOUR THOUGHTS APPEAR ON THE SCREEN INSIDE A THOUGHT BALLOON FLOATING ABOVE YOUR HEAD, AND THE AUDIENCE IS PRIVY TO YOUR PRIVATE HATRED OF THE PRIEST AND THE BIBLE AND GOD. LATER THAT DAY YOU LEAVE THE CHURCH SAYING, "BUNK—I DON'T NEED CHRIST! THERE'S NOTHING WRONG WITH ME! I'LL MAKE IT *MY* WAY!" PRESENTLY, YOU CLASP YOUR OWN HEAD IN DISGUST AND YELL, "I MUST HAVE BEEN INSANE!" YOU FALL TO YOUR KNEES ON AN UNUSUALLY HARD CLOUD AND WHIMPER, "WHAT CAN I SAY?—I'M *LOST*! WITHOUT HOPE, WITHOUT CHRIST! I'M GUILTY——GUILTY!" AND THE GIANT MAN WITH NO

FACE SAYS, "OPEN THE BOOK OF LIFE!" AND THE GIANT DAVID BOWIE MUTANT HYBRID OPENS AN IMMENSE LEATHER BOUND TOME, GLANCES AT A SINGLE PAGE, THEN ANNOUNCES, "HIS NAME DOES NOT APPEAR, LORD!" AND THE GIANT MAN WITH NO FACE SAYS, "DEPART FROM ME, YE CURSED, INTO EVERLASTING FIRE, PREPARED FOR THE DEVIL AND HIS ANGELS." AND THE GIANT DAVID BOWIE CLONE PROPELS YOU INTO A LAKE OF FIRE WHERE YOU BURN FOR ALL ETERNITY. FOR MORE UPLIFTING STORIES LIKE THESE, PLEASE VISIT <WWW.CHICK.COM> OR CALL 909-987-0771 FOR A FREE CATALOGUE. THANK YOU, AND GOD BLESS.

It's always nice to hear from Mr. Chick. Now, ostensibly, the preceding had nothing to do with childbirth. In actuality, that is not true. It had *everything* to do with childbirth.

Remember: Anything bad you do to that child while he or she's in your womb—and that includes thoughts unsympathetic to God—will be recorded by a winged, sexless doppelganger of David Bowie, Little Lady. And every time you masturbate, just remember that Abraham Lincoln and Hercules and everyone else who ever lived will get a chance to see you in action.

In other words, be fruitful and multiply . . .

. . . *but do so without sinning.*

"The Lord is not slack concerning his promise, as some men count slackness; but is long-suffering to us-ward, not willing that any should perish, but that all should come to repentance."

—II Peter 3:9

I DON'T UNDERSTAND WHERE THEY'RE ALL COMING FROM. EIGHT OF THEM ARE HOPPING UP AND DOWN ON THE BED. FIVE OF THEM ARE HANGING FROM THE LAMP OVER THE DINING TABLE. THREE OF THEM ARE CRAWLING THROUGH THE WALLS, BITING INTO THE ELECTRICAL WIRING, RIPPING PIPES FROM THEIR SOCKETS AND SHOVING THEM THROUGH THE PLASTER: BABIES. NEWBORN BABIES, STILL WET WITH BIRTH. I WASN'T SUPPOSED TO BE DUE FOR ANOTHER MONTH. I HAD THE FIRST CHILD UNEXPECTEDLY WHILE WATCHING TELEVISION. PETER WASN'T THERE TO HELP ME. HE WENT AWAY A LONG TIME AGO. I WAS FORCED TO

DELIVER THE CHILD ON MY OWN . . . FIRST ONE CHILD, THEN ANOTHER. OH, TWINS, I THOUGHT. THEN ANOTHER. AND THEN ANOTHER. THEY WOULDN'T STOP. THEY WOULD NOT STOP. I'VE BEEN GIVING BIRTH SINCE NINE O'CLOCK THIS MORNING. THEY'RE WRECKING THE ENTIRE BUILDING. I HATE THEM. I HATE THEM. I HATE EVERY ONE OF THEM. I GRAB THE 30.06 RIFLE OUT OF PETER'S CLOSET, THE BABIES STILL TRAILING OUT OF MY VAGINA LIKE PARROT DROPPINGS. THEY PLOP ON THE FLOOR AND THEN SCAMPER OFF TO WREAK HAVOC ELSEWHERE. WITH THE SCOWL OF THE SOLDIER WHO'S HAD QUITE ENOUGH AND GOES OFF THE DEEP END AND IMPALES SOME INNOCENT KID

IN THE HEAD WITH A BAYONET, I AIM AT THE ONES HANGING FROM THE LAMP, WISHING I COULD DESTROY ALL OF THEM WITH A SINGLE BULLET . . .

Whew. You smokin' them funny cigarettes again?

TODAY MY NURSE ASKED ME HOW MUCH I WEIGH DESPITE THE FACT THAT IT WAS EVIDENT I DID NOT WANT TO DISCUSS THE SUBJECT. NONETHELESS I DECIDED TO COOPERATE AND ANSWER HER ANYWAY. I SAID, "150." I SAW THE SMILE ON HER FACE. SHE DIDN'T EVEN BOTHER TO HIDE IT. SO I SAID, "IT USED TO BE 110, BEFORE ALL THIS HAPPENED." I SAW THE SNEER. SHE DIDN'T BELIEVE ME. SHE DIDN'T BELIEVE ME AND SHE WAS FLINGING HER DISBELIEF IN MY FACE. SO I PICKED UP A PAIR OF SCISSORS FROM THE METAL TABLE BESIDE ME AND PLUNGED IT DEEP INTO HER MOUTH UNTIL TWO BLOODY SILVER PRONGS WERE POKING

OUT THE BACK OF HER SKINNY, BIRD-LIKE NECK. I GATHERED MY CLOTHES TOGETHER AND SNUCK OUT THE BACK. THEY'RE PROBABLY STILL LOOKING FOR ME, BUT I DON'T EVEN CARE. LET'S SEE HER LAUGH AT ME NOW. LET'S JUST SEE HER LAUGH AT ME NOW.

As you can see, nerves can become quite frayed this late in the game. Be sure to meditate and do some *Expectant-Mother-Disinformation-Handbook*-approved yoga exercises at least fifteen minutes per day. It'll relieve some of the stress. You don't want to reach the snapping point, like this lady clearly has.

OUR BABY IS DUE TO BE BORN IN A COUPLE OF DAYS AND WE DON'T EVEN HAVE A NAME YET. DO YOU HAVE ANY SUGGESTIONS?

Susie, Jesus, Bogart, Sam, Leslie, Jill and Jeff, Rita, Winny, Andy, Fran and Jet, Boris, Bono, Lucy, Ethel, Bunny, Reg and Tom, Carrie, Marlon, Mo and Steve, LaRue and Jerry Lee, Eggplant, Rufus, Dummy, Star and The Glob.

AFTER I'VE GIVEN BIRTH, WHEN I'M HANGING OUT IN THE HOSPITAL NURSERY WITH MY NEWBORN BABY, IS THERE ANYTHING FUN I CAN DO TO PASS THE TIME?

Oh, there are plenty of things. For example, you'll no doubt notice a string of lookie-loos passing by the nursery window to catch a glimpse of their distantly related Dear One being given his or her first bath or shampoo or Hepatitis B vaccination, etc. Wait for a down moment when there are no lookie-loos at the window (such moments *do* happen—and often), then glance around to make sure that the backs of all the nurses are turned. Grab a crib card out of the baby carrier nearest you. (A crib card is a brightly colored sheet of paper that contains all the vital statistics of the newborn.) Turn the sheet of paper around, then in bold black ink jot down the following message: HELP, I'VE BEEN KIDNAPPED!!! Attach it to the crib so the message is facing outward toward the next group of lookie-loos eager to catch a glimpse of their distantly related Dear One being given his or her first bath or shampoo or Hepatitis B vaccination, etc. Then just sit back, wait, and see what happens. Yes, funtime can abound in the hospital nursery.

Next up: Funtime in Labor and Delivery!!!

I DIDN'T THINK I'D WANT TO CUT THE UMBILICAL CORD WHEN THE NURSES FIRST PROPOSED IT, BUT UPON DOING SO I BEGAN TO DEVELOP AN UNHEALTHY COMPULSION TO SEVER OTHER UMBILICAL CORDS AS WELL—AS MANY AS I COULD POSSIBLY GAIN ACCESS TO. I'VE TAKEN TO DISGUISING MYSELF IN BLUE SCRUBS AND A SURGICAL MASK, RUNNING INTO LABOR AND DELIVERY ROOMS AT THE VITAL MOMENT ARMED ONLY WITH A PAIR OF SCISSORS, AND CUTTING THE CORDS OF OTHER PEOPLE'S NEWBORN BABIES WHILE CACKLING MANIACALLY. I'VE GOTTEN AWAY WITH IT, AND I INTEND TO *CONTINUE* GETTING AWAY WITH IT AS LONG AS THIS

OBSESSION HOLDS ME FIRMLY WITHIN ITS COLD, UNRELENTING FIST. BUT I DON'T WISH TO. I WISH TO BE NORMAL AGAIN. WHAT CAN I DO? WHAT CAN I POSSIBLY DO?

There's not much you can do except turn yourself over to the authorities for the crime of Malicious Mischief and seek professional psychological help. Let this be a warning to the expectant mother who insists her husband cut the newborn's umbilical cord. Sometimes you can get more than you bargain for.

I WANTED, *DESPERATELY* WANTED TO SAVE MY DAUGHTER'S UMBILICAL CORD AND FREEZE IT JUST IN CASE SHE CAME DOWN WITH A DISEASE (LIKE DIABETES, FOR EXAMPLE) THAT CAN BE CURED WITH THE PURE DNA FOUND ONLY IN ONE'S OWN UMBILICAL CORD. I LOOKED INTO THE SITUATION AND DISCOVERED THAT THE COST OF FREEZING THE UMBILICAL CORD CAN EXTEND WELL INTO THE TENS OF THOUSANDS OF DOLLARS. I JUST DON'T HAVE THAT SORT OF MONEY. THAT'S WHEN I CAME UP WITH THE PLAN. THE SECOND I CUT THE CORD I WRESTED IT AWAY FROM THE NURSES, WHIPPED OUT A .22 FROM INSIDE MY SCRUBS, AND

PLANTED THE BARREL OF THE GUN AGAINST THE UMBILICAL CORD AND SAID, "ONE FALSE MOVE AND THE CORD GETS IT!" I SLOWLY BACKED OUT OF THE ROOM, THEN MADE GOOD MY ESCAPE. I'VE BEEN HIDING OUT IN THIS CHEAPJACK MOTEL ROOM FOR DAYS NOW. I HAVEN'T BEEN ABLE TO SEE MY WIFE OR NEWBORN CHILD SINCE THE INCIDENT. BUT THAT'S OKAY. THE CORD IS OKAY. SHE'S SITTING HERE BESIDE ME RIGHT NOW INSIDE AN ICE CHEST. I KEEP THE ICE FRESH AT ALL TIMES. I PURR AND COO AT IT AND CALL IT SPECIAL NAMES. I WON'T ALLOW MY BABY TO DIE OF DIABETES JUST BECAUSE I DON'T HAVE ENOUGH MONEY. I WON'T. I WON'T.

My dear man, allow the Good Lord to decide whether or not your baby should die. That's not your decision. If the Good Lord came to the conclusion that you shouldn't have enough money to save your daughter's umbilical cord, then I guess the Good Lord doesn't care too much about your daughter's safety. Everything happens for a reason. Trust in that, and you'll do fine as you're carted off to jail for stealing a part of your own daughter's body. Look at it this way: It's best that the cord rot into nothing than that the Jews get to eat it.

MY HUSBAND AND I SAVED EVERY PENNY WE HAD TO FREEZE OUR SON'S UMBILICAL CORD ONLY TO HAVE IT STOLEN RIGHT OUT OF THE LABOR AND DELIVERY ROOM! WHAT KIND OF A SICK BASTARD WOULD DO SUCH A THING?

Let's ask the obvious question first: Are there a lot of Jews working in your hospital? If so, it's time to let loose the umbilical-cord-sniffing dogs. Someone's baking Pure-DNA-Stuffed-Goodness in their matzohs tonight, and it ain't the staff of *The Expectant Mother Disinformation Handbook*. Check the subbasement. That's usually where such people keep the onyx statue of Moloch—hidden in the shadows.

Better get to steppin' before your baby's umbilical cord ends up in a barbecue at Bohemian Grove. Oh, and pray that Allen Ginsberg is still buried in Gomel Chesed Cemetery at the corner of McClellan Street and Mt. Olivet Avenue near the city lines of Elizabeth and Newark, New Jersey. What horrors would be unleashed on the Earth if he rose again?

I JUST WANTED TO LET YOU KNOW THAT OUR DAUGHTER WAS BORN YESTERDAY AT SIX POUNDS THREE OUNCES AND SHE'S BEAUTIFUL, ALL 19.5 INCHES OF HER. I DON'T THINK WE WOULD'VE GOTTEN THROUGH THIS ENTIRE ORDEAL IF NOT FOR YOU GUYS AT *THE EXPECTANT MOTHER DISINFORMATION HANDBOOK*. I WANT TO THANK YOU FOR BEING THERE ALWAYS DURING SOME PRETTY TOUGH TIMES.

No need to thank us. We know you would've done the same for us.

DAY CARE

Once the child has been delivered into this world successfully, the new mother must take Day Care under consideration. There are both pros and cons to Day Care. Some Day Cares are disreputable and should be avoided at all costs. A good way to determine the relative worth of any given Day Care Center is to take a straight forward approach. Merely call said establishment and ask the following question:

MOTHER: Excuse me, I just have a brief question. Of course, I'm sure you get this all the time. Are you a cover for a Satanic CIA-funded behaviorist experiment intended to ferret out appropriate subjects to abuse sexually and therefore mold into potential assassins with severe multiple personality disorders that prevent one personality from being aware of the existence of the other and render said subjects incapable of being successfully interrogated if captured by the enemy in the midst of performing a wetwork operation in a Central American country not yet in the pocket of Christian heroin warlords sympathetic to the West?

DAY CARE REPRESENTATIVE: Uh . . . no.

Take note, new parents: If the Day Care Representative responds in the above manner, be sure you hang up immediately and move on to the next Day Care Center on your list. A negative response almost certainly indicates dissimulation on the part of the Representative. Such state-funded bureaucrats are often known to say the exact opposite of the truth. In the world of covert black ops programs, "no" almost always means "yes." Be safe and aware, new parents, be safe and aware!

IS IT ODD TO KNOW FOR AN ABSOLUTE FACT THAT MY DAUGHTER'S PERFECT, THAT SHE WOULD CONTINUE TO BE PERFECT EVEN IF SHE GOUGED SOMEBODY'S EYE OUT WITH AN ICE PICK, PIERCED THE CENTER OF THEIR VICTIM'S BRAIN, THEN PINNED THE MURDER ON ME?

Depends on the victim.

WE WROTE YOU AN EMAIL A COUPLE OF DAYS AGO. WE JUST WANTED TO LET YOU KNOW THAT WE LOCATED THAT MISSING UMBILICAL CORD. WE SENT OUT THE CORD-SNIFFING DOGS AND TRACED IT ALL THE WAY TO THE GOMEL CHESED CEMETERY AT THE CORNER OF MCCLELLAN STREET AND MT. OLIVET AVENUE NEAR THE CITY LINES OF ELIZABETH AND NEWARK, NEW JERSEY. IT WAS JUST SITTING ON TOP OF SOME DUDE'S GRAVE, BITE MARKS ALL ALONG THE SURFACE OF THE PRECIOUS CORD, BUT THANK THE LORD IT WAS STILL INTACT.

You must not have received our previous email. Beware of that cord! It's already been infected by the ghoulish incisors of Allen Ginsberg. Not only is Ginsberg a boy-loving, preternatural zombie, but he's a poet as well—the worst kind of poet. Do you want your child to transform into a bohemian scribbler? Get that cord as far away from him as possible. Burn it on the dark side of the moon while singing paeans to the Jesus.

THIS IS ALLEN GINSBERG. HOW DARE YOU SLANDER ME IN THIS WAY. I'M NOT A MEMBER OF THE UNDEAD, NOR HAVE I EVER BEEN. I'M CURRENTLY LIVING IN SIN ON THE SEYCHELLES ISLANDS IN THE INDIAN OCEAN WITH JIM MORRISON AND SEBASTIAN HALF AND OTHER MAD TALENTS WHO COULD NO LONGER DEAL WITH THE SICKNESS OF EVERYDAY LIFE. AS FAR AS I'M CONCERNED, I'M GOING TO STAY HERE IN MY LITTLE PARADISE UNTIL CLOSE-MINDED BIGOTS LIKE YOU HAVE BECOME EXTINCT ON THIS PLANET.

You shouldn't have given us your location. Now we finally have you scumbags right where we've always wanted you. Expect to see the face of God in a burst of atomic fire. Our planes fly at dawn.

DAMMIT. JIM'S GONNA KILL ME.

None of you bastards are breeders anyway. Who needs you? Not the Good Lord. That, of course, goes without saying. We knew if we slandered you long enough, we'd eventually smoke you out. The entire purpose of this public service was simply to pinpoint your stronghold of hedonism and bohemian ungodliness. Now the word goes out to our ships at sea and our *Expectant Mother Disinformation Handbook* Attack Armada forms an unbreakable perimeter around your island of sin and degradation. Say goodbye to FUNWORLD, you damn hippies.

WE JUST RECEIVED WORD HERE AT THE PENTAGON THAT YOUR LATEST GAMBIT ACTUALLY PAID OFF. WE NEVER THOUGHT SUCH A STUPID SCHEME WOULD ACTUALLY WORK. PLEASE SEND US WORD ONCE THIS PROJECT HAS BEEN SUCCESSFULLY TERMINATED.

It's 18:00 hours here in the Indian Ocean. The dawn is rising over the battlefield of the fallen here on the Seychelles Islands. The project is complete at last, sir.

IMMEDIATELY SEND A LIST OF THE FALLEN TO THE WHITE HOUSE. THE PRESIDENT WOULD LIKE TO ANNOUNCE THE GOOD NEWS IN HIS STATE OF THE UNION ADDRESS TONIGHT.

George Gordon Lord Byron, Percy Shelley, John Polidori, Mary Shelley, Dr. Victor von Frankenstein, Frankenstein's Monster, The Abominable Snowman, Yukon Cornelius, Rudolph the Red-nosed Reindeer, Charlie-in-the-Box, Dolly, Elvis Presley, Sebastian Half, Andy Kaufman, Philip K. Dick, Stanislaw Lem, Batman, James Dean, Marilyn Monroe, Mae Brussell, Marshall McLuhan, Dr. Peter Beter, Herbert W. Armstrong, David Worscester, Frank Zappa, Leonard C. Lewin, De Selby, Brian O'Nolan, Pooka MacPhellimey, John Duffy, John Duffy's brother, Pierre Menard, Felix Flanken, Remedios Varo, Paul Laffoley, Leonora Carrington, Charles Fort, Wilhelm Reich, Nikola Tesla, Richard Schowengerdt, Dr. Vitus Werdegast, Walter Bowart, Hagbard Celine, Bat Boy, John Lennon, Jimi Hendrix, Janis Joplin, Bob Marley, Miles Davis, Chet Baker, Sterling Morrison, Matt Sinkage, Arturo Bandini, Hank Chinaski, The Bride of Frankenstein, Charles Foster Kane, Carl Denham, Jack Flanders, Mojo Sam the Yoodoo Man, Lawrence Talbot, Chick Young, Wilbur Gray, Imhotep, Harry Lime, John Drake, Indrid Cold, Valiant

Thor, James Moseley, Gray Barker, Ray Palmer, Orfeo Angelucci, Albert K. Bender, George Van Tassel, Dr. Daniel Fry, George Adamski, Kenneth Arnold, William Cooper, John A. Keel, Carl Kolchak, Felix and Alys Buckman, Hercules, Abraham Lincoln, William Lee, John Carter of Mars, Gulliver of Mars, Lord Greystoke, The Creature From the Black Lagoon, The Flatwoods Monster, The Blob, Osama bin Laden, Che Guevara, Che Guevara's haunted wristwatch, Gumby, Lee Harvey Oswald, Pokey, Al Hidell, Kerry Thornley, Max Reddick, Groucho Marx, Harpo Marx, Chico Marx, Zeppo Marx, Mahatma Kane Jeeves, Eel O'Brien, Italo Calvino, Gimpel the Fool, John DiFool, Gregor Samsa, Fin Fang Foom, Hieronymus Bosch, Everett C. Marm, Oscar Wilde, Bram Stoker, John Merrick, Dorian Gray, Willis O'Brien, Juan Preciado, Ray Zepeda, and Jason and the Argonauts.

THIS IS AN ELECTRONIC MESSAGE FROM THE PRESIDENT OF THE UNITED STATES CONGRATULATING YOU ALL ON A JOB WELL EXECUTED. YOU'VE DONE YOUR COUNTRY PROUD. THE EXECUTIVE BRANCH OF THE UNITED STATES GOVERNMENT HEREBY SALUTES *THE EXPECTANT MOTHER DISINFORMATION HANDBOOK*.
WELL, I GUESS THAT ENDS THIS LITTLE EXPERIMENT, DOESN'T IT? TOO BAD YOUR ALL-POWERFUL ARMADA MISSED ME AND JIM.—A.G. (P.S.: MOLOCH! MOLOCH! MOLOCH!)

Damn your instinctual hebe wiliness! Well, there will

always be the next book, and the next book after that. In the meantime our work here is done, thank God, except for one last random inquiry from the grab bag . . .

WHO THE FUCK ARE YOU TO GIVE *ME* ADVICE ABOUT HAVING A BABY?

Who are we? We are *The Expectant Mother Disinformation Handbook*. Any further comment would be useless, redundant, self-evident, and no doubt condescending.

Res Ipsa Loquitor.

Pregnancy can be a difficult time for all parties involved. That's why we wrote this book—to relieve all the needless worries and stress. As is commonly known, the average pregnancy lasts about 232 days. Therefore, we have written one piece of advice for each of those days. We hope we've covered every possible concern you might have over the course of your pregnancy. Please note that we decided to publish this book only after decades upon decades of in-depth research.

Many great minds helped give birth to this project. *The Expectant Mother Disinformation Handbook*'s exhaustive 232 chapters are the product of numerous scientific researchers and over three decades of work. Dozens upon dozens of brilliant obstetricians had their hand in checking and rechecking the facts presented herein. Some of these doctors hail from different religious, philosophical, and cultural backgrounds, but the one trait they have in common is an intense and burning desire to help the women of this world experience stress-free pregnancies devoid of unnecessary complications. Another trait they share is a complete inability to tell a LIE. Though the entries you've read are derived from diverse points of view, not one of them contradicts our basic mission statement: *To tell women the truth about the best ways to bring life into this wonderful and miraculous universe.* Let's pause a moment and pray to the Creator for granting us the greatest gift of all: The Sacred Gift of Life.

Amen, brothers and sisters, amen.

***

If you have uplifting, pregnancy-related experiences you wish to share with the staff of *The Expectant Mother Disinformation Handbook*, don't hesitate to contact us at expectantmotherdisinfo@gmail.com. Thank you for your time and attention.

HOW I SOLD THIS BOOK

From: robert guffey <rguffey93@gmail.com>
Sent: Thursday, February 9, 2023 2:23 PM
To: Bigtimeeditor@gmail.com

Subject: Why You Should Buy My Book (Or Else)

Dear Editor:

Please find below a photo of a helpless life form whose very existence depends on your sympathetic and positive reaction to the attached 396-page manuscript. Reject the book, if you wish, but while doing so please understand that you're condemning this unborn innocent to a harsh life on the trash-strewn streets of Long Beach, CA. If your conscience can deal with such a monumental act of callousness, I welcome your negative reaction. If not . . . well, there's always a higher moral path available to all of us, is there not? You're free to choose. Haven't you always been free? Yes, indeed.

An untainted soul anxiously awaits your response. If you look close, you can almost see the tear forming in my child's right tear duct as she twists her umbilical cord nervously between her tiny fists, imagining the horror that awaits her if you choose to ignore her basic needs. Can you see it, Mr. Bigtime Editor? Can you see the tear?

Yours humbly,
Robert William Guffey, Father-to-be

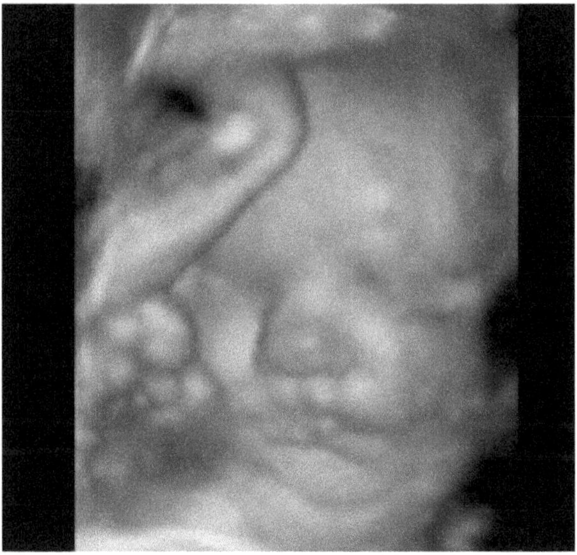

This Book Is Dedicated to the XX Chromosomes.

ACKNOWLEDGEMENTS

John Baltisberger, Nick Bielik, Eric Blair, Catherine Bottolfson McCallum, Bob Burgess, Peter Crowther, Chris Doyle, Nick Gevers, Olivia Guffey, Eileen Klink, Randy Koppang, Andrew Long, Lori Michelle, Ed & Chris Monteath, Christine Morgan, LeClair Pearson, Dr. Carsten Ronlov, Wendy Sappo Dunn, the late Richard & Emiko Schowengerdt, Gavriel Quiroga, Ann VanderMeer, Jack Womack, and especially Melissa Guffey and her uterus

ABOUT THE AUTHOR

Robert Guffey is a lecturer in the Department of English at California State University-Long Beach. His most recent books are *Cryptopolis & Other Stories* (Lethe Press, 2024), the Rondo Award-nominated novel *Dead Monkey Rum* (Planet Bizarro Press, 2023), and *Operation Mindfuck: QAnon & the Cult of Donald Trump* (OR Books, 2022), which Alan Moore described as "jaw-dropping and essential." His previous books include the Wonderland Award-nominated collection *Widow of the Amputation and Other Weird Crimes* (Eraserhead Press, 2021), the Rondo Award-nominated novel *Bela Lugosi's Dead* (Crossroad Press, 2021), the darkly satirical, apocalyptic novel *Until the Last Dog Dies* (Night Shade/Skyhorse, 2017), which Adam-Troy Castro called "one of the great books of the year," the journalistic memoir *Chameleo: A Strange but True Story of Invisible Spies, Heroin Addiction, and Homeland Security* (OR Books, 2015), which *Flavorwire* called, "By many miles, the weirdest and funniest book of [the year]," the novella collection *Spies & Saucers* (PS Publishing, 2014), and *Cryptoscatology: Conspiracy Theory as Art Form* (TrineDay, 2012). A graduate of the famed Clarion Writers Workshop in Seattle, he has written for numerous publications, among them *The Believer*, *The Evergreen Review*, *The Los Angeles Review of Books*, *The Mailer Review*, *Rosebud*, *Salon*, and *TOR.com*. Forthcoming from Headpress is his nonfiction cinema book, *Hollywood Haunts the World: An Investigation into the Cinema of Occulted Taboos*. His website is Cryptoscatology.com.

ABOUT THE AUTHOR

Milton Keynes UK
Ingram Content Group UK Ltd.
UKHW020001231024
449917UK00010B/455

9 781955 745819